WOMEN'S
HISTORY
IN
MINNESOTA

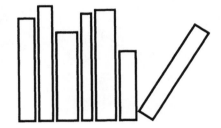

WOMEN'S HISTORY IN MINNESOTA

A Survey of Published Sources and Dissertations

COMPILED BY JO BLATTI

MINNESOTA HISTORICAL SOCIETY PRESS • ST. PAUL

MINNESOTA HISTORICAL SOCIETY PRESS
St. Paul 55102

Copyright 1993 by the Minnesota Historical Society
All rights reserved

Manufactured in the United States of America
10 9 8 7 6 5 4 3 2 1

International Standard Book Number 0–87351–291-X

♾ The paper used in this publication meets the minimum requirements of the American National Standard for Information Sciences—Permanence for Printed Library Materials, ANSI Z39.48–1984.

Library of Congress Cataloging-in-Publication Data
Blatti, Jo.
    Women's history in Minnesota : a survey of published sources and dissertations / Jo Blatti, compiler.
       p.   cm.
    Includes index.
    ISBN 0–87351–291-X (alk. paper)
    1. Women—Minnesota—History—Bibliography. I. Title.
Z7964.U5M563 1993
[HQ1438]
016.3054'09776—dc20   93–15751

ⅢⅢⅣ CONTENTS

CONTENTS

⫿⫾/ Foreword

Women's History in Minnesota: A Survey of Published Sources and Dissertations is a product of the Women's History Research and Grants Project administered by the Research Department of the Minnesota Historical Society. The project received initial funding from the Minnesota State Legislature in 1989 and has also been supported by the Society's Publications and Research Division. Research Supervisor Deborah L. Miller has served as the project's administrative supervisor.

Project Director Jo Blatti designed this bibliography in consultation with Society staff members and a statewide advisory group of scholars and citizens. She was assisted in its compilation by Lynn McCarthy, research clerk, and by many others who are named in the acknowledgments. The advisers and their affiliations are Annette Atkins, St. John's University; Clarke Chambers, University of Minnesota (retired); Yvonne Condell, Moorhead State University; Andrea Hinding, YMCA Archives, St. Paul; L. DeAne Lagerquist, St. Olaf College; Shelley McIntire, Minnesota Indian Women's Resource Center; Kathleen Ridder, St. Paul; Janet Spector, University of Minnesota; Barbara Stuhler, University of Minnesota (retired); State Representative Steve Trimble, St. Paul; Angie Velasco, St. Louis Park; and Anne Webb, Metropolitan State University.

In 1991 the Women's History Research and Grants Project awarded nineteen grants in support of re-search and writing on women's history. Recipients were selected from a field of forty-seven applicants by a committee representing the project advisory group and the Society's staff. Among the subject areas covered by the grant-supported projects are Asian-American, African-American, American-Indian, Finnish, German, Hispanic, and Jewish women; women in sports, the labor movement, the nursing profession, fashion retailing, radical politics, immigrant and ethnic communities, and the cooperative movement; and those who were transient and poor. The grant recipients are producing a richly informative array of oral histories, articles, books, public performances, photographic exhibits, and radio programs.

Widespread interest and active participation generated by both the bibliography work and the grants program have been gratifying. They are also convincing evidence that the need for new and substantive efforts in the field of women's history in Minnesota continues. We hope that this bibliography of primarily published sources on women's history encourages and facilitates those efforts.

JEAN A. BROOKINS
*Assistant Director
for Publications and
Research*

▙▚▞ Introduction

"What I will be offering you is not novel sights,
but different views."[1]

Sooner or later, almost everyone in the Upper Midwest region of the country has the experience, at once exhilarating and disorienting, of seeing utterly familiar landscapes transformed by mountains of snow—erasing some landmarks and changing our perspectives on others. So it is, in a sense, with this women's history bibliography, which provides a view of Minnesota as seen through the experiences of its women residents.

The bibliography includes 844 citations of works describing the lives and activities of Minnesota women—recent Hmong and Soviet Jewish migrants to the Twin Cities metropolitan area, farm women, teachers, homemakers, bankers, clubwomen, Ojibway lacemakers, newspaper editors, painters, Lutheran deaconesses, welfare activists, businesswomen, suffragists, antisuffragists, and many more. Previously published bibliographies describe various aspects of Minnesota's political, geographical, and institutional history. Yet the voices of women—half the population—are heard relatively rarely for reasons that are many and at this point, perhaps, familiar. Earlier views of history emphasized public activity in which women seldom held official or recognized power. Often uncataloged, women's history sources were hard to locate, and the content of those sources was often seen as unconventional or indirect. Last, but by no means least, few imagined that women's voices could communicate much that was necessary to know of our collective history in this place.

Times have changed. Among the most pronounced changes in daily life since World War II for Minnesotans and other Americans is the increased participation of women in the paid work force. The roles and contributions of women have provided a major topic for public planning and research in Minnesota since the mid-1960s. A generation of scholarship, based on existing and new sources, has explored greater diversity in women's experiences, greater participation in economic and civic affairs, and more complex views of domestic arrangements than had been previously documented. Recent women's history scholarship has also pioneered flexible and subtle interpretive models acknowledging complex interactions between private and public life.

This bibliography was conceived as a companion piece to existing bibliographies that would make this recent history accessible. Our purposes in undertaking the project were threefold:

1. To identify books, articles, pamphlets, and dissertations describing women's roles and experiences in all periods and cultures of Minnesota history;

2. To produce a bibliography for use in classrooms and other formal and informal learning programs that rely on readily available works;

3. To encourage additional research and writing on women's history topics in our region.

In many cases, our findings are heartening. Life histories of such diverse and accomplished individuals as portraitist Frances Cranmer Greenman, nursing educator Katharine Densford Dreves, suffragist Sarah Tarleton Colvin, Sister Mary Seraphine of the Sisters of St. Joseph of Carondelet, and labor organizer Sabrie G. Akin illustrate some of the many arenas women have successfully occupied. The publications of countless civic and social-welfare organizations document women's participation in the formation of public policy over the past 150 years. Works as varied as the Reverend J. S. Boyd's commemorative poem about the women's fund-raising at the Presbyterian church in Greenleafton and historian Joan R. Gundersen's analytic studies of All Saints Episcopal Church in Northfield demonstrate significant women's roles in church finance and governance. Dozens of titles describe farm and rural life, ethnic identity, and community conditions in the state's developing towns and cities.

There is sobering news as well. Numerous women,

INTRODUCTION

such as farm wife Mary E. Carpenter and Ojibway author Ignatia Broker, chronicle hard lives in the settlement period and displacement among American-Indian people. The extensive reports produced by the Minnesota Commission on the Economic Status of Women document persistent economic and occupational inequities for women workers from the 1960s to the present. A diverse group of studies tells us that overall opportunities for women have declined in many areas of education, a field believed to be hospitable to women. Violence against women has led to numerous contemporary public policy reports and family studies, more than many of us expected or thought possible. As is the case with all histories, however, we need access to the fullest possible records of the past to understand our present and to imagine our future.

CONTENTS AND PRINCIPLES OF SELECTION

The project team producing this bibliography faced two major questions. The first was how to delimit the universe of books, articles, and other published works that might be included. The second was how best to report our findings. In the end, we designed an original subject bibliography, based on many resources and examples available to us. Because others approaching women's history from a state or regional perspective will face the same questions, we discuss assumptions and chosen options at some length below.

This bibliography describes nonfiction books, articles, pamphlets, and dissertations about women in all periods and cultures of Minnesota history. Although some works about American-Indian women, in particular, may describe individuals, events, and ways of life dating to the sixteenth century, the majority of the titles focus on women in the nineteenth and twentieth centuries.

The bibliography is based on surveys of collections in the Minnesota Historical Society, the library system at the University of Minnesota–Twin Cities, and the Twin Cities metropolitan area Cooperating Libraries in Consortium or CLIC (James J. Hill Reference Library, Macalester College, College of St. Catherine, University of St. Thomas, Augsburg College, Concordia College, and Hamline University). We also searched the *America: History and Life* indexes and *Dissertation Abstracts* for women's history titles on Minnesota subjects. Outside the metropolitan area, we surveyed county historical societies, the Regional Research Centers, and college and university libraries by mail questionnaire, and through interlibrary loan we examined titles identified by those institutions. We acknowledge that these surveys produced a preliminary selection of works and not a complete one.

We used four principles of selection for inclusion in the bibliography:

1. Is this a *published* work? That is, is it printed and bound and sold or distributed in some manner as opposed to being a typescript or manuscript?

2. Is the focus of the work broadly historical? Does it describe or analyze women's experiences at a specific moment or over a period of time? We included sociology, anthropology, American studies, women's studies, archaeology, folklore, and cultural studies in our definition of "historical." We also included medical and psychological studies in which the social contexts of women's illness or wellness are a primary focus. However, physiological studies and fiction were excluded.

3. Is women's experience central to the work? Does the main exposition add substantially to our knowledge of women's lives and roles?

4. Is the locale Minnesota or a contiguous state or province? Most works contained in this bibliography describe individuals and situations within the borders of the state. Important exceptions or extensions include works on American-Indian life that describe social movement in multistate regions of the Upper Midwest; comparative work on ethnic and cultural groups in several locations, such as Finnish communities in Minnesota and Michigan or Hmong settlements in Minneapolis and Kansas City; and recent scholarship about rural women's lives in northern Iowa and the eastern Dakotas that may be extended to southern Minnesota and the Red River valley of western Minnesota.

While some works include sections in European and American-Indian languages, this is principally an English-language bibliography.

One major exception to our "published work" criterion was the decision to survey doctoral dissertations at the University of Minnesota–Twin Cities for women's history content. Although these technically are unpublished works, we believe the potential resources at Minnesota's major and only public doctoral-level institution should not be ignored. Of approximately 300 dissertations examined, 142 are included in this bibliography. Available time did not permit equally thorough examination of master's theses collections at the University of Minnesota or other graduate programs in the state. We have, however, included some master's and undergraduate honors papers, which were found by computer-assisted searches, because these papers often treat topics not considered in other sources. Also, the project undertook a survey of the University of Minnesota index for master's theses focusing on women. This list is accessible through the Women's History Research and Grants Project Papers housed in the MHS Archives at the Minnesota Historical Society.

This bibliography does not consider manuscripts or other primary source materials, such as letters, diaries, and government documents. For these, readers are referred to the Minnesota Historical Society, the Social Welfare History Archives and the Immigration History Research Center at the University of Minnesota–Twin Cities, and county historical society and Regional Research Center collections. Government documents can be located through the reference departments of major research libraries in the metropolitan area and regional repositories in both the Minnesota State University system and the Minnesota public libraries. This bibliography also does not include oral history and audio-visual materials. Whenever available, published guides to primary sources—such as Andrea Hinding's *Women's History Sources: A Guide to Archives and Manuscript Collections in the United States* and guides to the Minnesota Historical Society collections and to other archives—are included in the reference section of this bibliography. Readers with specific research questions should make direct inquiries at the various repositories. Reference staff can, for example, help locate the numerous published works that exist in manuscript collections in the Minnesota Historical Society and elsewhere that we could not survey in our limited time.

ORGANIZATION OF CONTENTS

Like so much else in women's history, this bibliography was made to order—not to fit one woman's dimensions but to encompass the many women whose lives are recognized in its pages. Numerous models and options lay before us as we considered the task of organizing the research—other bibliographies produced by the Society and by a handful of women's projects across the country, the Library of Congress cataloging system, and feminist critiques of existing cataloging structures and language.[2] The resulting work reflects a series of decisions made by project staff and advisers:

1. We wanted to use a form of topical organization, believing that the significance of this bibliography lay in part in providing the opportunity to see like works in relation to one another.

2. While valuable in other ways, existing Minnesota history bibliographies—organized principally around settlement patterns, American-Indian relations with European Americans, and cultural geography—did not represent women's experiences adequately.

3. An intentionally constructed set of subject categories based on close observation of women's documents and life patterns was of greater value than the Library of Congress categories and other existing, essentially indirect and reactive, cataloging systems.

In identifying these assumptions, we are deeply indebted to the counsel of our project advisers, particularly Annette Atkins and Anne Webb, and to the pioneering work of Joan Marshall, Ruth Dickstein, and Mary Ellen S. Capek on alternative cataloging structures and language.[3]

Although its thirteen major categories and numerous subheadings sit on the page in neat columns, this bibliography's effective shape is one of webs or threads weaving back and forth among private and public spaces or commitments. The work opens with Surveys and Works of Reference and then moves through Cultural, Ethnic, and Group Affiliation and Life History sections to questions of personal and collective identity. The Social Life and Natural Sciences and Health categories function as a middle ground—a place where personal identity engages social or environmental structures, such as marriage, parenthood, social class, genetic inheritance, or the physical world. This is nature/nurture territory, particularly fertile ground in women's history as we increasingly recognize how much public work of the culture is carried on in ostensibly private family and domestic settings. The bibliography then moves toward the more formal public sphere through Organizations and Clubs—all kinds of social, cultural, religious, professional, reform, and activist groups—and then to State and Local History and Regional Studies categories that recognize place as a central factor in social life. Three categories—Religion and Philosophy, Visual, Literary, and Performing Arts, and Education—maintain a focus on public activities and contributions to a collective creative life. The Economics and Employment and Law and Government categories—seemingly the most public of all—actually function as mediators, sharing many index entries with the Social Life and Natural Sciences and Health sections. In one of many possible examples, the title *Economic Problems of Families in Transition* (no. 797) is located under the "legal rights" subcategory and is also indexed under "marriage" and "family and kinship."

Taken altogether, what does the completed bibliography reveal about women's historical experiences in Minnesota? In a sense, readers will supply the best answers to that question in their uses of the bibliography, but the distribution of entries suggests many avenues of inquiry. Several subsection headings that we anticipated would be useful had to be omitted for lack of suitable entries. Among them were Métis, biological sciences, philosophy and ethics, mythology, nursery and day-care programs, kindergarten, and extension education. Works that touch on these subjects, however, can be found by consulting the index.

Only two citations appear under the "environment and ecology" subsection, yet it hints at interesting changes in the literature of twentieth-century women's relationship to the natural world. Early writings cross-referenced to the environment and dated about 1910 recount honeymoon or retreat journeys of adventurous, progressive couples; more recent publications are just as likely to describe wilderness as a testing ground for individual mettle or as the site for collective outings by groups of women.

While some work has been undertaken on most major ethnic and cultural groups in Minnesota, the majority of titles concern American-Indian and European-American women. Interestingly, some recently arrived Asian-Pacific immigrants have been the subject of as much work as have African-American and Hispanic women who have been residents for several generations. Surprisingly little material appears under "foods" and "folk and domestic arts." This occurs in part because material that might have been placed there in earlier periods or in another schema has been integrated into productive work categories in this bibliography.

Categories containing the most citations underscore the fidelity of Minnesota resources to a larger, national picture. Three clusters of entries—life histories (including biographies and autobiographies), organizations, and economics and employment—account for 424 of the 844 entries in this bibliography. While this is not surprising—contemporary scholars of women's history have identified all three as fundamental areas of research—it is useful to consider the historiographic implications of these dominant forms. Some women's historians have identified the life history and personal narrative as distinctive feminine forms that tell of domestic, emotional, and social life (as well as interior monologues) customarily omitted from mainstream histories.[4] Many readers will recognize the national women's club movement as the locus for a great deal of work on relationships among private and public spheres in nineteenth- and twentieth-century life. Similarly, in the area of work, contemporary feminist historians have pioneered new definitions of productive labor in homes and farms that accommodate both paid jobs and unpaid tasks that support family life.

OPPORTUNITIES FOR RESEARCH, TEACHING, AND PUBLIC PROGRAMMING

Possible extensions and applications of this bibliography appear to be almost endless. Its contents document many connections among people and ideas that merit further exploration. For instance, in addition to her involvement with the woman suffrage movement, Clara Hampson Ueland was instrumental in organizing the first kindergarten association in Minneapolis. Sketches of Ueland, the autobiography of her daughter Brenda Ueland, and the reminiscences of pioneering kindergarten teacher Stella Louise Wood all provide perspectives on early childhood education. An imaginative classroom or museum-program exercise based on existing sources might use role-playing to explore this subject from the perspectives of parent, teacher, and child.

The same materials, examined with others identified in the bibliography (such as *Women and the State,* the proceedings of the 1915 meeting of the Minnesota Academy of Social Sciences, no. 644), could provide the point of entry for original research into the relationships among various social reforms, including education and the commitments of activist women associated with pro- and antisuffrage organizations. Florence Wells Carpenter and other articulate antisuffragists shared community volunteer profiles similar in many respects to those of Clara Ueland and other advocates of woman suffrage. When these materials are examined carefully, do particular issues or social concerns emerge as attractive to the two groups? Are there patterns in organizational and board memberships? Do women associated with pro- and antisuffrage groups participate jointly in "general purpose" organizations, such as the Women's City Club in St. Paul or the Woman's Club in Minneapolis? Biographical and organizational publications identified herein provide opportunities for case-study work that has not, to our knowledge, been undertaken in Minnesota.

The great number of women's organizations of all sorts documented in this bibliography suggests many avenues of approach. One research and discussion project for school or museum programs might be to investigate several years of records from women's clubs held by a single county historical society.[5] How many clubs existed simultaneously in a given area? Does overlapping membership appear to be common? What about rural/town allegiances? How do clubs' organizational missions, projects, and procedures compare with one another? Are changes in the structure or interests of community organizations discernible over time? Do comparable records exist for men's organizations in the same period?

A scholarly study might ask these and other questions in preparation of an analytical article or monograph on rural and urban women's organizations or the role of the club federation movement in creating a state and regional community based on local club memberships. In yet another application, surviving club yearbooks and programs could provide the basis for reenactments of club discussions and debates, a potential resource for classrooms and for museum interpretation and other public programs.

A final example of the bibliography's possible uses is offered by the entry entitled *Contributions of Black Women to Minnesota History* (no. 105). Little known outside the African-American community, the collection was published in 1977 as a bicentennial project by the National Council of Negro Women, Minnesota Section. The work suggests an important series of questions about what it means to be a notable woman as defined by other members of the same community. Exploring these ideas with students might be one application. Using other resources identified in the bibliography, a scholar of women's history might develop a comparative analysis. To what extent do similar themes, ideas, or biographic presentation strategies arise in *Contributions of Black Women to Minnesota History* and other collective biographies of women from other ethnic or cultural groups, such as *Souvenir "Norse-American Women," 1825–1925* (no. 53) or *Women Who Dared: The History of Finnish American Women* (no. 58), and in works representing the culture at large, such as *Who's Who Among Minnesota Women* (no. 81)? Or is each a highly distinct collection with little apparent crossover? In either case, what does this suggest about the bases for public recognition of women's achievements?

HOW TO USE THIS BIBLIOGRAPHY

The entries in this bibliography are arranged alphabetically by author within subject categories. Each entry appears in only one place: under the subject category most closely related to its content. In the compilation process, however, all the entries received anywhere from one to six cross-references. Thus the index includes all subject categories used in the bibliography, additional subject headings, all proper and place names that appear in the annotations, and an entry for all periodicals. Given the interrelated and interdisciplinary qualities of this work, readers are urged to consult the index for complete subject entries and cross-references.

Each bibliographic entry moves from author (including notations for editor or compiler), to title,

place of publication, publisher, publication date, and number of pages. Following these basic elements, a couple of additional notations may appear if appropriate. One notes the existence of footnotes, bibliography, index, and illustrations. Another, enclosed in parentheses at the end of the citation, signifies the location of materials in uncataloged or special collections at the Minnesota Historical Society or the University of Minnesota. In these cases, the following abbreviations are used:

MHS - Minnesota Historical Society Research Center, St. Paul
U of M/Wil - University of Minnesota, Wilson Library, Minneapolis
U of M/Wal - University of Minnesota, Walter Library, Minneapolis

The research universe is relatively finite. The vast majority of the works in this bibliography may be located quickly by consulting computerized catalogs at the Minnesota Historical Society, the University of Minnesota, or any participating library in the CLIC system. Theses and dissertations will be found at the institutions for which they were produced or, in some cases, at the Minnesota Historical Society. Many titles may be available to researchers through interlibrary loan.

The annotations within the bibliography's entries provide synopses of the works and their focus; they do not evaluate the quality of the works. All place names mentioned are in Minnesota (often accompanied by county reference) unless they are nationally recognized cities that appear without further identification or local communities in other states, for which state abbreviations are given.

Our bibliography project could not explore the visual collections available to researchers, but we also could not resist the opportunity to add images of women to this published work. All the photographs that appear on the following pages are from the collection of the Minnesota Historical Society. They were selected by Deborah Miller, who properly, and ardently, advocates the use of photographs as rich research sources.

JO BLATTI
Project Director

NOTES

[1]Michael J. Bell used this phrase to describe his work on the Iowa Jewish heritage project, 1989–90, in "To Light Out for the Territories Ahead of the Rest," *Palimpsest* 71 (Winter 1990): 146.

INTRODUCTION

[2]See Teri Conrad, comp., *Women in the West: A Bibliography, 1984–1987* (Pullman: Coalition for Western Women's History, Washington State University, 1988); Nancy Baker Jones, comp., *Women and Texas History: An Archival Bibliography* (Austin: Texas State Historical Assn., 1990); and Andrea Timberlake et al., eds., *Women of Color and Southern Women: A Bibliography of Social Science Research, 1975–1988* (Memphis: Center for Research on Women, Memphis State University, 1988). Also, historian Karen J. Blair, Central Washington University, kindly shared the manuscript (in progress) of her annotated bibliography on women of the Pacific Northwest.

[3]Joan K. Marshall, comp., *On Equal Terms: A Thesaurus for Nonsexist Indexing and Cataloguing* (New York: Neal-Schuman, 1977); Ruth Dickstein et al., eds., *Women in LC's Terms: A Thesaurus of Library of Congress Subject Head-*

ings Relating to Women (New York: Oryx Press, 1988); and Mary Ellen S. Capek, ed., *A Women's Thesaurus: An Index of Language Used to Describe and Locate Information By and About Women* (New York: Harper and Row, 1987).

[4]Suzanne L. Bunkers, " 'Faithful Friend': Nineteenth-Century Midwestern American Women's Unpublished Diaries," *Women's Studies International Forum* 10, no. 1 (1987): 7–17; The Personal Narratives Group, *Interpreting Women's Lives: Feminist Theory and Personal Narratives* (Bloomington: Indiana University Press, 1989).

[5]This project probably could be done in any county, for numerous additional club yearbooks and programs exist in local collections. Our bibliography survey requested information on books and articles in library collections; yet many club materials are customarily cataloged with manuscripts and archival materials.

ⅢⅢⅣ Acknowledgments

Many persons contributed to the production of this bibliography. Jean A. Brookins, assistant director for publications and research at the Minnesota Historical Society, and her colleague Deborah L. Miller, research supervisor, proposed the idea for this bibliography and an associated grants program and provided support and encouragement over a two-year production period. Members of our statewide advisory committee gave generously of their time and expertise, particularly in the critically important stage of project design. Lynn McCarthy, research assistant and clerk for the Women's History Research and Grants Project, performed yeowoman service in mastering multiple word-processing programs as well as the repetitive yet precise demands of our research routine. Rosalie Weisman served as research assistant during McCarthy's maternity leave. Carol Jenson did a fine job adding the last entries to the compilation after this director's departure from the project. Alan Ominsky, production supervisor, and Kathy Mahoney and Gloria Haider, word processing secretaries, all at the Minnesota Historical Society Press, and Mark Hammons at the Social Welfare History Archives, University of Minnesota, supplied invaluable consultation on the fine (and sometimes sticky) points of our computer needs. Minnesota Historical Society Press editor Sarah P. Rubinstein provided continual editorial consultation and the benefit of extensive experience with earlier bibliography projects. Deborah Swanson, assistant editor, gave generously of her time and talent, and editor Elaine Carte also assisted. Sharon Ramirez spent much of the summer of 1990 working with us as a graduate intern, surveying dissertations at the University of Minnesota Archives for possible inclusion in this bibliography. Also in 1990, volunteer Doreen Holte checked the University of Minnesota master's thesis files for possible women's history materials.

We owe equally heartfelt thanks to the many librarians and archivists who assisted us. Barbara Jones, then head of reference at the Minnesota Historical Society, and Barbara Walden, subject bibliographer for history at the University of Minnesota, contributed greatly to our understanding of issues in library cataloging and women's history. The two archivists-bibliographers on our advisory committee, Shelley McIntire of the Minnesota Indian Women's Resource Center and Andrea Hinding of the YMCA Archives, generously shared their experiences and their findings. Dozens of librarians and archivists in greater Minnesota responded to our mail survey, ensuring the inclusion of materials located outside the Twin Cities metropolitan area. Patricia Harpole and the staff at the Minnesota Historical Society Research Center were unfailingly helpful and attentive. Society librarian Alissa Rosenberg, our often-appealed-to connection with interlibrary loan, assiduously shepherded our requests through that system. University Archivist Penelope Krosch and her colleagues Lois G. Hendrickson and Carol O'Brien provided a hospitable workplace for many hours spent with dissertations on deposit at the University of Minnesota. The University Archives staff also provided a meticulous master file of women's history sources in their repository. Many of its titles appear in this bibliography; the remainder are accessible to researchers through the Women's History Research and Grants Project Papers in the MHS Archives. George Swan and colleagues at the Subject Bibliography Unit, Wilson Library, University of Minnesota, provided an equally comfortable base for extended periods of work in that library complex.

To these and all others who have contributed to this bibliography, we send thanks.

IIII/ Surveys and Works of Reference

1. Brook, Michael, comp. *Reference Guide to Minnesota History: A Subject Bibliography of Books, Pamphlets, and Articles in English.* St. Paul: Minnesota Historical Society, 1974. 132 p. Index.

   The major statewide bibliography; based on collections of the Minnesota Historical Society. More than 3,700 entries. Women's history not extensively addressed in topical categories; however, considerable information about women's activities to be found within categories such as local history, social questions, the arts, religion, education, population and immigration, and Indians.

2. Brook, Michael, and Sarah P. Rubinstein, comps. *A Supplement to Reference Guide to Minnesota History: A Subject Bibliography, 1970–80.* St. Paul: Minnesota Historical Society Press, 1983. 69 p. Index.

   Sequel to the 1974 bibliography contains about 1,600 entries. Many are commemorative and local history contributions inspired by the national bicentennial celebration of 1976. Same basic organization as the 1974 volume.

3. Caron, Barbara, et al. *Ammunition for Women.* St. Paul: College of Saint Catherine, [1973?]. 7 p.

   Annotated bibliography of women's literature available at College of St. Catherine library about 1970. Includes sections on the contemporary woman, the psychology of womanhood, social history, the working woman, and women's liberation.

4. Chambers, Clarke A., and Judith Martin. *Woman in America.* Minneapolis: Department of Continuing Education for Women, University of Minnesota, 1972. 37 p.

   Bibliographic essay prepared for adult women students at the University of Minnesota–Twin Cities discusses historical views of women and issues raised by the second women's movement, 1960–72. Includes sections titled, "The Psycho-Sexual Argument," "Women in the Family," "General Accounts," "Political Histories," "Working Women," "Education," "Women and the Law,"

"Special Studies" (important, but difficult to categorize references), "Comparative Studies," "Symposia and Collected Essays," "The President's Report, 1963," "Primary Documents of Women's Rights," and "The Contemporary Debate."

5. College of Saint Catherine [St. Paul]. *Woman: A Bibliography.* St. Paul: Saint Catherine Library, 1967. 129 p. Index.

   Annotated bibliography describes 1,560 nonfiction books about women's status, opportunities, and responsibilities published from 1831 to 1967. Places special emphases on sociological and economic studies published in the early 20th century and on 1960s works on the psychological liberation of women. (Note: All titles held in St. Catherine's library.)

6. Fogerty, James E., comp. *Manuscripts Collections of the Minnesota Regional Research Centers: Guide Number 2.* St. Paul: Minnesota Historical Society, 1980. 79 p. Index. (MHS).

   Sequel to 1975 *Preliminary Guide* adds eighth center, Northeast Minnesota Historical Center at University of Minnesota-Duluth. Contains 858 entries, including 196 describing public records (mainly schools); 36 describing papers of individual women, including legislators and politicians; and 22 describing women's organizations. Additional information about women's roles and activities is located in church records and school records.

7. Fogerty, James E., comp. *Preliminary Guide to the Holdings of the Minnesota Regional Research Centers.* St. Paul: Minnesota Historical Society, 1975. 20 p. Geographical index.

   Guide to holdings of Regional Research Centers located at Bemidji, Mankato, Moorhead, St. Cloud, Southwest, and Winona state colleges. Materials range from mid-19th-century manuscripts and personal papers to mid-1970s oral histories. The guide is divided into two sections—manuscripts and oral history interviews. The oral history section is subdivided into four categories: Farm Holiday Association, Minnesota state legislators and politics, the 1930s depression in the Red River valley, and reminiscences. Women's entries describe farm and rural life, state legislative politics, teaching experience, and education.

8. Goff, Lila Johnson, and James E. Fogerty, comps. *The Oral History Collections of the Minnesota Historical Society.* St. Paul: Minnesota Historical Society Press, 1984. 121 p. Index.

Describes oral history holdings of Minnesota Historical Society in St. Paul and the Regional Research Centers' collections statewide. Includes 1,474 entries. Describes organizational collections such as Women's International League for Peace and Freedom in Minnesota and Women in Politics and Business in Duluth. Many individual interviews focus on women's roles and activities in domestic life, education, politics, and civic life.

9. Hinding, Andrea, ed. *Women's History Sources: A Guide to Archives and Manuscript Collections in the United States.* 2 vols. New York: R. R. Bowker Co., 1979. 1,114, 391 p.

Contains descriptions of 18,026 collections of unpublished sources pertaining to the history of women in the United States from the colonial period to the 1970s from 1,586 repositories. Arranged alphabetically by state and city. Volume one is devoted to collections, volume two to the index. The Minnesota section includes 1,139 entries—predominately personal papers, oral histories, and organizational records.

10. Holbert, Sue E. "Women's History Resources at the Minnesota Historical Society." *Minnesota History* 52 (Fall 1990): 112–18.

Presents an overview of materials that focus on the lives of women. These sources can be found in a variety of media, including museum artifacts, photographs, oral history tapes, manuscript collections, and books. The author notes that women's historical contributions have been obscured by prejudicial record keeping.

11. Jerabek, Esther, comp. *Check List of Minnesota State Documents, 1858–1923.* St. Paul: Minnesota Historical Society, 1972. 216 p.

This finding aid contains additions and corrections to an earlier bibliography of Minnesota territorial documents, 1849–58, plus a checklist of executive documents, 1858–1923. Entries of interest to women's history include superintendent of public instruction, normal schools, University of Min-

nesota, Department of Labor and Industries, Department of Education, and Bureau of Labor.

12. Kane, Lucile M., and Kathryn A. Johnson, comps. *Manuscripts Collections of the Minnesota Historical Society: Guide Number 2.* St. Paul: Minnesota Historical Society, 1955. 212 p. Index.

Sequel to *Guide* (1935). Organized alphabetically. Describes 1,189 collections, including many journals, letters, and organizational records concerning women's roles and activities, mid-19th century to 1950s.

13. Kane, Lucile M., comp. *Guide to the Public Affairs Collection of the Minnesota Historical Society.* St. Paul: Minnesota Historical Society, 1968. 46 p. Reference note.

Describes 158 groups of papers and 25 tape-recorded interviews. Organized alphabetically. Holdings include League of Women Voters materials and several suffrage organizations, plus papers of women active in mainstream and third-party politics.

14. Koske, Mary, comp. *Guide to the Minnesota Finnish American Family History Collection.* Minneapolis: Immigration History Research Center, University of Minnesota, 1985. 42 p. Appendixes.

Collected from 1979 to June 1981, more than 100 oral history interviews and written narratives document Finnish cultural and domestic life in Minnesota from mid-19th century to 1980s. Strong focus on women's and family history. Collection is organized alphabetically by author's or narrator's name.

15. Lucas, Lydia A., comp. *Manuscripts Collections of the Minnesota Historical Society: Guide Number 3.* St. Paul: Minnesota Historical Society, 1977. 189 p. Index.

Sequel to *Guide* (1935) and *Guide 2* (1955). Includes substantial additions to some collections previously described. Organized alphabetically, the 1,194 entries describe personal and family manuscripts and records of organizations for inventoried collections. Many concern women's lives and activities in areas including politics and civic affairs, social welfare, family life, World War I, and the Peace Corps.

16. Nute, Grace Lee, and Gertrude W. Ackermann, comps. *Guide to the Personal Papers in the Manuscript Collections of the Minnesota Historical Society.* St. Paul: Minnesota Historical Society, 1935. 146 p. Index.

Organized alphabetically, the 455 collections described are mostly professional papers, reminiscences, letters, and journals. Many by or about women's experiences in Minnesota, particularly territorial period and early decades of statehood.

17. Palmquist, Bonnie Beatson, comp. *Women in "Minnesota History," 1915–1990: An Annotated Bibliography of Articles Pertaining to Women.* St. Paul: Minnesota Historical Society Press, 1991. 8 p.
Briefly describes more than 150 articles published during a 75-year period. Topical categories include American-Indian women, the arts (except literature), crime, education, ethnicity, family and social life, labor, literature and journalism, material culture, medicine and sciences, occupations, politics, religion, social-welfare reforms, volunteers, and women's movements. Update of the author's article published in *Minnesota History,* Spring 1977.

18. Pinto, Patrick R., and Jeanne O. Buchmeier. *Problems and Issues in the Employment of Minority, Disadvantaged and Female Groups: An Annotated Bibliography.* Industrial Relations Center Bulletin 59. Minneapolis: University of Minnesota, 1973. 62 p.
Contains 548 entries for national and Minnesota sources, 1965–72. Includes reporting and abstract services, legal contexts, general readings concerning disadvantaged groups, and sections referring to African Americans, Hispanics, American Indians, women, age-related discrimination, prison records, and persons with physical or mental disabilities.

19. Sampson, Sister Ann Thomasine. *A Guide to Publications and Information about the Sisters of St. Joseph [of] Carondelet.* St. Paul: The Province, 1983. 4 p.
Lists books, pamphlets, articles, and manuscripts and typescripts, plus St. Paul collections that hold material about the Sisters of St. Joseph of Carondelet activities, 1850s-1980s. Includes research ideas for primary sources that may or may not be in collections.

20. Sampson, Sister Ann Thomasine. *Oral History Collection of Sisters of Saint Joseph of Carondelet.* St. Paul: The Province, [1983?]. 16 p.
Summary of community oral history project, 1975–83, focusing on educational activities of the Sisters of St. Joseph of Carondelet (including College of St. Catherine, St. Agatha's Conservatory, and other institutions), finances, governance within congregation prior to and following Vatican II; nursing and health care; liturgical celebrations; recruitment; and women's organizations and movements. Includes list of 196 interviews identified by subject.

21. Social Welfare History Archives, University of Minnesota. *Guide to Holdings.* Minneapolis: University of Minnesota, 1979. 55 p.
The archives collects records of national voluntary organizations in social welfare services and personal papers of their leaders. Significant local collections include United Way, Associated Family Services, and Abortion Rights Council—all of Minneapolis. Special collections include the Ephemera Collection (75,000 print and near-print publications of more than 2,000 social welfare organizations) and the Women's Movement Collection (240 periodicals and 1,500 miscellaneous publications).

22. Thomas, Evangeline, ed. *Women Religious History Sources: A Guide to Repositories in the United States.* New York: R. R. Bowker Co., 1983. 329 p. Index, bibliography.
Survey of collections concerning women's communities in Roman Catholic, Orthodox, Episcopal, Lutheran, Methodist, and Mennonite denominations. Capsule histories of organizations presented geographically by city and state and cross-referenced to bibliography. Multiple entries for Minnesota Roman Catholic congregations. Includes "biographical register of foundresses and major superiors."

􏰀 Cultural, Ethnic, and Group Affiliation

23. [Minnesota] Commission on the Economic Status of Women. *Minority Women in Minnesota.* St. Paul: The Organization, 1986. 51 p.

Describes social and economic characteristics of African-American, American-Indian, Asian-American, and Hispanic women. Includes educational attainment, marital status, living arrangements, labor force participation, income, and occupation data. Also features "portraits" of average African-American, American-Indian, Asian-American, and Hispanic women based on census data.

AFRICAN AMERICANS

24. Fairbanks, Evelyn. *The Days of Rondo.* St. Paul: Minnesota Historical Society Press, 1990. 182 p.

Memoir of childhood and young womanhood in St. Paul's African-American community in the 1930s and 1940s. Extensive information about the community and about life within an extended family that stretched to the southern U.S.

25. Green, William D. "The Summer Christmas Came to Minnesota: The Case of Eliza Winston, A Slave." *Law and Inequality: A Journal of Theory and Practice* 8 (November 1989): 151–77.

Legal essay concerning an 1860 Minnesota case in which Eliza Winston, the slave of a Mississippi planter vacationing in Minneapolis, was freed through the operations of local abolitionists and the courts. Contexts are abolition, the variable interpretations of 1857 *Dred Scott* decision, and the pre-Civil War history of the Falls of St. Anthony as a resort destination of Southern Americans.

26. Taylor, David Vassar, comp. *Blacks in Minnesota: A Preliminary Guide to Historical Sources.* St. Paul: Minnesota Historical Society, 1976. 33 p. Index.

Catalog for 1974–75 Minnesota Historical Society project documenting institutional and personal histories of African Americans in the Twin Cities

Audrey Thayer and her daughter, Nina Devlin, were photographed in 1991 by John Ratzloff on Ojibway tribal land near Bass Lake in Mahnomen County, on the White Earth Reservation.

Area (St. Paul especially), Duluth, Fergus Falls, and Rochester, from the 19th century to the 1970s. Includes primary and secondary sources. Organized topically around categories of history, government and politics, business and economics, race relations, social welfare, education, religion, organizations, the arts, oral interviews, photographs, and manuscript collections. Considerable material concerning women's lives and roles to be found in personal papers, oral history narratives, religion, and organizations categories.

27. Zalusky, J. W. "Eliza Winston: Slave Woman in Minnesota." *Hennepin County History* 24, no. 1 (Summer 1964): 17–18.

Summary of the Eliza Winston case of 1860 in which Winston, an enslaved woman brought to Minneapolis by a vacationing Mississippi family, appealed her status to local authorities on grounds that Minnesota was a free state. Her case proved controversial because abolitionist authorities ruled in Winston's favor in direct conflict to the *Dred Scott* precedent and because freedwoman Winston reportedly elected to continue a work relationship with her former owners.

AMERICAN INDIANS

28. Albers, Patricia, and Beatrice Medicine, eds. *The Hidden Half: Studies of Plains Indian Women*. Washington, D.C.: University Press of America, 1983. 280 p. Notes, bibliography.

Collection of papers, most presented originally at a 1977 symposium, "The Role and Status of Women in Plains Indian Cultures." Drawn from 19th- and 20th-century research in the Northern Plains region of the U.S. and Canada, these case studies are organized in sections entitled: images of women, women's work, and status of women and female identity. The collection offers an overview and critique of scholarship in the field and also suggests new approaches derived from anthropology and women's studies.

29. Emmerich, Lisa E. " 'To Respect and Love and Seek the Ways of White Women': Field Matrons, the Office of Indian Affairs, and Civilization Policy, 1890–1938." Ph.D. diss., University of Maryland, 1987. 346 p. Footnotes, bibliography. (MHS).

Discusses United States government program designed to make tribal women into forces of assimilation. The field matrons were sent to teach domestic skills to American-Indian women but gradually shifted their focus to dealing with health problems in order to make the program relevant to Indians' lives. The study is based in part on records in Bureau of Indian Affairs field offices, which include Minnesota, Wisconsin, North Dakota, and South Dakota tribes.

30. Green, Rayna. *Native American Women: A Contextual Bibliography*. Bloomington: Indiana University Press, 1983. 120 p. Date and subject indexes.

Bibliography of works concerning American-Indian women nationally from the 1600s to 1980 contains 672 entries organized alphabetically by author. Includes oral history plus media productions. Ojibway/Chippewa and Dakota/Sioux references relevant to Minnesota and immediately surrounding area. The volume introduction is a critical overview of the literature.

31. League of Women Voters. *American Indians of Minneapolis—An Update.* Minneapolis: The League, 1984. 32 p. Bibliography.

Sequel to earlier studies about American Indians in Minneapolis and Minnesota produced by the League in the 1960s and 1970s. Includes discussion of changing roles of Indian women, Indian child welfare issues, and health programs.

32. Smith, G. Hubert. "The Winona Legend." *Minnesota History* 13 (December 1932): 367–76.

Follows the Winona legend in explorers' accounts based on Dakota Indian oral tradition. According to the story, Winona was a Dakota woman who jumped from Maiden Rock into Lake Pepin on the Mississippi River because she was not allowed to marry the man she loved.

33. Tsosie, Rebecca. "Changing Women: The Cross-Currents of American Indian Feminine Identity." *American Indian Culture and Research Journal* 12 (1988): 1–37.

Analyzes historical studies and novels that focus on the gender roles of Indian women. Includes work on Ojibway, Oglala Lakota, Devil's Lake Sioux, Winnebago, and Menominee women.

Dakota/Sioux

34. "Old Bets." *Hennepin County History* 28, no. 4 (Spring 1969): 23.

Profile of the Dakota woman Aza-ya-man-ka-wan (Berry Picker), also known as Old Bets. Briefly chronicles her assistance to European Americans during Dakota War of 1862 and subsequent personal history, particularly in St. Paul.

35. Wa Mda Ska. "Old Betz, the Sioux Heroine." *Literary Northwest* 2 (January 1893): 175–80. (MHS).

Relates life story of Hazza aka Win, a Dakota woman also known as Old Betz (Old Bets). Beginning in the 1840s she lived at Kaposia, near present-day downtown St. Paul. According to this account, she assisted a number of white captives during the Dakota War of 1862 and also helped to convict the Indians hanged at Mankato. She died in 1873.

Lakota/Sioux

36. Medicine, Beatrice. "Indian Women and the Renaissance of Traditional Religion." In *Sioux Indian Religion,* edited by Raymond J. DeMallie and Douglas R. Parks, p. 159–72. Norman: University of Oklahoma Press, 1987. Bibliography.

Based on paper delivered at the 1982 symposium "American Indian Religion in the Dakotas: Historical and Contemporary Perspectives" in Bismarck, N.Dak. Writing as both a Lakota woman and an anthropologist, Medicine offers an overview of women's and men's ceremonies in Lakota tradition, the reemergence of the Sun Dance, the *wakan* power concept, and contemporary motivations for participation in ceremonies. See also "Christian Life Fellowship Church" by Mercy Poor Man and other articles in this collection for additional bicultural perspectives.

Ojibway/Chippewa

37. Broker, Ignatia. *Night Flying Woman: An Ojibway Narrative.* St. Paul: Minnesota Historical Society Press, 1983. 135 p. Glossary.

Childhood and young womanhood of author's great-grandmother in late 19th-century Minnesota. Principal focus is transition from traditional tribal culture to reservation system (White Earth) and selective adaptation of elements of European-American culture. Also of interest stylistically as an example of a woman's tale within Ojibway oral tradition.

38. Buffalohead, Priscilla K. "Farmers, Warriors, Traders: A Fresh Look at Ojibway Women." *Minnesota History* 48 (Summer 1983): 236–44.

Essay explores women's status in Ojibway culture of Minnesota and the Great Lakes region through reexamination of missionary and settlement narratives produced by European Americans. Presents fresh interpretation of original sources and also of contemporary feminist concerns through close examination of the complementary roles of women and men in tribal culture.

39. Densmore, Frances. "Notes and Documents: A Minnesota Missionary Journey of 1893." *Minnesota History* 20 (September 1939): 310–13.

Describes journey of Pauline Colby and others from St. Columba's Episcopal mission on the White Earth Reservation to Leech Lake to set up another station. Missionary Colby remained at Leech Lake until 1922 and instructed Ojibway women in lacemaking.

40. Duncan, Kate C. "American Indian Lace Making." *American Indian Art Magazine* 5, no. 3 (Summer 1980): 28–35, 80.

Describes activities of Episcopal missionary Sibyl Carter and the operations of the Sibyl Carter Indian Lace Association, 1890–1926. Chronicles development of Ojibway women's lacemaking at the White Earth Reservation in Minnesota and expansion of these "industrial" communities to tribal groups (including the Dakota in Minnesota) throughout the Midwest, Northeast, and Southwest. Analyzes piecework earnings, marketing, and use of both European and American-Indian design traditions in the craft.

41. Hart, Irving Harlow. "The Story of Beengwa, Daughter of a Chippewa Warrior." *Minnesota History* 9 (December 1928): 319–30.

Based on 1927 interview with 90-year-old Beengwa, daughter of Augenosh, who relates stories of her life with the Sandy Lake band of Ojibway.

42. Hilger, Sister M. Inez. *A Social Study of One Hundred Fifty Chippewa Indian Families of the White Earth Reservation of Minnesota.* Washington, D.C.: Catholic University of America Press, 1939. 251 p. Appendix, bibliography, index.

Ethnographic study analyzes relationships between living arrangements (particularly housing) and family values among reservation Ojibway. Based on 1938 fieldwork. Though not about women specifically, contains considerable information about sex roles in courtship, marriage, childrearing, and economic activities.

43. Kegg, Maude. *Gabekanaansing/At the End of the Trail.* Linguistics Series, Occasional Publications in Anthropology, no. 4. [Greeley, Colo.]: Museum of Anthropology, University of Northern Colorado, n.d.; Thunder Bay, Ont.: N.p., 1978. 85 p. Glossary.

Memories of a Chippewa childhood in Minnesota as told to John Nichols, editor and transcriber. Bilingual work in Ojibway and English includes complete text of "When I Was a Little Girl" (1976), plus additional memories of steamboat days, domestic life, snuff, and winter play.

44. Kegg, Maude. *Gii-ikwezensiwiyaan/When I Was a Little Girl,* edited and transcribed by John Nichols. Onamia, Minn.: Privately published, 1976. 29 p.

Bilingual account (English/Ojibway) of author's childhood activities in early 20th-century Mille Lacs region of Minnesota. Considerable information about springtime sugar camps and fishing operations run by women and the wild rice culture and harvest. Booklet prepared for visitors at the

Minnesota Historical Society's Mille Lacs Indian Museum.

45. Landes, Ruth. *The Ojibwa Woman.* New York: Columbia University Press, 1938. 247 p.

Cultural study based on fieldwork in Ojibway communities of western Ontario about 1930. Focuses on social behaviors of men and women as seen through author's observations and the life histories of Ojibway women. Discusses village and tribal life in sections entitled youth, marriage, occupations, abnormalities, and life histories.

46. Minnesota Chippewa Tribe. *Contemporary American Indian Women: Careers and Contributions.* Cass Lake, Minn.: The Tribe, 1983. 99 p. Bibliography, teacher's guide, publisher's guide, illustrations.

Profiles of more than 80 American-Indian women active during the 1970s in tribal government and politics, law, administration, education, communications, health, social services, the arts, and business. Most are Minnesota Ojibway but also includes women of other tribes and some national figures.

Winnebago

47. Mountain Wolf Woman. *Mountain Wolf Woman, Sister of Crashing Thunder: The Autobiography of a Winnebago Indian,* edited by Nancy Oestreich Lurie. Ann Arbor: University of Michigan Press, 1961. 142 p. Notes, appendixes, illustrations.

Mountain Wolf Woman (1884–1960), a Wisconsin resident in the Black River Falls area for much of her life, focuses on family and tribal affairs in context of rapidly changing conditions for Indian people. Includes discussion of peyote and other religious practices. Of interest to anthropologists as a companion text to Paul Radin's 1926 biography of Crashing Thunder.

ASIAN-PACIFIC AMERICANS

48. Mason, Sarah R. *Training Southeast Asian Refugee Women for Employment: Public Policies and Community Programs, 1975-1985.* Minneapolis: Center for Urban and Regional Affairs, University of Minnesota, 1986. 142 p. Notes, references, appendixes.

Contains overview essay on public policy and refugee training plus descriptions of national case studies. St. Paul training programs discussed include Family Living in America (1977–), Power Sewing and Apparel Arts for Refugee Women

(1983–85), Bilingual Training in Electronics Assembly (1983–85), Refugee Health Training Program (Minneapolis and St. Paul, 1984–86), and Hmong Craft Business Development Project (1982–83). Considerable information about individual refugee women's experiences throughout the work.

49. Tsuchida, Nobuya, ed. *Asian and Pacific American Experiences: Women's Perspectives.* Minneapolis: Asian/Pacific American Learning Resource Center and General College, University of Minnesota, 1982. 255 p. Notes.

Collection of 24 articles, essays, and oral histories by and about Asian-Pacific women in Midwest and on West Coast. Selections concerning mostly 20th-century Filipina, Chinese, and Southeast Asian residents of Minnesota. Includes "Occupational Profiles of Filipino Women in Minnesota" by Belen Andrada, "Interview with Belen Andrada" by Nobuya Tsuchida and Gail Thoen, "Family Structure and Acculturation in the Chinese Community in Minnesota" by Sarah R. Mason, "Prejudice Against Chinese as Seen from within American Society: The Experience of an Interracial Couple" by Linda M. Mealey, "Interview with Choua Thao" by Nobuya Tsuchida and Gail Thoen, and "Asian Women and the Law: Two Case Studies" by David R. Matsumoto.

Hmong

50. Graves, Susan. "Hmong Women Enrich Hennepin County's Folk Art Tradition." *Hennepin County History* 48, no. 4 (Fall 1989): 25–27.

Describes *pa ndau* (flower cloth) embroidery and applique tradition among immigrant Hmong women of Minneapolis, 1970s–80s. Pays particular attention to story blankets, a recent *pa ndau* form depicting village life, fairy tales, war, and escape experiences. Also notes nontraditional use of *pa ndau* for ornaments, decorative objects, and clothing produced for non-Hmong clientele.

51. Sartorius, Rolf E. *An Evaluation of the American Refugee Committee's First Steps for Women Project.* Minneapolis: American Refugee Committee, 1989. 17 p.

Report describes program designed to teach independent living skills to Hmong women in the Twin Cities. Includes perspectives of project participants and staff. Recommends changes in classroom instruction, the mentor program, and project administration to serve students better.

CULTURAL, ETHNIC, AND GROUP AFFILIATION

EUROPEAN AMERICANS

52. Alper, Deborah Pattison. "Freedom and the Self: Continuity and Change in the Lives of Soviet Women Immigrants in St. Paul." Master's thesis, University of Minnesota, 1988. 153 p. Notes, references.

Explores identity and adjustments to new cultural conditions through life histories of four Soviet Jewish women from Ukraine. Based on 1980s research. Provides considerable information about motivations for emigration and social services offered by the Jewish Community Center in St. Paul.

53. Guttersen, Alma A., and Regina Hilleboe Christensen, eds. *Souvenir "Norse-American Women," 1825–1925.* St. Paul: Lutheran Free Church Pub. Co., 1926. 454 p. Index.

Memorializes roles of Norwegian-American women in United States history through biographical sketches, prose, poetry, organizational notes, and newspaper features. Though the scope is national, many of the entries are specific to Minnesota. (Note: Some of the articles are written in Norwegian.)

54. Hought, Anna Guttormsen, with Florence Ekstrand. *Anna: Norse Roots in Homestead Soil.* Seattle: Welcome Press, 1986. 146 p. Illustrations.

Autobiography of Norwegian woman who emigrated to Montana in 1916. Hought homesteaded and later married and raised her family in Montana and western Minnesota.

55. Johnson, Judy, comp. *A Selected Bibliography of Primary and Secondary Sources About the Finnish Experience on the Iron Range.* Chisholm, Minn.: Iron Range Research Center, 1989. 44 p.

Includes oral histories; genealogies and family histories; audio-visual materials; microfilms; theses and dissertations; manuscripts, personal papers, and organizational records; and serials and pamphlet files. Considerable information about women's lives in the sections on family and community life; emigration and immigration; customs, culture, and ethnic consciousness; and organizational records.

56. Nordstrom, Byron J. "Evelina Månsson and the Memoir of an Urban Labor Migrant." *Swedish Pioneer History Quarterly* 31 (July 1980): 182–95.

Applies the history of Swedish migration patterns to the life of a young Swedish woman immigrant employed in Minneapolis during the years 1901–07. She worked at several unskilled and semi-skilled jobs in order to return to Sweden with a nest egg.

57. Ross, Carl. "Finnish-American Women in Transition, 1910–1920." In *Finnish Diaspora II: United States,* edited by Michael G. Karni, p. 239–55. Toronto: Multicultural History Society of Ontario, 1981. Reference notes.

Concludes that the influence of women on the Finnish-American community has been underestimated. The study focuses on young Finnish-American women who demonstrated their independence by hiring out as domestic workers. As a result they helped to define a new concept of women's social responsibility and participation in public affairs. The study includes material from Finnish settlements in Minnesota and Michigan.

58. Ross, Carl, and K. Marianne Wargelin-Brown, eds. *Women Who Dared: The History of Finnish American Women.* St. Paul: Immigration History Research Center, University of Minnesota, 1986. 164 p. Notes, illustrations.

Collections of essays considers experiences of individual Finnish-American women, their relationships to immigrant institutions, and their feminist activity—primarily in New York, Michigan, and Minnesota during the late 19th and early 20th centuries. Minnesota-specific works include "Milma Lappala: Unitarian Minister and Humanist" by Carol Hepokoski and the profile of Ida Pasanen contained in "Three 'Founding Mothers' of Finnish America" by K. Marianne Wargelin-Brown.

59. Wargelin-Brown, Marianne. "A Closer Look at Finnish-American Immigrant Women's Issues, 1890–1910." In *Finnish Diaspora II: United States,* edited by Michael G. Karni, p. 213–37. Toronto: Multicultural History Society of Ontario, 1981. Reference notes.

Argues that at the turn of the century the Finnish-American community was a complex and contradictory society. Although Finnish-American women were assertive politically and economically and community attitudes toward them appeared to be liberal, Finnish-American men held the final authority. Social taboos prevented women from challenging male authority. Finnish communities in Minnesota and Michigan served as the basis for much of this study.

HISPANICS

60. Guendelman, Sylvia. "The Incorporation of Mexican Women in Seasonal Migration: A Study of

Gender Differences.'' *Hispanic Journal of Behavioral Sciences* 9 (1987): 245–64.

Public health study (1983–86) compares sex differences in migratory behaviors, work patterns, and conjugal relations in a group of female and male workers who move seasonally between Mexico and the United States. Includes overview of current scholarship. Findings suggest that the immigration experience is significantly different for men and women. U.S. employment strengthens traditional breadwinner roles for men while leading to new roles for women as wage earners. Study also documents more egalitarian marriage relationships between working couples in the U.S. and more traditional ''parallel'' relationships in Mexico. (Note: Though this is based predominately on Mexico-California migration, the basic framework is of interest to seasonal migration in the Midwest.)

61. Guendelman, Sylvia, and Auristela Perez-Itriago. ''Double Lives: The Changing Role of Women in Seasonal Migration.'' *Women's Studies* 13 (1987): 249–71.

Study compares migration experiences of Mexican women who move seasonally between the U.S. and Mexico. Based on public health research conducted in Mexico, 1983–86. Findings suggest that migration is experienced differently by women who become wage earners in the U.S. and women who do not. Explores ''cooperative'' and ''dependent'' marriage roles based on women's work experiences.

62. Saucedo, Ramedo J., comp. *Mexican Americans in Minnesota: An Introduction to Historical Sources.* St. Paul: Minnesota Historical Society Press, 1977. 26 p. Index.

Bibliography for 1975–76 Minnesota Historical Society project documenting institutional and personal histories of Mexican Americans in the Twin Cities (primarily St. Paul) and rural regions of the state, 1900–70s. Focus of the project is on primary source material, including 74 oral histories; many of the project informants are women. The sourcebook categories include history, biographies, organizations, businesses, civil and human rights, education, religion, culture and heritage, and migrants.

LESBIANS

63. Meyer, Cynthia J. ''Social Support and Couple Closeness Among Lesbians.'' Ph.D. diss., University of Minnesota, 1988. 153 p. Bibliography, appendixes.

Psychology study explores emotional closeness and social support among lesbian couples. Based on 1980s research with Minnesota (primarily Twin Cities) informants. Findings report generally low levels of family support for lesbian couples and high levels of support from friends. Also reports varying rates of couple closeness relative to stage of the relationship and to support provided by friends and family.

⫿⫿⫿/ Life History

BIOGRAPHY

64. Albertson, Don L. "Sister Kenny's Legacy." *Hennepin County History* 37, no. 1 (Spring 1978): 3–14.

Describes the work of Australian nurse Sister Elizabeth Kenny (1886–1952) in Minnesota, 1940–50. Kenny pioneered heat and muscle reeducation therapies for polio and other paralysis patients during the period in which polio, in particular, was epidemic. The Sister Kenny Institute, foundeded in Minneapolis in 1942, became a showcase for her work in the U.S. Associated with Abbott-Northwestern Hospital in the 1990s, the institute remains a center for rehabilitation therapies and training in physical medicine.

65. Aldrich, Darragh. *Lady in Law: A Biography of Mabeth Hurd Paige.* Chicago: Ralph Fletcher Seymour, 1950. 347 p. Illustrations.

Describes career of longtime Minneapolis representative in the Minnesota legislature. First elected in 1922, along with three other women, Paige alone was reelected, and she served until 1944. In 1927 she became chair of the Committee on Public Welfare and Social Legislation, which coincided with her interests in civil rights and child labor and her earlier work with the Women's Christian Association.

66. American Mothers Committee, comp. *Mothers of Achievement in American History, 1776–1976.* Rutland, Vt.: Charles E. Tuttle Co., 1976. 636 p. Bibliography, index, illustrations.

Profiles of 500 notable mothers are organized by state. The Minnesota section includes the Dakota woman Aza-ya-man-ka-win (Berry Picker, Old Bets) of Mendota and St. Paul; missionary and educator Cornelia Wright Whipple of Faribault; writer and charitable volunteer Charlotte Clark Van Cleve of Minneapolis; civic activist Phebe Sutherland Fuller of Redwood Falls; Roseau County pioneer Mör Johnson Hetteen; suffragist and Farmer-Labor politician Susie W. Stageberg of Red Wing; homemaker and civic volunteer Irene Lyons Tib-

Rafaela Cortez, dressed for her marriage to Carlos Martin Garay, posed in 1947 on Woodward Street in an ethnically mixed neighborhood near St. Paul's Swede Hollow.

betts of Minneapolis; physician Lillian Bendeke Parson of Elbow Lake; homemaker and civic volunteer Mabel Olson Wolff of Buffalo; and charitable volunteer Verona Stubbs Devney of St. Paul.

67. Barsness, Diana. "Anna Ramsey: Shining Exemplar of the True Woman." *Minnesota History* 45 (Fall 1977): 258–72.

Uses the letters of Anna Jenks Ramsey to present her life as a reflection of upper-middle-class life during the mid-19th century. She adapted to husband Alexander Ramsey's active political career; administered home, family, and religious matters; and helped to form a cultured society in early St. Paul. Her correspondence reveals that she resented the hardships of early Minnesota and held very independent views about religion and social standards.

68. Beasley, Maurine Hoffman. "Lorena Hickok to Harry Hopkins, 1933: A Woman Reporter Views Prairie Hard Times." *Montana—The Magazine of Western History* 32, no. 2 (Spring 1982): 58–66.

Sketches Hickok's reports to the head of the Federal Emergency Relief Administration and to Eleanor and President Franklin Roosevelt, 1933–36. Also provides brief biography of Hickok (1893–1968), a journalist raised in Wisconsin, South Dakota, and other midwestern states, who worked for the *Minneapolis Tribune* before heading east in the 1920s to work for the New York *Daily Mirror* and the Associated Press. Later positions in government and politics and as a free-lance writer were due in part to the patronage of Eleanor Roosevelt.

69. Beito, Gretchen Urnes. "Coya Come Home." *Viking* 87, no. 3 (March 1990): 14–17.

Profiles Coya Gjesdal Knutson, Democratic-Farmer-Labor representative serving in the Minnesota legislature, 1950–55, and the U.S. House of Representatives, 1955–58. Focuses on relationships among family, civic responsibilities, and public attitudes—particularly regarding husband Andrew Knutson's demand that she abandon politics and return to Oklee, Red Lake County.

70. Beito, Gretchen Urnes. *Coya Come Home: A Congresswoman's Journey.* Los Angeles: Pomegranate Press, Ltd., 1990. 334 p. Notes and sources, index.

Biography of Coya Knutson, Minnesota's only elected female representative to Congress (1955–58), describes her early life on family farm, education at Concordia College in Moorhead, adult work as a teacher, homemaker, hotel manager, and Democratic-Farmer-Labor activist, and 1950s elections to Minnesota legislature and U.S. Congress. Detailed attention to the domestic and political tensions that ended her career as an elected official.

71. Bell, Marguerite N. *With Banners: A Biography of Stella L. Wood.* St. Paul: Macalester College Press, 1954. 163 p. Index, illustrations.

Profiles Wood (1865–1949), head of a well-regarded training program for kindergarten teachers in the Twin Cities, 1897–1948. Offered first through the Minneapolis Kindergarten Association and later through Miss Wood's School, the program merged with the Macalester College teacher training curriculum in 1948. Provides considerable information about the kindergarten movement, teaching as a career for women, and Stella Wood's family, social activities, and professional life.

72. Blegen, Theodore C. "Guri Endreson, Frontier Heroine." *Minnesota History* 10 (December 1929): 425–30.

Analysis and translation of a letter written in 1866 by a Norwegian immigrant woman who had survived an attack on her family in Kandiyohi County during the Dakota War of 1862.

73. Christie, Jean. " 'An Earnest Enthusiasm for Education': Sarah Christie Stevens, Schoolwoman." *Minnesota History* 48 (Summer 1983): 245–54.

Traces life of spirited, assertive woman who saw education as a source of strength for women. Born in 1844, she began what was to become a long-term teaching career in 1863 in a one-room school in Wisconsin. Between 1873 and 1875, she taught at Carleton College in Northfield and later married a Good Thunder farmer. She became active in the Northwestern Alliance and the Woman's Christian Temperance Union and in 1890 was elected to one two-year term as Blue Earth County superintendent of schools.

74. Cleeland, Sylvia Asplund. *Dalkulla Anna: A Swedish Maid from Dalarna.* Honolulu, Hawaii: Fisher Printing Co., 1984. 252 p. Appendixes.

Biography of the author's mother, Anna Jansson Lingman Asplund (1867–1957), an immigrant to the U.S. in the 1890s. Offers detailed information about girlhood in the Dalarna region of Sweden, experiences as a homemaker in St. Paul and Mankato, 1889–1904, and later life in the Central Valley of California. Of particular interest are circumstances of Asplund's two marriages, her roles as a parent, and her activities as a widowed head of household.

75. Coen, Rena N. "Eliza Dillon Taliaferro: Portrait of a Frontier Wife." *Minnesota History* 52 (Winter 1990): 146–53.

Profiles Eliza Taliaferro (1792?–1875), describing her ten-year residence at Fort Snelling, 1828–38, as spouse of Indian agent Lawrence Taliaferro, relatives in St. Louis, and the couple's return to her home in Bedford, Penn., for the remainder of their lives. Also discusses 1830s portrait of Taliaferro, possibly painted by the Missouri artist George Caleb Bingham, and visits to several local attractions, including Lake Calhoun and Lake Harriet.

76. Cohn, Victor. *Sister Kenny: The Woman Who Challenged the Doctors.* Minneapolis: University of Minnesota Press, 1975. 302 p. Selected bibliography, notes, index, illustrations.

Profiles Australian nurse Sister Elizabeth Kenny

(1880–1952) and the rehabilitation techniques she developed for polio treatment. Pays special attention to establishment of Kenny Institute in Minneapolis and its operations in the 1940s and 1950s.

77. Dees, Janis White. "Anna Schoen-René: Minnesota Musical Pioneer." *Minnesota History* 48 (Winter 1983): 332–38.

Describes Schoen-René's 16-year stay in the Twin Cities from 1893 to 1909. The German-born musician organized operas, founded the University of Minnesota Choral Union, laid the foundation for the Minneapolis Symphony Orchestra, and advised the Minneapolis public schools and Twin Cities convent schools on music curricula.

78. "Donna S. Lind: Serving 1970–." *Hennepin County History* 33, no. 2 (Spring 1974): 13.

Profile of museum staff member at Hennepin County Historical Society in the 1970s. Describes multifaceted duties on the job, plus personal interests.

79. "Florence Earle Wichman . . . Civic Leader, Talented Minneapolis Musician." *Hennepin County History* 18, no. 4 (Spring 1959): 11–12.

Profile of Hennepin County Historical Society board member. Details training and career as professional singer, plus volunteer activities with Hennepin County Historical Society, the Minneapolis Public Library, and the Thursday Musical, among other organizations.

80. "Forgotten Pioneers . . . IV." *Ramsey County History* 4, no. 2 (Fall 1967): 18–20.

Brief biographical sketches of early women settlers of St. Paul, 1838–50s. Includes information about Mrs. Abraham Perry and her daughters Rose Perry Clewett (Mrs. James R.) and Adele Perry Guerin (Mrs. Vetal), Mary Turpin Robert (Mrs. Louis), Matilda Rumsey Megee (Mrs. Alexander), Mrs. M. L. Stoakes, and Mrs. J. W. Selby.

81. Foster, Mary Dillon, comp. *Who's Who Among Minnesota Women.* [St. Paul?]: Privately published, 1924. 380 p. Index, illustrations.

Profiles, many accompanied by portraits, of hundreds of women and women's organizations throughout Minnesota. Though not exhaustive, the sketches are broadly inclusive on many counts: regional representation statewide; Protestant, Catholic, Jewish, and Colored [sic] women's clubs; business, professional, social welfare, and cultural activities. Focus is on World War I and suffrage generation, but many 19th-century women are included.

82. Frear, D. W. "Mrs. Jennie Atwood Pratt." *Hennepin County History* 4, no. 15 (July 1944): 7–8.

Profile of childhood settler in Minnetonka and Minneapolis area describes her New England origins, family's activities in territorial Minnesota, and her own subsequent marriage to James Pratt.

83. Glass, Lauren Kay. "Katharine Densford Dreves: Marching at the Head of the Parade." Ph.D. diss., University of Illinois at Chicago, 1983. 289 p. Appendixes, bibliography.

Profiles Dreves (1890–1978) and her contributions to changing conditions and educational agendas in the nursing profession, 1915–59. Pays special attention to her directorship of the University of Minnesota School of Nursing, 1939–59, and her style of leadership in the university, professional associations, and international health care politics. Also describes her status as a single, professional woman who married upon retirement.

84. Hanson, Cynthia A. "Catheryne Cooke Gilman and the Minneapolis Better Movie Movement." *Minnesota History* 51 (Summer 1989): 202–16.

Describes social activist's work on motion picture reform in Minneapolis and nationally during the 1920s. Focuses on issues of community values and censorship, Gilman's role as founder of the Better Movie Movement Plan with the Women's Co-Operative Alliance (1920), a brief episode of cooperation with the Hayes Office in 1922, and testimony before the U.S. House of Representatives Education Committee in 1926. Also provides considerable discussion of Better Movie Movement operations in Minneapolis and biographical data about Gilman.

85. Howard, Jane. "Between the Lines: Emilie Buchwald of Minneapolis, Minnesota." *Lear's,* October 1989, [p. 150–53?].

Profiles cofounder of Milkweed Editions, a Minneapolis nonprofit press (established in 1984) specializing in experimental writing and art.

86. Johnson, Dolores D. "Clara Hampson Ueland and Marian Lucy Le Sueur: A Comparative Biography." Typescript, [197–?]. 62 p. Bibliography, footnotes. (MHS).

Unpublished paper provides parallel sketches of Minneapolis suffragist and social welfare reformer Clara Hampson Ueland (1860–1927) and midwestern radical activist Marian Lucy Le Sueur (1877–1954). Brief conclusion offers comparative comments about the women's lives.

87. Johnston, Patricia Condon. "Nelle Palmer of Stillwater: Entertainer and Innkeeper." *Minnesota History* 48 (Spring 1983): 207–12.

Profiles Nelle Obrecht Palmer (1893–1970), describing childhood as a professional performer in her family's touring musical troupe, Obrecht's Juvenile Concert Company, and young adult career in vaudeville and stock productions. Discusses transition to hotel business with husband and fellow trouper Arthur V. Palmer as vaudeville succumbed to motion pictures in the 1920s and the couple's successful management of Stillwater's Lowell Inn, 1930–70, using their theatrical background and years of travel experience.

88. Johnston, Patricia Condon. "Reflected Glory: The Story of Ellen Ireland." *Minnesota History* 48 (Spring 1982): 13–23.

Sister Seraphine, the sister of Archbishop John Ireland, spent 72 years in the Roman Catholic religious order of the Sisters of St. Joseph of Carondelet. During her 39-year tenure as Mother Superior of the St. Paul Province, the order opened 30 schools, five hospitals, St. Agatha's Conservatory, and the College of St. Catherine.

89. Kennelly, Sister Karen. "The Dynamic Sister Antonia and the College of St. Catherine." *Ramsey County History* 14, no. 1 (Fall–Winter 1978): 3–18.

Profiles Sister Antonia (1873–1944, family name Anna McHugh), who served as dean and later president of College of St. Catherine in St. Paul, 1914–37. Includes family history in North Dakota, education at convent schools and the University of Chicago, religious vocation, and association with the Sisters of St. Joseph of Carondelet.

90. Knight, Ginny. *A Sampler of Women.* Robbinsdale, Minn.: Guild Press, 1984. 56 p. Illustrations.

Profiles nine women active in business and professions in the 1980s: college professor Ginny Allery, physician Barbara Armstrong, writer Hazel Clayton, records manager Ann Marie Hoffman, pastor Diane Koob, journalist Carole Larson, corporate executive Diane Martindale, lawyer Carolyn Sandberg, politician and nun Jackie Slater. Emphasizes feminist and multicultural values.

91. Kreuter, Gretchen. "Kate Donnelly and the 'Cult of True Womanhood'." *Ramsey County History* 13, no. 1 (Fall–Winter 1976): 14–18.

Biographical sketch of Kate Donnelly (1833–94) contrasts author's 1970s feminist interpretation with husband Ignatius Donnelly's 1895 memoir of his wife. Includes a general discussion of 19th-century ideals about women, particularly the "cult of true womanhood" and its persistence in 20th-century life.

92. Lacey, Alice, ed. *South Dakota's American Mother: The Life Story of Christina K. Lacey.* Sioux Falls, S.Dak.: Pheasant Press, 1989. 148 p. Appendix, bibliography, index, illustrations.

Reminiscences published as a tribute to Christina Lacey's long life, 1879–1972. Lacey grew up near Carroll, Iowa, moved to South Dakota to teach, and later became active in home extension work.

93. Lamson, Peggy. *Few Are Chosen: American Women in Political Life Today.* Boston: Houghton Mifflin Co., 1968. 240 p. Index, illustrations.

Case studies produced in commemoration of the 50th anniversary of women's suffrage analyze the careers of ten women prominent in national politics in the mid-20th century. Includes profile of Eugenie Anderson, Democratic-Farmer-Labor activist from Red Wing who became ambassador to Denmark, Bulgaria, and the United Nations.

94. Le Sueur, Meridel. *Crusaders: The Radical Legacy of Marian and Arthur Le Sueur.* New York: Blue Heron Press, 1955; St. Paul: Minnesota Historical Society Press, Borealis Books, 1984. 109 p. Index, illustrations.

Memoir of author's mother Marian Wharton Le Sueur (1877–1954) and stepfather Arthur Le Sueur (1867–1950). Treats the Le Sueurs' experiences in Socialist politics in the Midwest and nationally. Considerable attention to their base in Minneapolis–St. Paul beginning around 1917, family and friendships, and biographical information.

95. LeVesconte, Lillie Belle Gibbs. *Little Bird That Was Caught: A Story of the Early Years of Jane DeBow Gibbs.* N.p., 1924. 26 p. Reprint. [St. Paul]: Ramsey County Historical Society, 1968. 54 p.

Biographical sketch of the author's mother focuses on Jane Gibbs's childhood experiences as an adopted member of the Reverend Jedediah and Julie Eggleston Stevens family. The Stevenses traveled to and worked at Midwest trading centers and missions of the 1830s and 1840s (Mackinac [Mich.], Prairie du Chien [Wis.], Lake Harriet [now Minneapolis], and Wabasha [now Winona]). (Note: The St. Paul farm homesteaded by Jane and her husband Heman Gibbs in 1849 is a historic site operated by the Ramsey County Historical Society.)

96. Lief, Julia Wiech. "A Woman of Purpose: Julia B. Nelson." *Minnesota History* 47 (Winter 1981): 302–14.

Describes the life of Julia Bullard Nelson who, after she became a widow in 1869 at age 26, worked for the American Missionary Association teaching at freedmen's schools in Texas and Tennessee. She later returned to her Red Wing home and became a principal organizer for the Minnesota Woman Suffrage Association and the Minnesota Woman's Christian Temperance Union.

97. Lortie, Jeanne Marie. "Mother Scholastica Kerst—I." *American Benedictine Review* 34 (June 1983): 130–48.

Focuses on childhood and early religious career of Benedictine nun Sister Scholastica Kerst, 1847–89. Describes church-sponsored education at St. Gertrude's Convent in Shakopee, St. Joseph's Convent in St. Mary's, Penn., and St. Benedict's Convent in Erie, Penn., 1862–75. Recounts duties and institutional politics of Kerst's tenure as superior of St. Joseph's Convent (later St. Benedict's Convent and Academy in St. Joseph in Kittson County), 1880–89. Discusses roles of parents Anna and Peter Kerst, German immigrants to St. Paul, in supporting their daughter's religious vocation.

98. Lortie, Jeanne Marie. "Mother Scholastica Kerst—II." *American Benedictine Review* 34 (September 1983): 268–90.

Profile of Kerst (1847–1911) describes her role in establishing Benedictine schools and hospitals in the Duluth diocese, 1889–1911. Focuses on Sacred Heart Institute (established 1895), Villa St. Scholastica (1909), and Kerst's role in developing a unified school system for the diocese in the 1890s. Discusses anti-Catholic sentiment in Duluth mobilized through the local branch of the American Protective Association (1890s). Also includes information about St. Benedict Hospital in St. Cloud (established 1886) and St. Mary's Hospital in Duluth (1896).

99. McBride, Genevieve. "Theodora Winton Youmans and the Wisconsin Woman Movement." *Wisconsin Magazine of History* 71 (Summer 1988): 243–75.

Describes work of president of Wisconsin Woman Suffrage Association, 1913–20. Between 1911 and 1920, Youmans also wrote more than 400 columns on suffrage for the *Waukesha Freeman* and researched and wrote a history of the suffrage movement in Wisconsin. Her study was published in the *Wisconsin Magazine of History* in 1921 and in volume 6 of Ida Husted Harper, ed., *History of Woman Suffrage,* in 1922.

100. McDonald, Sister Grace. "A Catholic Newspaper Woman and Novelist of the Pioneer West." *Mid-America* 17, ser. 6 (January 1935): 30–36.

Profiles editor and writer Julia Amanda Sargent Wood (1825–99?) who also wrote under the name Minnie Mary Lee. Wood published impressions of daily life in the Sauk Rapids area in the nationally circulated *Arthur's Home Magazine* and *Peterson Magazine* in the 1850s and 1860s. She edited the *New Era,* a newspaper published by her husband William H. Wood in Sauk Rapids, 1859–63, contributing essays, fiction, and poetry to its pages. Following her conversion to Roman Catholicism in the 1870s, Wood wrote five proselytizing novels on the conversion theme. The widowed Wood remained active in midwestern newspaper publishing in company with her son Delacey Wood.

101. Mikulak, Ellen, comp. "Anna Ramsey's Letters." *Ramsey County History* 9, no. 2 (Fall 1972): 17–22. Bibliography, notes.

Anna Ramsey's (1826–84) letters to family members in 1860s and 1870s. Documents domestic life with daughter Marion and husband Alexander, religious and charitable interests in St. Paul, and 1870 trip to Europe. Considerable detail about activities and perspectives within prominent family.

102. *Minnesota Woman's Yearbook, 1978–79.* Minneapolis: Sprague Publications, 1978. 176 p. Illustrations, index.

First edition of an annual publication listing women's resources and profiling women of accomplishment. Primarily Twin Cities individuals and institutions.

103. *Minnesota Women 1984.* St. Paul: Blue Sky Marketing, 1983. 26 p. Illustrations.

First edition of a calendar featuring writer Meridel Le Sueur, American-Indian activist Patricia Bellanger, restaurateur Reiko Weston, and Lt. Gov. Marlene Johnson, among others. Produced in association with the Minnesota branch of the National Organization for Women.

104. *Minnesota Women 1985.* St. Paul: Blue Sky Marketing, 1984. 26 p. Illustrations.

Second edition of a calendar featuring violinist Chouhei Min, farmer Norma Lee Hanson, state legislator Karen Clark, and Rabbi Stacy Offner, among others. Produced in association with the Minnesota branch of the National Organization for Women.

105. Mitchell, Ethel V., ed. *Contributions of Black Women to Minnesota History*. St. Paul: Mason Publishing Co., 1977. 118 p. Illustrations.

Commemorative volume published by the Bicentennial Committee of the National Council of Negro Women, Minnesota Section. Contains brief biographies of 70 African-American women active in Twin Cities religion, professions, politics, civic affairs, and entertainment, 1900–70s.

106. Morton, Zylpha S. "Harriet Bishop: Frontier Teacher." *Minnesota History* 28 (June 1947): 132–41.

Describes formation of St. Paul's first school in 1847. Harriet Bishop received special training for frontier teaching in a course Catharine Beecher conducted for the Board of National Popular Education in Albany, New York.

107. "Mrs. George C. Christian." *Hennepin County History* 17, no. 67 (July 1954): 3, 6.

Brief sketch of Carolyn McKnight Christian (1875–1964), donor of the present home of the Hennepin County Historical Society, notes her commitment to the Citizens' Aid Society and other charitable organizations in Minneapolis.

108. Noun, Louise. "Making Her Mark: Nellie Verne Walker, Sculptor." *Palimpsest* 68 (Winter 1987): 161–73.

Describes life of Iowa native who gained national recognition during the first half of the 20th century with her sculptures, many of which are located in Minnesota, Iowa, and Wisconsin. Her work includes the Iowa Suffrage Memorial in the state capitol in Des Moines.

109. Nute, Grace Lee. "Wilderness Marthas." *Minnesota History* 8 (September 1927): 247–59.

Sketches of Hester Crooks Boutwell, Catherine Bissell Ely, and Lucy Lewis. All were wives, homemakers, and teachers in missionary families of the 1840s and 1850s in north-central Minnesota. Article is organized around comparisons of "savage" and "civilized" life. Gives considerable attention to Boutwell and Ely's status as "half-breeds."

110. Pfannenstiel, B. R. "Anna Rathbun and *The Park Region Pioneer*." *Women's History Newsletter* 1, no. 1 (January/February 1990): 4–6.

Analyzes Rathbun's editorial positions and financial concerns as publisher of the *Pioneer* in Pelican Rapids, Otter Tail County, 1887–91. Notes Rathbun's claim to head the only general interest newspaper of its time managed entirely by women. Also describes other activities tried by Rathbun and her

sister Hattie Rowe to support themselves, including sales of sewing machines and other items, music lessons, and operation of a lunchroom.

111. "Pioneer Woman Threatens Indian." *Hennepin County History* 6, no. 22 (April 1946): 3.

Incidental note recounts Susan Hays Burns's domestic encounter with an Indian man wishing to trade. Taken from biography of Mrs. Joseph Justad of St. Louis Park.

112. Pratt, Linda Ray. "Woman Writer in the CP: The Case of Meridel Le Sueur." *Women's Studies* 14 (February 1988): 247–64.

Analyzes Le Sueur's career since the 1920s as well as her continued Communist party membership, in contrast with many writers who left the party during the late 1930s. Concludes that radical politics provided Le Sueur with more opportunities for publishing her work but also led to her being blacklisted during the 1950s.

113. Pruitt, Mary C. " 'Lady Organizer': Sabrie G. Akin and the *Labor World*." *Minnesota History* 52 (Summer 1991): 206–19.

Profiles Sabrie Goodwin Akin, a labor leader, newspaper publisher, and socialist feminist active in Duluth, 1895–1900. Describes her role as a "bridge builder" among diverse reform movements, including elite women's, business, temperance, and labor groups.

114. Robertson, Shiela C., and Kathleen Ann O'Brien. *A Social History of Women: Linda James Benitt*. N.p.: Women Historians of the Midwest, 1981. 57 p. Bibliography.

Profile of Hastings farmer Linda James Benitt (1891–). Includes material on public health training and career, poultry and fruit farming from 1930 to 1958, and activities as a Minnesota leader and teacher in the Agricultural Adjustment Administration (AAA), a New Deal agency. One in a series of curriculum packets in women's history developed by WHOM (Women Historians of the Midwest); an accompanying poster portrait of Benitt also produced.

115. Robertson, Shiela C., and Kathleen Ann O'Brien. *A Social History of Women: Mary Longley Riggs*. N.p.: Women Historians of the Midwest, 1982. 53 p.

Profile of Mary Longley Riggs (1813–69), a teacher and missionary to the Dakota Indians at Lac qui Parle, Traverse des Sioux, and Hazelwood. Includes information about her courtship and marriage to Stephen R. Riggs, their children, and their activities as a missionary family. One in a series of curriculum packets in women's history developed by WHOM (Women Historians of the Midwest); an accompanying poster portrait of Riggs also produced.

116. Robertson, Sheila C., and Kathleen Ann O'Brien. *A Social History of Women: Mathilda Tolksdorf Shillock.* N.p.: Women Historians of the Midwest, 1981. 68 p.

Profile of immigrant Mathilda Tolksdorf Shillock (1826–1910), a musician and intellectual from East Prussia. Includes information about family stays in New England, Texas, and Wisconsin and final settlement in Minnesota, first in New Ulm and later in St. Paul–Minneapolis. Considerable information about her work as a music teacher and her experiences raising children. One in a series of curriculum packets in women's history developed by WHOM (Women Historians of the Midwest); an accompanying poster portrait of Shillock also produced.

117. Robertson, Sheila C., and Kathleen Ann O'Brien. *A Social History of Women: Theresa Ericksen.* N.p.: Women Historians of the Midwest, 1982. 39 p. Bibliography.

Profile of Theresa Ericksen (1867–1943), a military nurse who served in the Philipines during the Spanish-American War and in France during World War I. Includes information about immigration to Minnesota from Norway, public health nursing, and veteran status. One in a series of curriculum packets in women's history developed by WHOM (Women Historians of the Midwest); an accompanying poster portrait of Ericksen also produced.

118. "Ruth Zalusky Thorstensen: Serving 1970–." *Hennepin County History* 33, no. 2 (Spring 1974): 11.

Briefly profiles curator and historian of the Hennepin County Historical Society. Special mention of successful Sunday afternoon program series she developed at museum and of longtime volunteer work at the institution prior to paid work there.

119. Scholand, Sister M. Joseph Clare. *The Woman of the Strong Heart.* Fargo, N.Dak.: Red River Historical Society, [1965?]. 21 p. Illustrations.

Profiles Benedictine nun Mother Monica Forkey (1882–). Includes Forkey's reminiscences of childhood in the Grand Forks area, religious education at Sacred Heart Institute in Duluth, hospital duties in Brainerd and Bemidji, and return to the Red River valley to serve as administrator of Crookston hospitals operated by the order and as prioress of Mount St. Benedict Community. Also describes

mission to children of Hispanic migrant laborers in the sugar beet industry.

120. Schubert, Esther. *Women of Wright County: A Volume of Biographies.* Edited by Caroline T. Westrum. Buffalo, Minn.: Wright Way Graphics, 1983. 115 p. Footnotes, illustrations.

Contains more than 200 sketches of 19th- and 20th-century women. Includes an essay about American-Indian women's lives, a note on nursing in the area, and other special features. Table of contents provides an alphabetical index to the biographies.

121. Solberg, Winton U. "Martha G. Ripley: Pioneer Doctor and Social Reformer." *Minnesota History* 39 (Spring 1964): 1–17.

Profiles Ripley (1843–1912), a prominent suffragist, obstetrician, and social reformer in Minneapolis. Describes childhood home in northeastern Iowa, relocation through marriage to Massachusetts, suffrage activities there, medical education at Boston University, and subsequent practice in Minneapolis, including founding of Maternity Hospital.

122. "A Spry 80, Lincoln Kin Runs Odd Shop." *Hennepin County History* 25, no. 2 (Fall 1965): 27.

Profile of Minneapolis businesswoman Katherine Todd and her card, gift, and picture framing shop in the 1940s–60s, plus family connection to President Abraham Lincoln. Reprint from *Minneapolis Sunday Tribune.*

123. Stuhler, Barbara, and Gretchen Kreuter, eds. *Women of Minnesota: Selected Biographical Essays.* St. Paul: Minnesota Historical Society Press, 1977. 402 p. Index.

Sixteen essays on individual and group subjects, from settlement period to 1970s. Concluding chapter offers 100 brief biographies of other Minnesota women. Essays consider Harriet Bishop, Kate Donnelly, Jane Grey Swisshelm, Eva McDonald Valesh, Maria Louise Sanford, Frances Densmore, Mary Molloy, Alice O'Brien, Maud Hart Lovelace, Gratia Alta Countryman, Cathryne Cooke Gilman, Ada Comstock Notestein, Anna Dickie Olesen, women legislators, Fanny Brin, and sisters Agnes, Henrietta, and Nora Larson.

124. Sundberg, Sara Brooks. "A Farm Woman on the Minnesota Prairie: The Letters of Mary E. Carpenter." *Minnesota History* 51 (Spring 1989): 186–93.

Analyzes letters to family and friends written from the Carpenter family's homesteads in Cascade Township, Olmsted County, and Grandview

Township, Lyon County, 1870–88. Provides descriptions of farm wife's daily activities and family's efforts, never realized, to farm clear of debt in southeastern and southwestern Minnesota. Also charts changes in Carpenter's point of view; optimistic through many trials, she became discouraged in the late 1880s. Her death in 1889 at age 49 was attributed to melancholy.

125. Tapping, Minnie E. "Bloomington Centenarian Does Her Own Work." *Hennepin County History* 6, no. 24 (October 1946): 6–7.
Profiles Hattie Scott Spinnings Chadwick, an 1860s immigrant to Minnesota from Canada via New York. Focuses on her lifelong industry as a homemaker.

126. Wagner, Sally Roesch. "The Pioneer Daughters Collection of the South Dakota Federation of Women's Clubs." *South Dakota History* 19 (Spring 1989): 95–109.
Describes Pioneer Daughters collection, 4,000–6,000 women's biographies gathered by South Dakota Federation of Women's Clubs member Marie Drew, 1940s–80s, and now held at South Dakota State Historical Society. The biographies focus on the social history of everyday life in 19th- and 20th-century South Dakota, particularly the experiences of homesteading women. American Indians, missionaries, and career and professional women also included. Many of the autobiographies provide a "revisionist" view of Indian-white relations, emphasizing peaceableness and cooperation, not hostility.

127. Whitney, Helen. *Maria Sanford.* Minneapolis: University of Minnesota Press, 1922. 322 p. Illustrations.
Profiles Sanford (1836–1920) and her career as a professor of rhetoric at the University of Minnesota, 1880–1909. Chronicles family, early life in Connecticut, education, and teaching at Swarthmore College in Pennsylvania in addition to Minnesota activities. Also discusses Sanford's unfortunate financial investments and her struggle (successful late in life) to collect a salary commensurate with that of male professors. First chapter is Sanford's unfinished autobiography.

128. Women's History Month, Inc. *Women of Minnesota.* St. Paul: The Organization, 1987. 11 p.
Poster features biographical sketches of Dakota mixed-blood Susan Frénièr Brown (1820–1904), African-American civil rights activist Ethel Ray Nance (1899–), union leader and Democratic-

Farmer-Labor politician Myrtle Cain (1894–1980), African-American pioneer Mattie Porter Jackson (1854–1946), ethnomusicologist Frances Densmore (1867–1957), Ojibway informant to Densmore No dinens (c.1834–1919), and Mexican-American businesswoman and craftsperson Theresa Menchacu Muñoz (1919–). Also includes brief notes about 44 additional Minnesota women.

129. Wood, Sharon E. "My Life Is Not Quite Useless: The 1866 Diary of an Asylum Bookkeeper." *Palimpsest* 70 (Spring 1989): 2–13.
Rhoda Amanda Shelton's journal demonstrates the experience of an educated, middle-class woman employed at the Iowa Hospital for the Insane at Mount Pleasant. She describes her daily life, including contact with patients.

130. Woods, K. G., Shiela C. Robertson, and Kathleen Ann O'Brien. *A Social History of Women: Caroline Seabury.* N.p.: Women Historians of the Midwest, 1982. 45 p.
Profile of Caroline Seabury (1828–90?) based on diaries written from 1854 to 1862. Focuses on her experiences as a New Englander teaching in the South and mid-Civil War travels back to the North. She joined her brother Channing Seabury and his family in St. Paul later in the 1860s. One in a series of curriculum packets in women's history developed by WHOM (Women Historians of the Midwest); an accompanying poster portrait of Seabury also produced.

131. Young, Carrie. *Nothing to Do but Stay: My Pioneer Mother.* Iowa City: University of Iowa Press, 1991. 117 p. Illustrations.
Reminiscence about author's mother, Carrie Gafkjen Berg, a Norwegian immigrant who homesteaded near Williston, N.Dak., in 1904. The author reveals the struggles of prairie farm life during the depression of the 1930s, her parents' determined belief in the value of education, and a social life that centered on holiday celebrations.

AUTOBIOGRAPHY

132. Biesanz, Mavis Hiltunen. *Helmi Mavis, A Finnish-American Girlhood.* St. Cloud: North Star Press, 1989. 199 p. Illustrations, glossary of Finnish terms.
Memoir of girlhood in Finnish farming community of Vermilion Lake Township, St. Louis County, in the 1920s. Focuses on daily life, plus Finnish and American community events and institutions.

133. Bishop, Harriet E. *Floral Home; Or, First Years of Minnesota.* New York: Sheldon, Blakeman and Co., 1857. 342 p. Illustrations.

Memoir of schoolteacher and religious leader's first decade in St. Paul in the late 1840s and early 1850s combines reminiscence with travel writing and emigration tract. Includes detailed account of her journey west, early social life and customs, and educational activities.

134. Bliss, Olive Irene Hills. *The Miles of Yesterday: The Life Story of a Minnesota Woman.* St. Paul: Privately published, 1935. 43 p.

Describes childhood in Cannon City area (Rice County), schoolteaching in Rice County, education at Carleton College in Northfield, courtship and marriage to Alden Southworth Bliss, family life in various Wisconsin communities and St. Paul, widowhood, and extended journeys with adult children to the East Coast, Southwest, and other areas of the Midwest. Considerable detail throughout concerning social life and customs among business and professional people in her circle, 1860–1935. Also of interest due to frank discussion of family matters such as deaths of children and reactions to remarriage.

135. Bozarth-Campbell, Alla. *Womanpriest: A Personal Odyssey.* New York: Paulist Press, 1978. 229 p.

Reminiscence of author's intellectual and spiritual journey to become one of the first women priests in the Episcopal church when the Bishop of Minnesota recognized her priesthood in January 1978. The book relates the politics involved in the controversy over the ordination of women.

136. Bunkers, Suzanne L. " 'Faithful Friend': Nineteenth-Century Midwestern American Women's Unpublished Diaries." *Women's Studies International Forum* 10, no. 1 (1987): 7–17.

Explores theoretical and methodological questions regarding the writing and interpretation of women's diaries. Based on a study of manuscripts located in state, county, and local historical societies in Minnesota, Iowa, and Wisconsin.

137. Chase, Olivia Carpenter. "A Letter from a Pioneer." *Hennepin County History* 11, no. 44 (October 1951): 8–9.

Letter written to Maine relatives in 1854 describes early settlement conditions in St. Anthony (now Minneapolis) and Otsego Township in Wright County. Includes discussion of family connections in the area and hired girls' wages and availability.

138. Clapp, Louise Clements. "Portraits of Herstory: An Oral History of Four Midwest Women Who Survived the Great Depression." Honors thesis, Macalester College, 1985. 181 p.

Three of the four informants discuss daily life and work in the Yugoslav communities of St. Louis County. Anne Gelivich [Gerlovich] Hargrave of Duluth describes her childhood during the 1920s and 1930s and adult work experiences in labor and union circles, Democratic-Farmer-Labor politics, and nursing. Veda [Ponikvar] (note: family name not given in work) reminisces about growing up in a mining family in Chisholm, college education at Drake University in Iowa, participation in Democratic-Farmer-Labor politics, and founding the *Chisholm Free Press* (1947). Theresa (note: no surname given) remembers her 1929 marriage, family life on a small farm outside Gilbert in the 1930s, and relocation to St. Paul for husband's World War II factory job in 1942.

139. Colvin, Sarah Tarleton. *A Rebel in Thought.* New York: Island Press, 1944. 245 p.

Sarah Tarleton Colvin (1865–1949), a self-described feminist and nonconformist, was raised in the post-Civil War South and spent her adulthood working as a homemaker and volunteer in St. Paul. Includes descriptions of nursing training and employment in the 1890s, subsequent volunteer activities in the health field, local and national participation in the suffrage movement, and state board of education work in 1930s. Includes considerable information about dynamics and communication within author's marriage to physician Alexander Colvin.

140. Douglas, Bessie Pettit. *Call Back Yesterday.* Minneapolis: Privately printed, 1949. 362 p. Index, illustrations.

Memoir of author's childhood and young womanhood in Minneapolis, 1870s–90s. Includes extensive descriptions of prosperous and socially active family's home, social activities, and recreational travel. Frequent references to father Curtis Pettit's business affairs (grain and lumber) relative to family budget and scale of activities. Concludes with courtship and marriage to lawyer George Perkins Douglas in 1899.

141. Edelman, Edith Linoff. *The Wisdom of Love.* Minneapolis: EMLE, 1981. 222 p. Illustrations.

Autobiography of volunteer active in Jewish community affairs in Minneapolis, 1930s–. Describes emigration from Russia in 1922, education and early work experiences in St. Paul, and subsequent marriage(s) and family life in Minneapolis.

142. Elsmith, Dorothy Olcott. "Lake Superior Memories." *Inland Seas* 36, no. 2 (Summer 1980): 96–100.
Reminiscence of girlhood in Duluth in the 1890s and early 1900s. Describes social life and customs among wealthy families associated with mining, railroading, and shipping interests. Includes accounts of a ship's christening, a debutante party that coincided with a shipwreck, and Great Lakes cruises on ore boats fitted with luxurious passenger accommodations.

143. Franklin, Penelope, ed. *Private Pages: Diaries of American Women, 1830s–1970s.* New York: Ballantine Books, 1986. 490 p. Illustrations.
Collection of edited diaries written by 13 women across the country, 1830s–1970s, is organized via life cycle—youth through old age. The writers focus on everyday experiences and on inner dialogues with themselves and/or future readers. Includes journals of Minneapolis social worker Martha Lavell, 1926–38. Her writings describe college education at Mills College in California and the University of Minnesota, family life with mother and sister, early jobs, and attitudes concerning courtship and sexuality.

144. Furness, Marion Ramsey. "Recollections of Old St. Paul." *Minnesota History* 29 (June 1948): 114–29.
Contains reminiscences gathered in 1934 by the daughter of Alexander and Anna Ramsey in preparation for a talk at St. Paul's New Century Club. Her recollections include her childhood in St. Paul in the late 1850s, her first trip to Europe in 1869, and the visit of President Rutherford B. Hayes to the Ramsey house in 1878.

145. Gág, Wanda. *Growing Pains: Diaries and Drawings for the Years 1908–1917.* New York: Coward McCann, 1940; St. Paul: Minnesota Historical Society Press, Borealis Books, 1984. 475 p. Illustrations.
Edited journal covers Gág's life from ages 15 to 24, spanning girlhood in New Ulm and art studies in Minneapolis and St. Paul. Extensive descriptions of family arrangements and activities (including straitened circumstances), as well as artistic interests and education.

146. Gluck, Sherna, ed. *From Parlor to Prison: Five American Suffragists Talk About Their Lives.* New York: Octagon, 1976. 285 p. Bibliography, illustrations.
Includes information on the life of Sylvie Thygeson, who arrived in St. Paul in the late 1880s and, along with others, later organized the Woman's Welfare League to educate women about suffrage and birth control. By 1917 she and several other prominent St. Paul women had organized a birth control clinic, which encountered difficulty with Minnesota's strict law against distributing contraceptive information. The chapter on Sylvie Thygeson is based on two interviews made with her in 1972 when she was 104 years old.

147. Green, Anne Bosanko. *One Woman's War: Letters Home from the Women's Army Corps, 1944–1946.* St. Paul: Minnesota Historical Society Press, 1989. 308 p. Illustrations.
Author's correspondence reveals her experiences in basic training at Fort Des Moines, Iowa, and her life as a surgical technician working at U.S. Army hospitals in a variety of locations throughout the country. Excerpts from her parents' letters reflect wartime life in Minneapolis. A foreword by military historian D'Ann Campbell places the letters in historical context.

148. Green, Anne Bosanko. "Private Bosanko Goes to Basic: A Minnesota Woman in World War II." *Minnesota History* 51 (Fall 1989): 246–58.
Includes letters to and from Minneapolis native Anne Bosanko who joined the Women's Army Corps on her 20th birthday in 1944. She relates stories of basic training and social life at Fort Des Moines, Iowa.

149. Greenman, Frances Cranmer. *Higher Than the Sky.* New York: Harper and Brothers, 1954. 305 p. Illustrations.
Wry autobiography of Minneapolis portraitist Frances Cranmer Greenman (1890–1981). Includes reminiscences of childhood in South Dakota, East Coast art education, social life and portrait commissions in Minneapolis, 1920s–50s, and lifelong international travel. Youthful adventures include a painting expedition to the Ojibway communities of north-central Minnesota. Considerable attention given to balance between family and professional responsibilities throughout the memoir.

150. Hiscock, Jennie Isabelle. "I Remember: Fond Recollections of a Long and Interesting Life." *Hennepin County History* 38, no. 4 (Winter 1979–80): 3–12.
Author's reminiscence of girlhood in southeast Minneapolis during the 1880s. Describes daily activities of a prosperous family, neighbors, and children's games.

151. Jaques, Florence Page. *Canoe Country.* Minneapolis: University of Minnesota Press, 1938; St. Paul:

Minnesota Historical Society Press, Borealis Books, 1989. 78 p. Illustrations.

> Chronicles 1927 trip, the author's honeymoon with artist-naturalist husband Francis Lee Jaques, in the area that became the Boundary Waters Canoe Area of Minnesota and Canada. Provides autobiographical and natural history perspectives.

152. Jaques, Florence Page. *Snowshoe Country.* Minneapolis: University of Minnesota Press, 1944; St. Paul: Minnesota Historical Society Press, Borealis Books, 1989. 110 p. Illustrations.

> Describes trip to Basswood and Gunflint lakes in the area that became the Boundary Waters Canoe Area of Minnesota and Canada in the winter of 1942. Focuses on changing seasons and wildlife habitat. Includes a description of Justine and Bill Kerfoot's Gunflint Lodge as well as other resources and individuals in the region.

153. Jellison, Katherine. " 'Sunshine and Rain in Iowa': Using Women's Autobiography as a Historical Source." *Annals of Iowa* 49 (Winter 1989): 591–99.

> Discusses diary of Ada Mae Brinton (1891–1977?) of Stuart, Iowa, as a historical source. Focuses on interpretive aspects of the diary, its record of daily life during World War II, and descriptions of women's roles in family and public affairs.

154. Kerfoot, Justine. *Woman of the Boundary Waters: Canoeing, Guiding, Mushing and Surviving.* Grand Marais, Minn.: Women's Times Publishing, 1986. 200 p. Index, illustrations, glossary.

> Reminiscence of the author's activities as operator of a resort, citizen, and outdoor writer from Gunflint Lake in the Boundary Waters Canoe Area, 1927–85. Includes considerable information about family, friends, natural history, and recreation.

155. "The Laycocks, Pioneers of St. Louis Park." *Hennepin County History* 5, no. 19 (July 1945): 5.

> Incidental historical note includes Mrs. Laycock's reminiscences concerning female friendships and a runaway oxen adventure in the early settlement period of Hennepin County. (Note: No first names given.)

156. Mann, Ruth H. "Fifty Years in Retrospect: My Life 1921–1971." *Hennepin County History* 32, no. 3 (Summer 1973): 14–16.

> Memoir of activities in mixed rural/suburban community of Minnewashta, Hennepin County, 1920s–70, focuses on author's experiences with domestic responsibilities, Minnewashta Congregational Church, substitute teaching, and later antique business.

157. Månsson, Evelina. *Amerika Minnen: Upplevelsen ock iakttagelser från en 6-årig vistelse i U.S.A.* Hvetlanda, Sweden: Svenska Allmogeförlaget, 1930. 109 p.

> Personal account of young Swedish woman who migrated to Minnesota and remigrated in the early 20th century. She describes her journey and her life as a domestic in Hector, Renville County. She soon moved to Minneapolis where she worked as a cleaning woman in the Metropolitan Building and the Phoenix Building and as a seamstress at the Sterling Manufacturing Company and the Weum Watt Company. She also recalls her social life in Minneapolis, particularly in the Elliot Park neighborhood.

158. McCarthy, Mary. *Memories of a Catholic Girlhood.* New York: Harcourt, Brace and Co., 1946. 245 p. Illustrations.

> Orphaned as a result of the influenza epidemic of 1918, the author describes five difficult years spent with harsh Irish Catholic relatives in Minneapolis, 1918–23. Provides considerable detail concerning child-rearing practices and attitudes under relatively uncommon circumstances.

159. Meusberger, Joanne Wilson. "Farm Girl: Part 1." *Palimpsest* 68 (Winter 1987): 146–59.

> Describes Sac County, Iowa, farm life in late 1930s and the 1940s with a focus on play, holidays, and special occasions.

160. Meusberger, Joanne Wilson. "Farm Girl: Part 2." *Palimpsest* 69 (Spring 1988): 35–48.

> Provides picture of Sac County, Iowa, farm life in 1940s and 1950s with an emphasis on 4-H projects, threshing, and other work.

161. Micka, Mary Virginia. *Climbing Light.* St. Paul: Privately published, 1990. 30 p.

> Selections from journals written in 1982–84 by woman religious and teacher of literature at College of St. Catherine in St. Paul. Topics include teaching responsibilities, balance between writing ambitions and congregational claims, and continuing reinterpretations of personal and family history.

162. Micka, Mary Virginia. *See You in the Morning.* St. Paul: Privately published, 1986. 24 p.

> Selections from 1982 journal written by woman religious and teacher of literature at College of St. Catherine in St. Paul while on sabbatical in Cazenovia, N.Y. Topics include women's experience of aging, relationship of spiritual life to daily occupations, and writing career.

163. Mitchell, Mary Atkinson. "Growing Up at 'Overlook'." *Hennepin County History* 48, no. 4 (Fall 1989): 11–20.

Reminiscence of author's childhood in Groveland Terrace, an affluent Minneapolis neighborhood, 1916–29. Includes descriptions of family home, domestic help, neighbors, and some social and educational activities.

164. Newson, Mary Jeannette. "Memories of Fort Snelling in Civil War Days." *Minnesota History* 15 (December 1934): 395–404.

Childhood reminiscence of life at the fort while her father ran the commissary. Her recollections include the arrival of the first train at Mendota, a gala dinner party, and the jubilation at hearing word of Lee's surrender.

165. "Postscripts." *Minnesota History* 49 (Spring 1985): 202–3.

Olga Marie Gustafson's reminiscence of her experience as an American Red Cross relief worker in Duluth at the time of the October 12, 1918, Cloquet forest fire.

166. Redeen, Hilda. "Hilda . . . Still Sews, Knits and Crochets." *Hennepin County History* 30, no. 4 (Spring–Summer 1971): 14–20.

Author's recollections of her childhood as member of a poor Swedish immigrant family in communities of Carver and Hopkins, her apprenticeship to a Minneapolis seamstress in 1896, and her long career as a seamstress with a Minneapolis and suburban Hennepin County clientele.

167. Rice, Matilda W. "The 4th of July in the 1850s." *Minnesota History* 49 (Summer 1984): 54–55.

In an account written for the June 27, 1895, *St. Paul Dispatch,* the author describes a less-than-elegant ball held at St. Paul's American House hotel in the early 1850s.

168. Richards, Eva L. Alvey. "Child Pioneer." *Minnesota History* 33 (Summer 1952): 72–76.

Childhood reminiscence of the summer of 1894 in St. Louis County. The author focuses on her eventual success in convincing her parents to allow her to remain at home and attend a local school with Ojibway children.

169. Richards, Eva L. Alvey. "Schoolgirl of the Indian Frontier." *Minnesota History* 33 (Autumn 1952): 105–11.

Autobiographical account describes 1894–95 school year in rural St. Louis County. The author recounts daily trip with neighboring Ojibway children and the culture shock of the Indian children in the segregated classroom.

170. Riley, Glenda. "Women's History from Women's Sources: Three Examples from Northern Dakota." *North Dakota History* 52, no. 2 (Spring 1985): 2–9.

Reviews stereotypes of western women—"gentle tamers," "calamity janes," "fighting feminists," and so on. Offers contrasting data from documents written by women describing their daily lives. Includes excerpts from the 1885 diary of Mary Hetty Bonar, a Wadena schoolteacher whose summer adventure was cooking for a cattle drive in North Dakota; Ellen Stebbins Emery's 1889 letter to relatives describing a destructive fire on the family farm near Emerado, N.Dak.; and Emily Lindstrom's reminiscence of her childhood in a Swedish-American community in rural Grand Forks County, N.Dak., in the 1870s.

171. Schoen-René, Anna Eugénie. *America's Musical Inheritance: Memories and Reminiscences.* New York: G. P. Putnam's Sons, 1941. 244 p. Index, illustrations.

Reminiscence of German-born singer and voice teacher. Section on her life in Minneapolis, ca. 1893–1909, includes descriptions of music education at the University of Minnesota and in Minneapolis public schools, her own conducting experiences, her role in bringing touring European musical artists to the Midwest, and her role in organizing a permanent symphony orchestra in Minneapolis.

172. Swisshelm, Jane Grey. *Crusader and Feminist: Letters of Jane Grey Swisshelm, 1858–1865.* Edited by Arthur J. Larsen. St. Paul: Minnesota Historical Society, 1934. 327 p. Index.

Selected letters to the *St. Cloud Democrat* by St. Cloud editor Jane Grey Swisshelm. Many of the letters were written in the course of Minnesota speaking tours devoted to antislavery and feminist causes. These describe local communities, hospitality, and personalities in addition to state and national politics.

173. Thompson, Era Bell. *American Daughter.* Chicago: University of Chicago Press, 1946; St. Paul: Minnesota Historical Society Press, Borealis Books, 1986. 296 p.

Memoir of African-American girlhood in Driscoll, Bismarck, and Mandan, N.Dak., and St. Paul, 1910s–20s. Includes education at University of North Dakota and Morningside College in Sioux City, Iowa, and experiences as college graduate in

Chicago during the 1930s. Provides comparative perspectives regarding life with and without the support of a large African-American community.

174. Ueland, Brenda. *Me.* New York: G. P. Putnam's Sons, 1939; St. Paul: The Schubert Club, 1983. 351 p.

Describes writer Brenda Ueland's (1891–1983) Minneapolis childhood in home of parents, Judge Andreas Ueland and suffragist-reformer Clara Hampson Ueland, and her East Coast education, work experiences, and marriages. Includes her return to Minnesota in the 1930s and participation in the intellectual life of the Twin Cities.

175. Ullmann, Amelia. "Pioneer Homemaker." *Minnesota History* 34 (Autumn 1954): 96–105.

Reminiscence of life in St. Paul, 1855–65. The author joined her husband, who had established a fur and hide business, and encountered numerous difficulties, including crowded and bedbug-infested living quarters, poor-quality food, and less-than-adequate schools. Although this article does not discuss the subject of religion, it should be noted that members of the Ullmann family were leaders within the Jewish community.

176. Wakefield, Sarah F. *Six Weeks in the Sioux Tepees; A Narrative of Indian Captivity.* Shakopee, Minn.: Argus Book and Job Printing Office, 1864; Fairfield, Wash.: Ye Galleon Press, 1988. 90 p. Index, illustrations.

Describes events of Dakota War of 1862 in the vicinity of the Yellow Medicine (Upper Sioux) Agency, including author's capture and that of her children. Detailed account of their captivity, defense of the Dakota who assisted them, and selective critique of later investigation and executions. Of interest as personal narrative and as discussion of attitudes toward the Dakota at that time.

177. Woodward, Mary Dodge. *The Checkered Years: A Bonanza Farm Diary, 1884–88.* Edited by Mary Boynton Cowdrey. Caldwell, Idaho: Caxton Printers, Ltd., 1937; St. Paul: Minnesota Historical Society Press, Borealis Books, 1989. 265 p. Illustrations.

Diary kept by Mary Dodge Woodward, 1884–88, principal homemaker on a North Dakota wheat farm managed by her son Walter Woodward. Focuses on daily work and recreational activities of family and harvest crews, weather and growing conditions, family and friends in Wisconsin, and the author's situation as widowed mother of adult children. New introduction by Elizabeth Jameson.

⊪/ Social Life

FAMILY AND KINSHIP

178. Bell, Ida Pickett. "A Pioneer Family of the Middle Border." *Minnesota History* 14 (September 1933): 303–15.

Pioneer reminiscence focuses on family life in Itasca, Freeborn County, 1860–65, from a child's point of view. Describes emigration from Wisconsin, friends and relatives in Minnesota, homemaking and farming, and effects of the Dakota War of 1862 and the Civil War.

179. Buehler, Cheryl Ann. "The Divorce Transition and Family Functioning." Ph.D. diss., University of Minnesota, 1983. 206 p. Bibliography, appendixes.

Study investigates family experiences of divorced parents two years after final decree issued. Considers economic, housing, legal, coparental, and remarriage dimensions. Based on early 1970s research in Twin Cities metropolitan area. Identifies marked differences in women's and men's concerns. For women, economic well-being was primary; for men, parental visitation and functioning were paramount.

180. Byrum, Mildred L. "Mother-Child Interaction in Test Anxious Boys." Ph.D. diss., University of Minnesota, 1965. 85 p. References, appendixes.

Psychology study investigates mother-child interaction as a component of test anxiety. Based on 1960s research conducted with elementary students in a suburban St. Paul school district. Findings suggest that mothers of test-anxious boys evaluate their children's performance more negatively than mothers of low-anxiety participants.

181. Critchfield, Richard. *Those Days: An American Album.* Garden City, N.Y.: Doubleday, Anchor Press, 1986. 419 p. Illustrations, notes on sources.

Social history of a middle-class family (the author's own) in small towns in Iowa and North Dakota, 1880–1940. Focus is on family history and dynamics, particularly the marriage of parents Anna Louise Williams and James Critchfield, amidst changing culture and technology.

182. Doyle, Patrick M. "Child Custody and Mediation: A Two Year Follow-Up." Ph.D. diss., University of Minnesota, 1984. 258 p. Appendix, bibliography.

Exploratory study of families contesting child custody rulings as part of divorce action. Based on 1978–81 research with Hennepin County families referred to custody mediation. Documents several styles of parental response to divorce and custody disputes, including self-determination of custody and visitation rights and joint custody.

183. Geiger, Steven Paul. "Perceived Stressor Events and Life Changes of Spouses of Licensed Peace Officers." Ph.D. diss., University of Minnesota, 1983. 93 p. Bibliography, appendixes.

Explores stresses affecting families. Based on 1982 research with spouses of urban, suburban, and rural peace officers' in Minnesota. Considerable information about domestic and family life.

184. Hopmann, Marita Raubitschek. "Conversations with Young Children: Mothers and Fathers as Playmates and Teachers." Ph.D. diss., University of Minnesota, 1984. 226 p. References, bibliography.

Child psychology study exploring the nature of parent-child conversations with particular attention to possible differences in the ways that mothers versus fathers talk with their toddlers. Based on 1980s research at the Institute for Child Development, University of Minnesota. This study finds diversity in parental conversational techniques and outcomes, but it is not gender based.

185. Howell, Mary Catherine. "Some Effects of Chronic Illness on Children and Their Mothers." Ph.D. diss., University of Minnesota, 1962. 93 p.

Comparative study of psychological differences between ill and well children and their mothers conducted at University of Minnesota Hospitals in Minneapolis in the early 1960s.

Lee Ngook Kum Huie and her son, Wing Young Huie, smiled for a snapshot about 1959 in their home in Duluth, where Huie family members have long been respected businesspeople.

186. Jones, Thelma. "From the Diary of Mary Ann Fogelsanger, Long Lake Pioneer." *Hennepin County History* [19, no. 4] (Spring 1960): 6–9.

Diary entries written between 1868 and 1872 describe daily tasks, home medications, illness and death of infant son, husband's illness and recovery, and social and recreational activities within Long Lake community.

187. *Minnesota Governor's Conference on Families.* [St. Paul]: Minnesota State Planning Agency and the Council on the Economic Status of Women, 1978. 28 p. Appendix.

Summarizes proceedings of May 1978 conference convened to give policy makers and service providers an opportunity to examine pressures on contemporary families. Discusses financial matters, diverse family structures, racial and ethnic diversity, and support systems.

188. Scott, Winifred Joanna. "Attachment and Child Abuse: A Study of Social History Indicators Among Mothers of Abused Children." Ph.D. diss., University of Minnesota, 1974. 67 p. References, appendix.

Study of personal histories of mothers of abused children. Based on research with families referred to Ramsey County Child Abuse Team, 1970–74. Documents correlation between trauma in mothers' childhoods and incidence of abuse in later child rearing.

189. Spaulding, Patricia Parlin. "Perception of Family Work Roles: Couple Preference Patterns, Contextual Variables and Resource Adequacy." Ph.D. diss., University of Minnesota, 1988. 171 p. Appendixes, bibliography.

Study explores family work allocation between wives and husbands in selected Twin Cities households in 1983. Findings report a significant desire on the part of women and some men respondents for greater participation of men in family work. Also suggests that relative youth is single most important predictor of desire for change in family routines.

190. Thompson, Judith Rann. "Coping Patterns of Mothers Who Have Given Birth to a Child with Disabilities." Ph.D. diss., University of Minnesota, 1983. 161 p. References, appendixes.

Educational psychology study explores emotions and behaviors reported by mothers of children with disabilities. Focus is on developmental rather than physical disabilities. Based on 1982–83 research in Twin Cities metropolitan area. Findings document chronic trauma and grief, often in conjunction with acceptance among participating parents. Suggests that medical doctors are often slower than mothers to acknowledge disabilities. Also notes association between disability and divorce.

191. United States War Department. *Pilgrimage for the Mothers and Widows of Soldiers, Sailors, and Marines of the American Forces Now Interred in the Cemeteries of Europe.* Washington, D.C.: GPO, 1930. 339 p.

Organized by state, this national directory lists names and addresses of World War I decedents' survivors eligible to participate in the pilgrimage and describes program costs. Contains entries from 80 Minnesota counties.

192. Ward, Mary Josephine. "Maternal Behavior with Firstborns and Secondborns in the Same Family: Evidence for Consistency in Family Relations." Ph.D. diss., University of Minnesota, 1983. 201 p. References, tables, appendixes.

Developmental psychology study investigates mother-child interaction. Based on early 1980s research with working class and disadvantaged families using Minneapolis prenatal clinics. Findings report high degree of competence among participating mothers generally and suggest that these mothers gained experience and confidence with first-born children that was later applied to second-borns.

193. Watts, Janine Ann. "Stress and Satisfaction in Adult Child-Parent Relationships as Reported by Daughters and Mothers." Ph.D. diss., University of Minnesota, 1983. 164 p. References, appendixes.

Family-life study explores factors that contribute, positively or negatively, to mother-young adult daughter relationships and the congruence within mothers' and daughters' descriptions of their relationships. Based on 1982 research with students at University of Minnesota–Duluth and their mothers. Findings report life-style decisions on part of parents and children as source of greatest stress and independent decision making and shared activities as source of greatest pleasure.

MARRIAGE

194. Asher, Ramona Marie. "Ambivalence, Moral Career and Ideology: A Sociological Analysis of the Lives of Women Married to Alcoholics." Ph.D. diss., University of Minnesota, 1988. 373 p. References, appendixes.

Sociology study analyzes wives' perspectives regarding their lives with alcoholic husbands. Based on 1980s(?) interviews with Twin Cities area informants. Focuses on processes of discovery and definition of "problem drinking" and its consequences in terms of marital and family life, treatment, and broader social life.

195. Bruce, John Allen. "Maternal Involvement in the Courtship of Daughters." Ph.D. diss., University of Minnesota, 1972. 261 p. Bibliography, appendix.

Sociological study compares widely held belief that parents should not or do not participate in children's courtships with actual family behaviors. Identifies mothers and daughters as the family members most directly involved in the "marital launching" process. Findings report that mothers who work outside the home are less involved in daughters' courtships and suggest that these mothers may see work as an alternative social placement to marriage. Based on 1970 research with Minnesota mothers and daughters.

196. Budd, Linda Gail Stevenson. "Problems, Disclosure, and Commitment of Cohabiting and Married Couples." Ph.D. diss., University of Minnesota, 1976. 161 p. Bibliography, appendixes.

Study exploring cohabitation and its potential effects on marriage. Based on comparative research with cohabiting and married couples in the Twin Cities area in the mid-1970s. Specifically concerned with existence of problems, expression of commitment, and communication among cohabiting couples.

197. Cheek, Gael Frances. "Power and Ideology in Marriage: A Reexamination of Resource and Normative Theory Using Multiple Measures of Power." Ph.D. diss., University of Minnesota, 1987. 178 p. Bibliography, appendixes.

Investigates balance of power in marriage. Based on 1983 research with adult women students at the University of Minnesota and their husbands. Describes multiple dimensions of power, focusing on "outcomes" and "processes" in marital decision-making. Reports positive relationship between "liberal" beliefs held by wife and husband and women's power in marriage.

198. Duke, Joan Evelyn Mayer. "An Investigation of Perceived Equity in Dual-Earner Marriages." Ph.D. diss., University of Minnesota, 1988. 204 p. References, appendixes.

Counseling study investigates the occurrence and the interpretation of household task-sharing among Twin Cities area married couples. Based on 1986 research, the study examines the concept of equity (defined as fairness) rather than equality of task division. Findings indicate that there is significant male participation, particularly in child care and "masculine" tasks such as lawn mowing and household repairs. Reports of equity are more closely linked to positive marital adjustment than to specific task performance.

199. Henze, Diane Lee. "Equity in Family Work Role Among Dual Career Couples: The Relationship of Demographic, Socioeconomic, Attitudinal and Personality Factors." Ph.D. diss., University of Minnesota, 1984. 218 p. References, appendixes.

Study investigates household task division among two-career couples in relationship to age, education, income, job hours, family stage, continuity of wife's employment, sex role attitudes, and selected personality factors. Based on 1983 research with professional couples in the Minneapolis–St. Paul region. Context is women's greater participation in household and family maintenance. Men's participation in household tasks most clearly linked to positive attitudes toward women's rights and to income parity on part of wife.

200. Hudgens, Alletta Jervey. "Toward a Theory of Human Energy in Couples." Ph.D. diss., University of Minnesota, 1982. 128 p. Bibliography, appendixes.

Study explores human energy among dual-career and "traditional" middle-class couples. Considerable information about daily routines and marriage styles within the two groups. Finds significant differences in the ways women and men locate and describe energy resources.

201. Maher, Michael. "Letters to Fannie Higgins: The Courtship of Patrick O'Brien." *Ramsey County History* 14, no. 2 (1979): 3–11.

Discusses the 1870s courtship conducted largely by correspondence between Hudson, Wis., dressmaker Fannie Higgins and St. Paul postal worker Patrick O'Brien. Focuses on O'Brien's experiences and self-presentation. Considerable information about dynamics between the two people and social patterns of courtship.

202. Maher, Michael. "The Liberated Woman Patrick O'Brien Married." *Ramsey County History* 14, no. 2 (1979): 12–15.

Discusses the 1870s courtship conducted largely by correspondence between Hudson, Wis., dress-

maker Fannie Higgins and St. Paul postal worker Patrick O'Brien. Includes information about Hudson business, Higgins's family, daily activities, and speculation as to Higgins's actions and feelings in areas not covered by letters.

203. Robinson, Beatrice Ellen. "Former Spouse Conflict: During Marriage, Divorce, and Postdivorce." Ph.D. diss., University of Minnesota, 1983. 141 p. Appendixes, reference notes, bibliography, footnotes.

Family social sciences study investigates conflict in marriage, divorce, and postdivorce relationships among former spouses who share continuing child-care responsibilities. Based on 1970–73 research with Anoka, Ramsey, and Hennepin county divorce records. Findings suggest that argumentative couples continue to argue following legal dissolution of marriage; child discipline is a major area of disagreement for participants in this study.

LIFE CYCLES

204. Anderson, Roxanne Marie. "Mothers and Daughters: Their Adult Relationship." Ph.D. diss., University of Minnesota, 1982. 113 p. Appendixes, bibliography.

Study explores continuing bond between mothers and their adult daughters. Pays particular attention to separateness and independence in the relationship. Based on 1981 research with 38 mother-daughter pairs in Twin Cities area.

205. Deno, Evelyn Dreier. "Changes in the Home Activities of Junior High School Girls Over a Twenty-Seven Year Period." Ph.D. diss., University of Minnesota, 1958. 277 p. Notes, bibliography, appendixes.

Child psychology study documents changes in home responsibilities and family activity patterns of seventh, eighth, and ninth grade girls in Minnesota. Work is based on home economics surveys administered in urban and rural classrooms in 1929, 1934, and 1956. Considerable comparative information about urban and rural settings and effects of social class.

206. Fitzpatrick, Lawrence Joseph. "Tool-using in Children from 16 to 24 Months of Age: The Relationship of Age, Frustration, and Sex to Patterns of Tool Use." Ph.D. diss., University of Minnesota, 1978. 191 p. Reference notes, appendixes.

Study explores behavior mechanisms involved in the development of simple tool-using skills. Based on 1970s research with female and male two-year-olds at the Institute for Child Development,

University of Minnesota. Findings report that age (16, 20, 24 months) is the most significant factor in children's performance. Females and males did not differ in important ways.

207. Hilger, Sister M. Inez. *Chippewa Child Life and Its Cultural Background.* Smithsonian Institution, Bureau of American Ethnology Bulletin no. 146. Washington, D.C.: GPO, 1951; St. Paul: Minnesota Historical Society Press, Borealis Books, 1992. 204 p. Bibliography, index, illustrations.

Describes traditional child-rearing customs, domestic life, and cultural training among reservation Ojibway of Minnesota, Wisconisn, and Michigan. Based on fieldwork conducted 1932–40.

SOCIAL AND ECONOMIC CLASS

208. Hertz, Susan Handley. "A Study of the Organization and Politics of the Welfare Mothers Movement in Minnesota." Ph.D. diss., University of Minnesota, 1974. 371 p. Footnotes, appendixes, bibliography.

Describes and analyzes the welfare mothers movement in Minneapolis, 1964–71. Focuses on organizational and political development locally and nationally. Considerable attention to organizational process and to roles of ministers, lawyers, and other professionals as mediators among the AFDC League, the Welfare Rights Organization, and Hennepin County social service agencies. Author's approach is derived from political anthropology and social change theory.

209. Hubert H. Humphrey Institute of Public Affairs. *A Statistical Look at the Economic Status of Women in Minnesota and the United States.* Minneapolis: Women, Public Policy and Development Project, Hubert H. Humphrey Institute of Public Affairs, University of Minnesota, 1983. 4 p.

Analyzes state and national figures under headings of welfare, employment, income, child support, older women, female-headed households, and women in the population. Documents pronounced economic disparities between women's and men's incomes.

SOCIAL LIFE AND CUSTOMS (including holidays, recreation, and travel)

210. "Full of Surprises . . . Was Mrs. Dorilus Morrison's Famous Rose Fete on July 1, 1892." *Hennepin County History,* Fall 1961, p. 7–10.

Detailed account of elaborate festivities held at

Villa Rosa, one-time home of Mrs. Dorilus Morrison and family, now the site of the Minneapolis Insititute of Arts and Fair Oaks Park in Minneapolis. Includes considerable information about guest list, fashionable women's attire, and the entertainments offered.

211. *Happy New Year 1879: List of Entertainers.* Minneapolis: The Tribune, 1878. 4 p. (MHS).

A list of hostesses holding New Year's Day open houses, Minneapolis, 1879.

212. *Home Life in College Dwellings: The Story of a Venture in Co-operative Cottages for Women at the University of Minnesota.* Minneapolis: University of Minnesota, [1924?]. 8 p. Illustrations.

Pamphlet describes rationale and costs for women's living plan in dwellings acquired for planned development at the university, 1914–24. Includes mention of individual benefactors, faculty women's club, and alumnae support. Proposes replacement of the cottages with new construction as the original dwellings are razed.

213. Ledray, Linda E. *The Single Woman's Vacation Guide.* New York: Ballantine Books, 1988. 506 p. Index, illustrations.

Guide to solo travel strategies for women— national and international—includes description of northeastern Minnesota dog-sledding excursion.

214. Martin, Janet Letnes, and Allen Todnem. *Lutheran Church Basement Women.* Hastings, Minn.: Redbird Productions, 1992. 191 p. Illustrations.

An amusing portrayal of the work of Lutheran women's organizations, particularly in rural churches. This account uses photographs, recipes, songs, and poetry to present a social history of an important element in the lives of many persons of Scandinavian or German heritage.

215. Meier, Peg. *The Last of the Tearoom Ladies and Other Minnesota Tales.* Minneapolis: Neighbors Publishing, 1990. 240 p. Illustrations, index.

Features articles orginally published in the Minneapolis *Star Tribune,* 1985–90. Many profile women, and many have a historical aspect—"Deb Davis and Lillie Gibbs LeVesconte, A Tale of Two Mothers," "Narum's Foursome, 40 Years of Togetherness," "Mizinokamigok, Knitter of Ojibway Ways," among others.

216. *MW.* Minneapolis: Minneapolis Woman, 1989–90.

Bimonthly illustrated periodical covering Twin Cities personalities, social and cultural events, travel, cooking, fashion, and general interest features. Geared to business and professional women. (Note: Name changed to *Metropolitan Woman*.)

217. Shaw, Marian. *World's Fair Notes: A Woman Journalist Views Chicago's 1893 Columbian Exposition*. [St. Paul]: Pogo Press, 1992. 108 p. Index, notes, bibliography, illustrations.

A collection of 12 articles describing the exhibits and discussing the purpose of the fair, originally published in the Fargo, N.Dak., *Argus* in 1893. The author taught in the Minneapolis public schools from 1873 until her death in 1901. The book concludes with an analytical essay, "Women and the Press at the 1893 World's Columbian Exposition," written by Ann Feldman, cultural historian and world's fair scholar.

218. Weiner, Lynn. " 'Our Sister's Keepers': The Minneapolis Woman's Christian Association and Housing for Working Women." *Minnesota History* 46 (Spring 1979): 189–200.

Describes jobs, wages, and living conditions for female workers with special reference to boarding clubs operated by the Woman's Christian Association, 1874–1920. Provides information about transient and more permanent facilities, amenities, and rules in these "substitute domestic environments."

STEREOTYPING AND PERCEPTUAL BIAS

219. Anderson, Mary Roberdeau. "A Descriptive Study of Values and Interests of Four Groups of Graduate Women at the University of Minnesota." Ph.D. diss., University of Minnesota, 1952. 134 p. Notes, bibliography, appendixes.

Research in educational psychology that examines usefulness of men's and women's versions of standard occupational testing instruments in use in the 1940s. Specific concern is occupational counseling for women. Test population is women enrolled in the graduate school, law school, medical school, and medical technology program at the University of Minnesota in 1949. Provides descriptions of previous studies in this area and discussion of ideas concerning women's participation in the work force in the post-World War II period.

220. Beito, Gretchen. " 'I Am a Farmer's Wife, Not a Farmerette': Letters to the *Nonpartisan Leader*, 1917–1920." *Plainswoman* 5, no. 2 (October 1981): 4–5, 17.

Quotes and analyzes women readers' complaints

regarding recipes and household hints in the weekly newspaper published by the Nonpartisan League in the 1910s. The gist of these comments, which appeared as letters to the editor, was that the writers' interests in the League focused on matters of social policy and equity.

221. Evans, Sara M. "Toward a Usable Past: Feminism as History and Politics." *Minnesota History* 48 (Summer 1983): 230–35.

Explores the historical frameworks used by historians of women. The author uses examples, some of them from Minnesota history, to illustrate a movement toward historical exposition that more fully represents women's experiences.

222. Gilman, Rhoda R. " 'Women's History?—Do They Have Any?' " *Minnesota History* 44 (Winter 1975): 309–10.

Analyzes the 1975 Women Historians of the Midwest conference on women's history. The author explains the importance of examining basic assumptions about power, property, and periodization so that the study of women's history can expand beyond an emphasis on prominent persons and a narrow emphasis on women's rights.

223. Haugen, Nancy Mayo. "Attitudes of Registered Nurses in Minnesota Toward Women: Implications for Practice." Master's thesis, University of Minnesota, 1985. 94 p. References, appendixes.

Explores issues of stereotyping and perceptual bias in the nursing profession, particularly in the ways registered nurses (predominately female) relate to women patients (majority of consumers of health care). Based on 1985 survey of Minnesota nurses. Documents "traditional" attitudes toward women among majority of respondents. Also suggests that nurses' attitudes become more "liberal" with additional nursing education. Recommends continuing education and research.

224. McInerney, Claire F. *Educational Equity in the Third Wave: Technology Education for Women and Minorities*. St. Paul: Minnesota Department of Education, 1986. 14 p. Bibliography, footnotes.

Discusses effects of sex-role and ethnic stereotyping on computer access and related technology in the classroom. Recommends integrated approach to change through teacher education, administrative programs, and parent guidance.

225. Merchant, Helen K. "Women in Administration: Issues, Expectations, and Challenges." Master's thesis, College of St. Thomas, 1989. 100 p. References, appendixes.

Education study surveys women school administrators' perceptions regarding the impact of sex discrimination and networking on their own careers. Based on 1988–89 research with women administrators licensed in Minnesota. Findings report perceptions that sex discrimination operates on both overt and subtle levels in candidate selection and daily activities. Also women's professional networks in education are reported as less extensive and less supportive than men's.

226. Mook, Amy Wolf. "Attitudes Toward Women Administrators by Minnesota Secondary Principals, Boards of Education, and Superintendents." Ph.D. diss., University of Iowa, 1981. 125 p. Footnotes, appendixes.

This research was prompted by the decline in the number of women administrators in Minnesota secondary schools during the 1970s, despite the fact that the total number of administrative positions had increased. The study used a survey questionnaire to evaluate the attitudes of the supervisors of the 50 women secondary school administrators employed in Minnesota during the 1979–80 academic year. The results found principals and superintendents to be more favorable than school board members toward women administrators.

227. Nelson, Karen Knutson. "An Investigation of Counselor Attitudes Toward Roles of Women." Ph.D. diss., University of Minnesota, 1982. 217 p. Reference note, references, appendixes.

Study explores aspects of "counselor sexism," particularly sex-role attitudes. Author's motivation is to identify and eliminate sex bias in the counseling profession. Based on 1981 research with female and male counselors throughout Minnesota. Findings show that male counselors are more traditional in their attitudes; the personality factor dogmatism is associated with more traditional attitudes; more knowledgable counselors proved to be more liberal in attitudes.

228. Schneidler, Gwendolyn G. "Further Studies in Clerical Aptitude." Ph.D. diss., University of Minnesota, 1940. 125 p. Bibliography, appendixes.

Psychological study focusing on aptitude measurement, specifically the development of norms for Minnesota Vocational Test for Clerical Workers. Discussion based on test administered to 4,000 St. Paul high school students in late 1930s. Considerable attention to sex differences in aptitude scores and possible explanations.

229. Sorenson, Joan Ardis. "Factors Which Superintendents and School Board Chairpersons Perceive Affecting Women's Employment in School Administration." Ph.D. diss., University of Minnesota, 1983. 153 p. Bibliography, appendixes.

Education study examines the relatively low proportion of women holding administrative positions in public schools and factors that may inhibit superintendents and school board chairs from hiring women. Based on 1981–82 research in Minnesota school districts statewide. Findings identify seniority as an important consideration for school boards and superintendents, a perception of a lack of available qualified women on the part of outstate chairs, and a possible bias against women administrators generally in outstate regions. Also superintendents appear more willing to promote women than are school board chairs.

230. Tjosvold, Mary Margaret. "An Analysis of Selected Factors in Personnel Management Decisions which Superintendents Perceive As Affecting the Employment and Promotion of Women in Public School Administration in Minnesota." Ph.D. diss., University of Minnesota, 1975. 174 p. Bibliography, appendixes.

Study exploring male administrators' attitudes toward employment and promotion of women in Minnesota public schools. Based on 1973–74 survey of 80 superintendents statewide. Findings include existence of sex stereotyping and relatively low rates of administrative certification among women as factors in underrepresentation. Includes overview of women's representation in public school administration nationally.

231. Wain, Judith Elaine Anderson. "Attitudes of Teachers Toward Women School Administrators and the Aspirations of Teachers for Administrative Positions in the State of Minnesota." Ph.D. diss., University of Minnesota, 1975. 200 p. Bibliography, appendixes.

Study of women's participation in school administration based on 1975 research into attitudes and aspirations of female and male teachers in Minnesota public schools K-12. Findings include widespread acceptance of women administrators on the part of female and male teachers and also widespread assumption that job-related sex stereotyping stands in the way of prospective women administrators. Features extensive discussion of professional literature concerning women's abilities and opportunities in education.

VIOLENCE AGAINST WOMEN

232. Baunach, Phyllis Jo. "Physical Attractiveness and Attribution of Victim Responsiblity for

Attractiveness-Related and Attractiveness-Unrelated Crimes: Who Blames Beauty and When?'' Ph.D. diss., University of Minnesota, 1974. 80 p. References, footnotes, appendixes.

Experimental psychology study conducted at University of Minnesota in 1970s explores attitudes toward women victims of crimes. For the purposes of this study, rape, seduction, and abduction were defined as attractiveness-related crimes; assault, grand larceny, and arson were not. The principal finding was that attractive women appeared to be blamed in some measure for rape and other attractiveness-related crimes, especially by unattractive women.

233. Burkett, Linda Padou. "Parenting Behaviors of Women Who Were Sexually Abused as Children in Their Families of Origin." Ph.D. diss., University of Minnesota, 1985. 210 p. Appendixes, references.

Identifies two major patterns among previously abused women: "under-functioning," an inability to focus on their children's needs and inexperience, and "crusaders," who seem overinvolved in their parental role. Both patterns suggest an overdependence upon children for emotional support. Recommends further research exploring types of abuse and adult parental behavior. Also suggests therapeutic approaches that may break multigenerational patterns characteristic of family abuse. Based on 1980s fieldwork in the Twin Cities area.

234. Burt, Marti, et al., comps. *Handbook on Rape.* Minneapolis: State Task Force on Rape, National Organization for Women, 1974. 88 p. Bibliography, community resource list.

Includes sections on support for the victim, rights and expectations, personal testimony, and resources. Focus is on Twin Cities audience and institutions. Additional resources listed for Mankato, Rochester, and Duluth.

235. Community Planning Organization, Inc. *Battered Women: The Hidden Problem.* St. Paul: The Organization, 1976. 46 p. Notes, bibliography, appendixes.

First report to investigate physical abuse of women in the Twin Cities area. Details available social and legal assistance. Recommends changes in community attitudes and assistance available to women who are battered.

236. Consortium on Battered Women. *Resources for Battered Women.* [St. Paul?]: The Organization, 1980. 7 p.

Booklet lists food, financial, emergency housing, clothing, counseling, and legal resources in St. Paul.

237. D'Aurora, James Joseph, Jr. "Family Sexual Abuse: An Exploratory Study Examining the Psychological Differences of Women Victims in Therapy." Ph.D. diss., University of Minnesota, 1984. 188 p. References, appendixes.

Psychology study explores characteristics of women victims of incest. Contains considerable information about nature and circumstances of abuse. Based on 1982 research with Twin Cities area individuals in therapy. Findings suggest the existence of several distinct clinical profiles associated with family abuse.

238. *Family Violence: How the Systems Respond.* Minneapolis: League of Women Voters of Minneapolis, 1978. 42 p. Appendixes, bibliography.

Report on Minneapolis court, governmental, and private resources available to spouses and children subject to family violence in late 1970s. Describes programs for children and battered women, criminal sanctions, counseling, family shelters, and medical services.

239. Frazier, Patricia Ann. "Attributions and Adjustment to Rape." Ph.D. diss., University of Minnesota, 1988. 450 p. References, footnotes, appendixes.

Study investigates victim's assignment of blame and post-traumatic stress following rape. Based on 1,420 case histories documenting rape of adult women who were treated at Hennepin County Medical Center in Minneapolis, 1981–87. Principal findings are that the women generally do not blame themselves, attributing the rape to the rapist rather than to personal behavior or character, and the experience (though not the incidence) of depression following rape varies considerably in relation to factors such as identity (acquaintance or stranger) of rapist and severity of the assault.

240. Fredrickson, Renee Marie. "Incest: Family Sexual Abuse and Its Relationship to Pathology, Sex Role Orientation, Attitudes Toward Women and Authoritarianism." Ph.D. diss., University of Minnesota, 1981. 193 p. Bibliography, appendixes.

Study of incest offenders and their wives based on research with families in Washington and Anoka counties and Chicago, about 1980. Focuses on personality characteristics, masculinity and femininity, attitudes towards women as measured in standard psychological tests, and the implications of test data in understanding theory and clinical observations of the father-daughter incest phenomenon.

241. Ledray, Linda E. "The Impact of Rape and the Relative Efficacy of [a] Guide to Goals and Supportive Counseling as Treatment Models for Rape Victims." Ph.D. diss., University of Minnesota, 1984. 131 p. Bibliography.

Examines usefulness of two therapeutic approaches—goal setting directed by the client and crisis counseling delivered by a trained therapist. Based on 1980s research at Hennepin County Medical Center Emergency Department. Contains overview of rape circumstances and statistics in Minneapolis. Findings suggest that both treatment approaches are helpful; the goal-setting approach appears to be somewhat more effective.

242. Minnesota Department of Corrections. *Battered Women: An Effective Response.* St. Paul: The Department, 1979. [134 p.]

Educational manual prepared for professionals and grass-roots organizations providing services to women who are abused. Includes comparative discussion of women's culture among whites, African Americans, Hispanics, and American Indians; an analysis of available legal and medical systems; and suggestions for development of community resources. Bound with report to the legislature detailing the department's implementation of services for women who are battered.

243. Minnesota Department of Corrections. *Minnesota Programs for Battered Women, 1981 Update.* St. Paul: The Department, 1981. 64 p. Appendixes.

Report to the legislature describes statewide programs, including data collection on the incidence of violence against women, activities of the Task Force on Battered Women, and the operations of shelters and of nonresidential treatment, counseling, and educational centers.

244. NIP [Neighborhood Involvement Program], Rape and Sexual Assault Center. *For Your Protection . . . Rape Prevention Tactics.* Minneapolis: The Center, [1976?]. 6 p.

Self-protection pamphlet prepared for women by Neighborhood Involvement Program of Minneapolis in the 1970s. Covers home, street, hitchhiking, personal auto situations, and children's precautions.

245. Syers, Maryann. "Women Who Leave Violent Relationships." *CURA Reporter* (Center for Urban and Regional Affairs, University of Minnesota, Minneapolis) 20, no. 2 (April 1990): 6–10.

Reports findings from a 1980s(?) study of problems and adjustments facing battered women after leaving violent partners. Discusses informal social support from family and friends; institutional resources provided by the women's community, the courts, and social service agencies; counseling and self-help groups; and economic and educational opportunities. Based on in-depth interviews with 15 Twin Cities(?) women. Contains overview figures for victims of abuse for Minnesota statewide.

246. Syers-McNairy, Maryann. "Women Who Leave Violent Relationships: Getting On with Life." Ph.D. diss., University of Minnesota, 1990. 2 vols. 351 p. Charts, appendixes, bibliography.

Social work research based on intensive interviews with abuse victims, conducted between April 1987 and February 1988. The interview subjects were recruited through several Twin Cities organizations: the Minnesota Coalition for Battered Women, Chrysalis, and the Domestic Abuse Project. The author attempted to identify the changes that occur when a woman leaves a violent relationship to begin a new life. She concluded that these women needed a complex system of help, which included a social support network of family and friends; a legal network of police, judges, and attorneys; educational and informational resources; mental health assistance; and economic support.

247. United Way Task Force on Battered Women. *Battered Women: A Study of Physical Abuse of Women.* Minneapolis: Community Planning and Research Division, United Way of Minneapolis, 1977. 96 p. Bibliography, appendixes.

Documents incidence of violence against women through Hennepin County hospital, social service agency, and counseling center records. Describes characteristics of "battered" women and their attackers. Recommends training and education measures concerning family violence. Includes list of community resources.

248. Women's Advocates [St. Paul]. *Women's Advocates: The Story of a Shelter.* St. Paul: The Organization, 1980. 98 p. Illustrations.

Describes facilities and programs at St. Paul shelter for battered women and their children founded in 1972. Includes discussion of security, child care, organization of collective work, community education, relevant legislation, and fund raising. Functions in part as a "how-to" manual for groups planning similar endeavors.

SEX ROLES

249. Best, Joel. "Looking Evil in the Face: Being an Examination of Vice and Respectability in St. Paul as Seen in the City's Press, 1865–83." *Minnesota History* 50 (Summer 1987): 241–51.

Assesses newspaper accounts as a forum for the debate of vice policy. A number of prominent madams—including Mary E. Robinson, Kate Hutton, Maggie Morse, and Henrietta Charles—paid monthly fines in what amounted to a licensing system. The author concludes that the press maintained a double standard in reporting by identifying the women involved but not the men.

250. Bielefeld, Robert James. "The Constructs of Masculinity and Femininity as Measured by the Personality Inventory for Children." Ph.D. diss., University of Minnesota, 1971. 135 p. References, appendixes.

Psychology study investigates femininity and masculinity as seen by 7- to 12-year-old children. Based on 1958–62 and 1969–70 research in Minneapolis and Roseville public schools. Findings indicate that femininity is related most strongly to "good conduct," masculinity to activity or impulsivity. Also, masculinity and femininity are separate qualities associated with the behavior of females and males rather than items on a single bipolar continuum.

251. Hauff, Elaine. "The Relationship Between Sex Role Orientation and Gender-Related Judgments." Ph.D. diss., University of Minnesota, 1985. 105 p. Appendixes, references.

Educational psychology study asks: do people make differential judgments based on the gender of participants in a social situation? Based on 1980s research conducted in a Minneapolis community college. Findings show generally the same degree of approval to both sexes. The two exceptions involved situations of hiring and electing a candidate; in both cases, the female was preferred two to one.

252. Lavenda, Robert H. "Minnesota Queen Pageants: Play, Fun, and Dead Seriousness in a Festive Mode." *Journal of American Folklore* 101, no. 400 (April–June 1988): 168–75.

Report on folklore fieldwork about small-town beauty pageants in rural Minnesota communities in the 1980s. Explores pageants as an activity, candidates' family and community connections, and ideals of femininity expressed in the competitions.

253. Phillips, Roy D. *Woman's Place.* St. Paul: Unity Church, 1972. 5 p.

Published sermon concerning the women's liberation movement delivered at Unity Unitarian Universalist Church in St. Paul. Supports general moral argument of women's liberation while rejecting the "silly screaming" and "offensive . . . vigor" of the "shock troops" about 1972.

254. Smith, Marcia Jacobs. "Measurement of Masculinity-Femininity in an Adolescent Population." Ph.D. diss., University of Minnesota, 1973. 147 p. References, appendixes.

Psychology study investigates sex-role stereotypes and masculinity-femininity measurement. Based on early 1970s research with adolescents in four suburban school districts in the Twin Cities metropolitan area. Findings, which conformed to many commonly held stereotypes, generally were consistent with other research conducted in the same period.

255. Stedman, Rose Edith. "The Relationship of Masculinity-Femininity to Perception of Self, Chosen Occupation, and College Teaching among University Honor Students." Ph.D. diss., University of Minnesota, 1963. 169 p. Notes, bibliography, appendixes.

Educational study conducted with University of Minnesota students in 1960 explores college women's potential to participate in professional and technical careers. Context is labor shortage; focus of study is attitudes toward femininity-masculinity and vocational choice. Considerable discussion of attitudes concerning vocation, marriage, and child rearing.

256. *Women's Liberation Newsletter.* Minneapolis: Women's Liberation Group, University of Minnesota, 1969–.

Newsletter published by the Minneapolis Women's Liberation Group located at the University of Minnesota. Contains announcements, course offerings, and cultural notes for events on and off campus. Continues as *Female Liberation Newsletter.*

257. Woods, Thomas A. "The Editor's Page: Varying Versions of the Real: Toward a Socially Responsible Public History." *Minnesota History* 51 (Spring 1989): 178–85.

Focuses on problems in interpretation of women's roles in 19th-century agriculture. Author concludes that most scholars have found distinct rural gender roles when research is based on women's diaries and letters.

SOCIALIZATION

258. Benoist, Irving Royster. "An Investigation of the Relationship Between Sex-Role Attitudes and Expressive Behavior." Ph.D. diss., University of Minnesota, 1974. 168 p. References, appendixes.

Study explores how self-reported attributes, specifically femininity and masculinity, are reflected in nonverbal behaviors. Based on 1970s research with University of Minnesota psychology students. Documents considerable stereotyping in judgment of sex differences, particularly those concerning women.

259. Dermer, Marshall. "When Beauty Fails." Ph.D. diss., University of Minnesota, 1973. 52 p. References, footnotes, tables, appendix.

Study explores attitudes toward physical attractiveness of women. Based on early 1970s research with women students at University of Iowa and University of Minnesota. Results identify high correlations between physical attractiveness and good grades, dating popularity, and satisfaction with physical appearance. Neither "beauty" nor "physical attractiveness" is defined in this study although both qualities are used to explain diverse achievements and activities that might be attributed to values, motivation, or work habits in other theoretical systems.

260. Goldsmith, Susan Patricia Nelson. "Personality, Ego Development, and Moral Reasoning Differences Between Feminists and Nonfeminists." Ph.D. diss., University of Minnesota, 1978. 127 p. References, appendix.

Study explores differences between feminists and "more traditional" women through standardized psychological test instruments. Findings document higher levels of intelligence among feminist women, pronounced analytical tendencies, complexity and flexibility in their thinking, and a high tolerance for ambiguity and role conflict. Based on 1978 research with self-described feminists and nonfeminists in the Twin Cities.

261. Haas, Mary Helen. "A Study of Certain Factors Related to the Vocational Activity of Home Economics Education Graduates." Ph.D. diss., University of Minnesota, 1957. 232 p. Bibliography, appendixes, notes.

Educational study conducted with 162 alumnae of the University of Minnesota Home Economics Department, 1937–57. Context is state and national shortage of teachers and investigation of possible remedies within ranks of educated women engaged in full-time homemaking. Discusses attitudes concerning homemaking, careers, and family finances.

262. Marsh, Cynthia Elaine. "The Relationship of Values, Abilities and Selected Demographic Characteristics to Career Orientation in Adult Women: A Multidimensional Contingency Analysis." Ph.D. diss., University of Minnesota, 1981. 284 p. References, bibliography.

Study explores implications of personal values, ability, age, education, marital status, presence of children, career or homemaker orientation, and nontraditional or traditional orientation for career counseling of women. Based on 1978 research with clients of Vocational Assessment Clinic at University of Minnesota–Twin Cities campus.

263. Rossmann, Jack Eugene. "An Investigation of Maternal Employment among College Women—A Twenty-Five Year Follow-Up." Ph.D. diss., University of Minnesota, 1963. 193 p. Bibliography, appendixes.

Educational psychology study conducted in early 1960s investigates financial, social service, and psychological motivations of working mothers. Based on the experiences of 240 college-educated women who were students at the University of Minnesota in the 1930s.

ᴵᴵᴵᴵᴵ/ Natural Sciences and Health

264. *Newsletter/Midwest Health Center for Women.* Minneapolis: The Center, 1976–.

Newsletter reporting on reproductive counseling and services at Center facilities in Twin Cities and Duluth, plus additional national and international features.

HEALTH SCIENCES

265. Barsness, Nellie N. "Highlights in Careers of Women Physicians in Pioneer Minnesota." *Journal of American Medical Women's Association* 13, no. 1 (January 1958): 19–23.

Provides overview and brief sketches of 26 of the 518 women known to have practiced medicine in the state, 1880s–1940s. (Note: MHS copy bound with "Record of Early Minnesota Medical Women" by Annah Hurd, 1 p.)

266. Clifford, Eileen Jean. "The History and Impact of Selected Organizations on Health Education in the State of Minnesota." Ph.D. diss., University of Minnesota, 1986. 240 p. Appendixes, bibliography.

Study explores the contributions of volunteer and professional groups to community health in Minnesota, 1870s–1920s. Includes material on the Woman's Christian Temperance Union's successful campaign to institute compulsory public school curriculum concerning alcohol abuse, operations of school and visiting nurse programs, home demonstration projects conducted through Agriculture Extension, and physical education and other programs of the YWCA.

267. Curlee, Joan Ethelyn. "A Comparision of Male and Female Patients at an Alcoholism Treatment Center." Ph.D. diss., University of Minnesota, 1968. 116 p. References, appendixes.

Study based on 1960s research with patients at Hazelden, a private treatment center near Center City. Suggests that experience of alcoholism differs for women and men. Questions the idea that

women are "sicker" than men. Also notes element of "protest" in women's drinking, possibly linked to "conflicts about conventional feminine roles." Indicates that differing treatment methods—individually based for women and collective for men—may be more effective.

268. Evans, Kay Sara Webb, and Diane Wilson. *Women's Health Care in the Twin Cities: A Handbook and Directory.* Minneapolis: Minnesota Public Interest Research Group, 1980. 39 p. Illustrations.

Handbook describes routine women's health care procedures and common gynecological conditions and diseases. Includes resource list of Twin Cities clinics.

269. Madden, Mary Jane. "The Symbolic World of Obesity: A Study of the Rhetorical Visions of Obese Women." Ph.D. diss., University of Minnesota, 1982. 164 p. Bibliography, appendixes.

Study investigates the psychology of obesity. Based on early 1980s research with participants located through 12 nonprofit weight-loss programs in the Twin Cities area. Findings suggest that the vocabularies and fantasies of obese individuals offer new approaches to weight loss and maintenance.

270. Minnesota Viavi Co. *Book of Health for Mothers and Daughters: Their Needs, Diseases, and How They Should Be Treated.* Minneapolis: The Company, [1897?]. 48 p.

Pamphlet published by patent medicine company describes douche and salve treatments for various diseases of the womb and vagina. Includes many testimonials.

271. Phelan, Phyllis White. "Toward a Social Cognitive Model of Bulimia: The Role of Salient Beliefs, Self-Efficacy and Self-Schema." Ph.D. diss., University of Minnesota, 1984. 208 p. Notes, references, appendixes.

Study documents psychological characteristics associated with bulimia, an eating disorder experienced predominately by women in which binge eating is accompanied by purging via vomiting or laxatives or by fasting. Also explores social and cognitive (as distinct from physical) treatment methods. Based on 1983 research with Minnesota women.

272. Wright, Sara Elizabeth. "Premenstrual Syndrome (PMS) and Perceived Marital Inequity." Ph.D. diss., University of Minnesota, 1985. 143 p. Appendixes, bibliography.

Psychology study investigates premenstrual syndrome (diagnosed as moderate to severe) and its effects on marriage relationships. Based on 1980s research with couples located through the PMS Clinic of Minneapolis. Findings report significant effects in all cases studied, ranging from threat to marriage to a strengthening influence. Also discusses perceptions of marital equity reported by couples affected by PMS disorder.

MENTAL HEALTH

273. Andersen, Lauren Kay. "The Careers of Adult Women: Psychological Profiles from a Developmental Perspective." Ph.D. diss., University of Minnesota, 1980. 178 p. Bibliography, appendixes.

Study investigates the role of career in the psychological development of women. Based on 1974 research with employed women located through East Coast corporations and nonemployed women located through Continuing Education office of the University of Minnesota. Results show significant differences in developmental characteristics of the two groups. Author suggests potential applications to counseling and training programs.

274. Angle, Marilyn Ditzen. "The Relationship of Perceived Competence to Subjective Well-Being, Fear of Aging, and Sex-Role Orientation in Older Women." Ph.D. diss., University of Minnesota, 1988. 168 p. References, appendixes.

Psychology study investigates well-being and sense of competence in older women. Based on 1980s research with Minneapolis and suburban residents. Findings report a strong sense of well-being, little fear of aging, an egalitarian approach to sex roles, and a strong sense of personal competence among unusually healthy, well-educated, and financially secure informants.

275. Bradford, Jean Louise. "Sex Differences in Anxiety." Ph.D. diss., University of Minnesota, 1968. 139 p. Appendixes, references.

Psychology study explores gender as a factor in anxiety reactions among women and men. Based on 1960s research with undergraduate students at the University of Minnesota. Findings support hypothesis that females would report greater concern over situations of social threat, rejection, and embarrassment. However, fears of physical vulnerability were equally present in female and male participants; this outcome was unexpected and had been hypothesized as a "male" anxiety.

276. Clementson-Mohr, Judith. "Academic Women: Well-Being, Personality Variables and Attitudes toward Women." Ph.D. diss., University of Minnesota, 1978. 133 p. References, appendixes.

Psychology study based on 1978 research with women faculty at the University of Minnesota. Includes considerable comparative information concerning women in the general population and earlier, often longitudinal, studies of 20th-century professional women. Findings include high levels of well-being and markedly nontraditional attitudes toward women's roles among the individuals sampled.

277. Dollahite, David Curtis. "Familial Support Resources and Individual Coping Efforts in Economically Stressed Farm Men and Women." Ph.D. diss., University of Minnesota, 1988. 230 p. References, appendixes.

Psychology study is based on 1987 research with more than 200 families in south-central Minnesota who participated in mandatory farm credit mediation. Demonstrates a relationship between family support systems and individuals' abilities to handle economic stress. Also suggests differences between adult female and male coping strategies—women's are more likely to be socially based, men's to be individually based.

278. Faunce, Patricia Spencer. "Personality Characteristics and Vocational Interests Related to the College Persistence of Academically Gifted Women." Ph.D. diss., University of Minnesota, 1966. 588 p. References, appendixes.

Psychology study investigates the influences of personality characteristics and vocational interests on the persistence of academically gifted women. Based on research with College of Liberal Arts student records at the University of Minnesota, 1950–58. Overall, the student scores fell within normal ranges. However, nongraduates showed poor personal adjustment and relatively little insight regarding their difficulties with the problems of growing up. By contrast, graduate women reported relatively less trouble with personal problems and developments; their interests were more professional or academic in character, requiring degree completion to realize goals.

279. Hilgers, Karen Margaret. "Hardiness, Trauma Level and the Rape Victim." Ph.D. diss., University of Minnesota, 1987. 227 p. References, appendixes.

Psychology study investigates rape trauma and psychological hardiness. Based on 1980s research in the Twin Cities metropolitan area. Findings show significant relationships among rape recovery, hardiness, and family social support. Author suggests how these conditions may be extended via counseling to rape victims in need of these resources.

FOODS

280. Dingwall, Iva A. "Pioneers' Dinner Table." *Minnesota History* 34 (Summer 1954): 54–58.

The author, who was born in 1877, explains the food she ate as a child visiting her grandparents' farm near Elk River in Sherburne County. She describes varieties of fruits, vegetables, cakes, and desserts, as well as methods for pickling and preserving food.

281. Kreidberg, Marjorie. "Corn Bread, Portable Soup, and Wrinkle Cures." *Minnesota History* 41 (Fall 1968): 105–16.

Analyzes the social history of late 19th-century cookbooks and household manuals including works put together by church women, commercial promoters, and national book distributors.

282. Szathmary, Louis. *Along the Northern Border: Cookery in Idaho, Minnesota and North Dakota.* New York: Arno Press, 1973. 127 p. Illustrations.

Includes reprint editions (complete) of *Library Ann's Cook Book* (1928), compiled by the Minneapolis Public Library Staff Association, and the *Y.M.C.A. Cook Book* (1924), published in Grand Forks, N.Dak. The recipes and accompanying texts supply information about domestic equipment, consumption habits, migration patterns, and food folkways.

ATHLETICS

283. Ebbott, Elizabeth, and Jeannette Kahlenberg, eds. *What's the Score in Minnesota: A Summary Report on the Monitoring Project of the League of Women Voters of Minnesota.* St. Paul: The League, 1979. 19 p. Appendixes.

Report on equal opportunity for girls in organized, competitive athletics. Describes monitoring process for 69 school districts, private schools, and community recreation programs across the state. Summary focuses on public school district data, identifying instances of discrimination and suggesting remedies.

284. Graybeal, Elizabeth. "Measurement in Physical Education for Women." Ph.D. diss., University of Minnesota, 1935. 120 p. Bibliography, appendixes, charts.

Study conducted at University of Minnesota, 1932–34, compares experiences and achievements of women students actively engaged in physical education sports and exercises with others who took courses as lecture-film classes. Context for study is compulsory versus elective physical education credits in college curricula.

285. League of Women Voters of Minnesota. *Organizing a Community Look at Girls' Athletics.* St. Paul: The League, [1977?]. 41 p. Bibliography.

Procedural manual prepared for League of Women Voters groups monitoring equal opportunity for girls in athletics statewide in the 1970s. Provides organizational advice; relevant legal statutes and judicial interpretations; attitude surveys for students, teachers, and coaches; and a list of resource persons. Undertaken at the request of the State Department of Human Rights, the goal of this project was compliance through community awareness.

SEXUALITY

286. Maison, Sally. "Factors Affecting the Relationship Between Sexual and Marital Satisfaction." Ph.D. diss., University of Minnesota, 1981. 294 p. Bibliography, appendixes.

Study based on research with couples in the Twin Cities metropolitan area, about 1980. Looks at age, gender, education, years married, children, occupation, and impact of feminism as factors in informants' analyses.

287. Owings, Chloe. *The Effectiveness of a Particular Program in Parental Sex Education.* Minneapolis: University of Minnesota Press, 1931. 31 p. Appendix. (U of M/Wil).

Discusses knowledge of human reproduction and approaches to sex education among mothers participating in the study. Paper IV in a series of eight papers describing a joint project in family sex education undertaken by the Women's Co-operative Alliance of Minneapolis and the Social Hygiene Research Program at the University of Minnesota, 1925–31.

288. Schmitt, Gretchen Stein. "Congruence of Perception in the Sexual Experience." Ph.D. diss., University of Minnesota, 1985. 184 p. Bibliography, appendixes.

Psychology study investigates the ability of married couples to assess accurately what one another is perceiving in the sexual experience. Based on 1980s research with young married couples in Twin Cities metropolitan area. Documents subjective element of sexual experience and suggests ways in which these perceptions could contribute to communication between partners, within and outside of counseling situations.

BIRTH CONTROL AND ABORTION

289. Doyle, Marsha Vanderford. "In-House Rhetoric of Pro-Life and Pro-Choice Special Interest Groups in Minnesota: Motivation and Alienation." Ph.D. diss., University of Minnesota, 1982. 390 p. Bibliography, notes.

Encyclopedic analysis of the abortion controversy in Minnesota, 1960s–82, as seen through the activities of the principal special interest groups— the pro-choice Abortion Rights Council and pro-life Minnesota Citizens Concerned for Life. Includes detailed historical overview, plus close examination of pro-life and pro-choice language, ideas, and tactics over time. Particular attention to the impact of abortion controversy on politics and legislation statewide.

290. MacLeod, Charlotte M. "Community Reaction to the Establishment of an Abortion Clinic in Duluth, Minnesota." *North Dakota Quarterly* 52, no. 1 (Winter 1984): 34–47.

Chronicles planning and first-year operation in 1981–82 of the Midwest Health Center for Women–Duluth facility, which offers gynecological and obstetrical services, including abortion. Also describes protest organized by the Duluth Abortion Center Alert, a coalition of Roman Catholic, Protestant fundamentalist, and other critics of abortion services. Analyzes beliefs of clinic proponents and protesters and the political climate in Duluth that provided for both continued operation of the clinic and expressions of protest concerning its existence.

PREGNANCY AND CHILDBIRTH

291. Breitenbucher, Mary Catherine. "The Effects of Maternal Age Upon Quality of Child Care." Ph.D. diss., University of Minnesota, 1985. 98 p. Reference notes, references.

Explores psychological attributes teen-age mothers (15–19) bring to infant and child care. Describes some "negativity" on part of 17-to-18-year-olds. However, overall finding is that chronological age is less important than external variables, such as experience, personal growth, and the mother's social-support system. Based on 1980s research conducted at Minneapolis Public Health Infant and Child Care Clinic.

292. "Developing Understanding of the Needs of Mothers and Infants, October 10 and 11, 1951." Minneapolis: University of Minnesota Center for Continuation Study, 1951. [12 p.] Mimeo. (MHS).

Program for conference on pregnancy and childbirth lists schedule of events, presenters, and registrants. Focuses on social and psychological attitudes concerning birth and initial experiences of parenthood. Includes summaries of three papers: "Personality and Emotional Implications of Pregnancy and Labor" by Milton Abramson, "Problems of the Mother in the Postpartum Period" by Irwin H. Kaiser, and "Maternal Attitudes at the Time of Birth: Their Effects on the Child" by W. R. Heilig.

293. Halvorsen, Helen Olson, and Lorraine Fletcher. "19th Century Midwife: Some Recollections." *Oregon Historical Quarterly* 70, no. 1 ([Winter?] 1969): 39–49.

Focuses on Halvorsen's recollections of pregnancy and childbirth with her own eight children in western Wisconsin and Oregon, 1880s–90s. Contains detailed description of birthing practices.

294. League of Women Voters of Minneapolis. *Teenage Pregnancy and Parenting: A Community Concern.* Minneapolis: The League, 1986. 45 p. References, resource persons.

Discusses characteristics of pregnant adolescents in Minneapolis. Evaluates available educational services, health care, and social services. Also considers issues of male responsibility and prevention.

295. Lia-Hoagberg, Betty, et al. *Barriers and Motivators to Prenatal Care: Experiences of Low-Income Women.* Minneapolis: Urban Coalition of Minneapolis, 1988. 28 p. Illustrations.

Based on personal interviews with 211 women (white, African American, and American Indian) from lowest income areas of Minneapolis. Particu-

Marie Sarkipate Ericson was called "Minnesota's famous woman wilderness guide" by the Minnesota Tourist Bureau, which distributed this photograph taken near Ely in 1940.

lar concern: low birth weight as factor in infant health and mortality. Identifies factors such as maternal income, personal-family stress, depression and illness, feelings about the medical system, transportation, and child care responsibilities that influence access to prenatal care. Offers recommendations for improved care.

296. Lockwood, Elizabeth Karsen. "The Fallen Woman, The Maternity Home and the State." Master's thesis, University of Wisconsin–Madison, 1987. 151 p. Notes, bibliography.

Study of maternal health care for single women in Minnesota, 1870–1930. Describes Minnesota resources as pioneering in Progressive Era and more recent times. Includes historiographic overview, later 19th-century resources, Progressive Era changes via state regulation, and reaction and resistance within service institutions. Largely an exploration of Twin Cities-based institutions, although numerous references are made to alternative arrangements in outstate counties.

297. Lowry, Lisa Ann. "Developmental Effects of Teenage Childbearing on Children." Ph.D. diss., University of Minnesota, 1982. 149 p. Footnotes, reference notes, references, appendixes.

Comparative study of 90 first-born children of teen-age mothers (15–19) and older mothers (20–25) explores possible influence of maternal age on early childhood development. Based on 1970–80s research with women receiving prenatal care at Maternal and Infant Care Clinics, Minneapolis Health Department. Results show few differences among children in the two groups. Author suggests that external factors, such as the mother's support group, may be more important than mother's age.

298. Minnesota State Board of Health, Division of Child Hygiene. *Correspondence Study Course in the Hygiene of Maternity and Infancy, Course I, Lessons I-XV.* N.p.: The Board, 1923.

Provides detailed discussion of pregnancy and fetal development, maternal hygiene and preparations for delivery, delivery, infant feeding and care, childhood development, and common illnesses. Correspondence questions appear on last page of each lesson.

299. Sandven, Kari Ann. "Characteristics of Black Adolescent Mothers Who Choose Informal Adoption." Ph.D. diss., University of Minnesota, 1985. 138 p. References, appendix.

Psychology study investigates the child-rearing choices made by pregnant African-American adolescents in Minneapolis about 1985. Discusses three commonly chosen options: shared parenting with family of origin; "gift" arrangements whereby child is informally adopted by a relative or friend while mother retains legal custody; and exclusive parenting undertaken by the mother.

ENVIRONMENT AND ECOLOGY

300. Midwest Regional Conference. *Women in Natural Resources: Moving Toward the 90's.* St. Paul: The Organization, 1987. 96 p.

A collection of materials generated by a 1987 conference held at the University of Minnesota. A number of contributors evaluated their personal experiences and provided strategies for women seeking advancement in natural resources careers. Minnesota participants included Anne Kanten, then assistant commissioner of the Minnesota Department of Agriculture, and Francesca J. Cuthbert from the Department of Fisheries and Wildlife at the University of Minnesota in St. Paul.

301. Niemi, Judith, and Barbara Wieser, eds. *Rivers Running Free: Stories of Adventurous Women.* Minneapolis: Bergamot Books, 1987. 287 p. Bibliography, resource list.

Collection of essays concerning canoeing and wilderness travel by women, circa 1900 to the 1980s. Minnesota essays include "What Did Flies Matter When You Were Free" by Jesse Ford, "Not a Vacation: Mississippi River Notes" by Marsha Berry, "Quetico-Superior Honeymoon, 1925" by Hazel Rice, "Bear Story" by Heart Warrior Chosa, and "Woman of the Boundary Waters" by Justine Kerfoot.

ılılıl/ Organizations and Clubs

302. Minnesota Council on Foundations. *Inventory of Women's Services.* Minneapolis: The Council, 1978. 33 p. Appendix, index.

Statewide inventory in the mid-to-late 1970s. Divided into sections describing state agencies, education and employment, health, social services, victim services, arts groups, and membership organizations. Provides statement of purpose, percentage of female clients, number served annually, and sources of funding.

303. Oakey, Margaret Lansing. "Woman's Club Movement in Minnesota." Undergraduate paper, Department of History, University of Minnesota, 1931. 30 p. Notes, bibliography.

Undergraduate research paper discusses Minnesota women's clubs, 1870s–1900, in context of national women's club formation. Describes the activities of dozens of literary, educational, service, and pioneer clubs statewide. Also chronicles the origins and activities of the Minnesota Federation of Women's Clubs in the 1890s. Many primary source citations.

304. Remington, Judy. *The Need to Thrive: Women's Organizations in the Twin Cities.* St. Paul: Minnesota Women's Press, Inc., 1991. 76 p. Bibliography.

Describes late 20th-century women's groups including At the Foot of the Mountain Theater, Chrysalis, Harriet Tubman Center, CHART, Women's Art Registry of Minnesota, and others. Identifies three periods in these collective organizational histories: beginnings, 1965–75; growth and fruition, 1975–85; and stresses and change, 1985–90. Discusses power, victimization, the personal, solidarity and diversity, and organizational structure as factors in each period. Suggests that women's groups must define a new relation to power in order to continue to thrive.

305. Woman's Occupational Bureau, comp. *Minneapolis Women's Activities Yearbook, 1935–1936.* Minneapolis: Women's Week Exposition Committee, 1935. 52 p. (MHS).

Describes Women's Week Exposition portraying women's activities in business, the professions, the arts, and homemaking at the Minneapolis Auditorium in November 1934. Lists planning committee, out-of-town guests, and honored women (local and national). Also provides alphabetical listing of 59 currently active women's organizations, their officers, and objectives.

306. *Women's Network Directory.* Minneapolis: Women's Network, Inc., 1975. 262 p. Index, illustrations.

Provides descriptions of diverse women's resources, including education, employment, legal services, family, health, media and art, and religion throughout the Twin Cities metropolitan area in the 1970s.

SOCIAL, CULTURAL, AND EDUCATIONAL

307. *American Association of University Women, Minnesota State Division [Yearbook].* Minnesota: The Division, 1945–.

Statewide directories of AAUW chapters. Organized alphabetically by communities; include memberships lists, committee structure, and by-laws. (Note: Minnesota Historical Society collection includes 1945–76.)

308. American Association of University Women, St. Paul. *Bulletin—St. Paul College Club.* St. Paul: The Organization, 1927–50.

Monthly bulletin of the St. Paul branch of AAUW. Reports on social and educational activities locally and nationally. Continued as *Bulletin of the St. Paul Branch,* 1950–51, *Bulletin of the St. Paul College Club,* 1952–56, and *Bulletin—AAUW, St. Paul Branch,* 1956–61.

309. Anderson, Rebecca. " 'The Door of Opportunity': A Study of the Minneapolis YWCA Membership during the Great Depression." Honors thesis, Macalester College, 1984. 69 p. Select bibliography.

Historical study describes Minneapolis YWCA in relation to the national organization and to local conditions during the 1930s. Focuses on middle-class and fellowship aspects of the program through discussion of three clubs—Business and Professional Women, Industrial Girls, and Young Matrons.

310. Bessesen, Mrs. A. N., Jr., ed. *Convention Bulletin, May 1933.* Minneapolis: Minneapolis College Women's Club, 1933. 22 p. (MHS).

Describes programs and arrangements for the Eighth Biennial Convention of the American Association of University Women held at the Nicollet Hotel in Minneapolis, May 17–19, 1933, and the Fifth Biennial Convention of the Minnesota State Division of the AAUW, held at the Women's City Club of St. Paul, May 20, 1933. Also details special events at the Minneapolis Women's College Club associated with the national and state conventions and documents planning undertaken by Twin Cities members for these consecutive meetings.

311. Book Lovers' Club, Paynesville, Minn. *Yearbook.* Paynesville: The Organization, 1910/11–1917/18, 1919/20–1920/21, 1923/24–1925/26, 1927/28, 1933/34, 1937/38–1941/42.

Lists officers, members, and presentation topics for twice-monthly meetings of group organized in 1908 and federated in 1910. Gradually topics moved from historical and literary themes to current events and miscellaneous.

312. Buchanan Bible Study Club, Minneapolis. *Yearbook.* Minneapolis: The Organization, 1920/21–1953/54. (MHS).

Mrs. John C. Buchanan organized this group on March 5, 1920, to meet twice a month for Bible study centered on an annual theme, such as the prophets or women of the Bible. Yearbooks include lists of officers and committees; names, addresses, and phone numbers of members; and program topics. The collection includes a copy of the constitution and bylaws.

313. Burns, Inella. "Ladies of the Club." *Blue Earth County Historical Society Newsletter.* November 1984. 2 p.

Describes four women's clubs established in Mankato in the 1890s: the Tourist Club (geographical and literary), the Clio Club (literature and politics), the Mankato Art History Club, and Zetetic Club (culture and community welfare). As of 1984, only the Clio Club had disbanded.

314. Callister, Beulah. *Literary Guild of Kenyon, 1930–1980.* [Kenyon, Minn.: The Guild?], 1980. 19 p. (MHS).

Compilation of ongoing club activities in Kenyon, Goodhue County, 1930–80. Describes mixed program of book reviews, cultural and political discussions, and travel (local, national, and international).

315. *"Circle E" Citizenship and Civic Club, 1936–1937.* Minneapolis: The Organization, 1936. 12 p. (MHS).

Yearbook provides 1936–37 calendar of events for civic and social club founded in Minneapolis in 1924. Identifies officers, committees, and general membership. Includes constitution and bylaws. (Note: Yearbooks for 1939–40 and 1941–42 also held in Minnesota Historical Society collection.)

316. Clio Club, Hastings. *Yearbook.* Hastings, Minn.: The Organization, 1899. 28 p. (MHS).

Lists 1899 meeting dates and topics for social and educational club founded in 1892. Also includes officer and program committee rosters.

317. Columbian Club, Minneapolis. *Yearbook.* Minneapolis: The Organization, 1899/1901, 1901/02–1902/03, 1905/06, 1920/21, 1929/30, 1930/31–1934/35, 1936/37, 1938/39–1946/47. (MHS).

Organized in 1892 as the Columbian Study Class, the group changed its name by 1901. It met twice monthly to study literature and history. The yearbooks include lists of officers, names and addresses of members, and the topics for discussion at each meeting.

318. Cooper, Lois. *Thursday Musical: The First Century, 1892–1992.* [Minneapolis]: Thursday Musical, 1992. 149 p. Appendixes, illustrations.

Describes the development of the preeminent Minneapolis musical organization founded by a group of young women in 1892 to promote musical culture in the city. Originally members were required to perform, but in the late 1890s associate membership was extended to nonperformers and to students. Through the years the organization presented a variety of musical programs, which included guest artists as well as local performers, and developed student events and contests.

319. Cosmopolitan Club of Merriam Park, St. Paul. *Yearbook.* St. Paul: The Organization, 1898/99, 1901/02, 1907/08, 1915/16–1916/17, 1926/27, 1929/30–1930/31, 1934/35, 1945/46. (MHS).

Includes lists of officers and committee members as well as names and addresses of club members after 1915. They organized in 1885 in St. Paul and focused primarily on literary and historical themes. The yearbooks after 1915 indicate the members usually brought in male speakers for the academic subjects, and they relied on women members for presentations dealing with house and garden.

320. Coterie, Minneapolis. *Yearbook*. Minneapolis: The Organization, 1883/84–1918/19 (incomplete), 1920/21–1921/22, 1923/24–1924/25, 1926/27–1927/28, 1929/30–1932/33, 1934/35–1935/36. (MHS).

Yearbooks include officers' names and program topics for Minneapolis women's club organized in 1880. After 1892/93 each issue includes a directory of members' names and addresses. Members consistently studied history and a variety of literary topics, including works by German, Norse, Spanish, and Jewish authors. (Note: From 1885 to 1912/13, the organization issued two yearbooks per year; and the months covered by each yearbook varied, thereby creating a very confusing numbering system.)

321. *The Courant*. Minneapolis: The Courant Co., 1899–1914. Advertisements, illustrations.

Originated on May 4, 1899, as a weekly attempt to inform and entertain its readers about art, literature, and current history, as well as to report on social events in the Twin Cities area. Its supporters included a number of prominent persons, such as Mrs. Thomas Lowry, Mrs. Thomas G. Winter, Mrs. William D. Washburn, and Dr. James K. Hosmer. In September 1899 the magazine changed its publication schedule to two issues a month, and by June 1900 it had become a monthly publication with ties to the Women's Club movement in the Twin Cities and statewide. By 1902 the publication described itself as "The Official Bulletin of the Wisconsin, Minnesota, and North Dakota Federations of Women's Clubs" and later added South Dakota, Montana, and Wyoming to its territory. (Note: There are several issues missing from the Minnesota Historical Society holdings.)

322. *Courant Directory of Federation of Women's Clubs of Minnesota, Wisconsin, North and South Dakota*. St. Paul: Courant Directory Co., 1904. 485 p.

Provides an alphabetical listing of clubs by city within each state. Members and officers as well as post-office addresses are listed within each club section. The Minnesota Federation organized in 1895 with 15 clubs and included 190 clubs by 1904. Contains numerous advertisements with index.

323. Covell, Mrs. F. E., and Mrs. J. C. Armstrong. *Historical Pageant Depicting the Unfolding of the 'Club Idea' as Exemplified by the Federated Clubs of the Fifth District, Minnesota*. Minneapolis: Minnesota Federation of Women's Clubs, 1923. 16 p. (MHS).

Souvenir program includes complete script of the pageant, list of players, music, and hostesses for its performance at the New Garrick Theatre [*sic*] in Minneapolis for the midwinter meeting of the Minnesota Federation of Women's Clubs, February 9, 1923. Pageant script features specific mention of selected clubs—the Tuesday Club, the Woman's Club, Linden Hills Study Club, and Buchanan Bible Study Club.

324. Current Events and Literary Society, Minneapolis. *Yearbook*. Minneapolis: The Organization, 1892/93, 1898/99, 1901/02–1919/20. (MHS).

Study group organized in May 1892 met on alternate Thursdays, October to May. Includes constitution and bylaws and lists of program topics for 1893/94 to 1900/01. After 1902/03 many volumes include names and addresses of members. During 1918/19 members discussed a number of topics related to World War I.

325. Delphian Past Presidents' Club, Minneapolis. *Yearbook*. Minneapolis: The Organization, 1932/33–1949/50. (MHS).

Includes names of officers and committee chairs as well as names and addresses of members. Study topics focused on an annual theme such as Alaska, Mexico, or world problems and world personalities. Members included past presidents of accredited Delphian chapters who were at some point members of the Minneapolis chapter of Delphians.

326. Earl, Fanny Kennish. "The Women's Clubs of Minnesota." *Midland Monthly* 5 (January 1896): 18–23.

Gives overview of clubs active in Minnesota in 1890s. Includes sketches of individual clubs and clubwomen in St. Paul and Minneapolis and a list of cultural and civic groups statewide.

327. Educational and Industrial Union, St. Paul. *The Woman's Record*. St. Paul: The Organization, July 1890, September–November 1890, January–February 1891. Illustrations.

Published monthly by a staff of women. Presents an array of materials, including current affairs, advice columns, poetry, timely quotations, recipes, and advertisements.

328. Eradelphian Club. St. Paul. *Yearbook*. St. Paul: The Organization, 1910/11–1920/21, 1922/23–

1937/38, 1939/40–1944/45, 1946/47–1952/53, 1954/55. (MHS).

Includes members' names and addresses as well as lists of officers and federation delegates. Study club, organized in 1893, focused on a wide variety of topics, ranging from Maria Sanford to oriental rugs. Collection also includes brief synopsis of programs for 1893/94–1909/10.

329. Erickson, Judith B. " 'Bless Its Pink Pages': The *Minneapolis Journal* and the Schoolchildren in the Northwest." *Minnesota History* 50 (Summer 1986): 47–62.

Discusses Mae Harris Anson and her work with the *Journal Junior* clubs, which from 1898 until 1913 encouraged a number of young writers whose work was featured in the *Minneapolis Journal.* Participants included Fannie Kilbourne, Elizabeth Olds, Borghild Dahl, and Wanda Gág.

330. Fortnightly Study Club, St. Paul. *Yearbook.* St. Paul: The Organization, 1915–54. (MHS).

Lists annual program events on literary and social topics for study club established in 1914. Includes lists of members, officers, committees, and bylaws.

331. Friday History Club, Minneapolis. *Yearbook.* Minneapolis: The Organization, 1897/98, 1899/1900–1929/30, 1933/34–1942/43. (MHS).

Yearbooks list officers and program committees, members' names and addresses, as well as semimonthly presentation topics on a common annual theme, such as French history, Japan, or Holland. The group organized in 1896. As years passed it became more social and featured current events and book reviews.

332. Frohlicher, Vera Hanawalt. *The Minnesota Division of the American Association of University Women, 1923–1953.* N.p., 1954. 85 p. Appendix.

Sketches history of the state AAUW and its "collegiate alumnae" precursors, 1889–1953. Includes chapters on community action initiatives and financial assistance to students and an appendix listing branches, awards programs, state presidents and conventions, and charter members.

333. Girls Liberty League, Minneapolis. *Community Journal.* Minneapolis: The Organization, 1918–20.

Weekly newsletter published for members of federated girls clubs and organizations in Minneapolis. Established to promote community service and citizenship during World War I. Features news of volunteer opportunities and educational

and social activities. (Note: Title varies; published as *The Weekly News,* August–November 1918.)

334. Gradatim Club, Sauk Centre. *Year Book.* Sauk Centre, Minn.: The Organization, 1938–39. 8 p. (MHS).

Lists meeting dates and topics for social and cultural club founded in 1895. Also includes officers' roster and lists objectives of the organization.

335. Hamline Fortnightly Club, St. Paul. *Yearbook.* [St. Paul?]: The Organization, 1897/98–1949/50, 1970–77. (MHS).

Lists monthly book review programs and hostess assignments for study club organized in 1892. Also gives names and addresses for active and honorary members.

336. Inter Nos Study Club, Minneapolis. *Yearbook.* Minneapolis: The Organization, 1907/08–1916/17.

Volumes include lists of officers' names, directories of members' names and addresses, and meeting schedules with program topics. During early years members' studies focused on common themes such as Scotland, Holland, or Italy, but in later years the members turned to miscellaneous topics.

337. Kenwood Monday Club, Minneapolis. *Yearbook.* Minneapolis: The Organization, 1907/08, 1909/10–1917/18, 1919/20–1926/27, 1928/29–1929/30. (MHS).

Yearbooks list officers and program committee members as well as semimonthly presentations, focusing most often on a literary or historical theme—modern drama, South America, and so on.

338. Kiwanis Camp Auxiliary, St. Paul. *Yearbook.* [St. Paul?]: The Organization, 1936/37. 12 p. (MHS).

Lists meeting dates and events for social and service club in St. Paul. Also includes officers' roster and general membership list (with telephone numbers and addresses). Additional editions also published in 1937–38 and 1938–39.

339. Korsgaard, Kara Marie. "The Meeting Adjourned and Tea Was Served: The Organizational Lives of Elite Women in Late 19th Century St. Paul." Master's thesis, Hamline University, 1988. 160 p. Bibliography, notes, appendix.

Explores public lives of St. Paul women through the organizations they created. Uses New Century Club (NCC) as cornerstone for discussion. Also gives brief synopses of women's clubs throughout the Protestant community and a membership roster for NCC members, 1887–92, listing all known organizational affiliations.

340. Ladies Shakespeare Club, Minneapolis. *Yearbook*. Minneapolis: The Organization, 1896/97, 1898/99, 1900/01–1901/02, 1904/05–1915/16, 1917/18–1919/20, 1921/22–1922/23, 1924/25–1925/26. (MHS).

Yearbooks for study club, organized in 1891 and federated in 1895, which met semimonthly to discuss Shakespeare-related topics, such as history, scenes, and characters. Includes officers' and members' names and addresses after 1900. Issue for 1901/02 contains bylaws. Annual banquet programs included for 1903–05, 1907–11, 1914–15, 1917, 1923–25. During World War I focused on current events and Red Cross work.

341. Long, Lily A. *The New Century Club, 1887–1922*. [St. Paul]: The Organization, 1922. 14 p. (MHS). A brief history of the organization written to mark its 35th anniversary. The club began in St. Paul on August 25, 1887, with Marion Furness, the daughter of Anna and Alexander Ramsey, among the charter members. After three years the club changed from monthly to twice-monthly meetings to pursue miscellaneous topics as well as a literary course that they later broadened to include history and social issues. The group joined the General Federation of Women's Clubs but later withdrew because some members opposed the federation's social reform agenda. The New Century Club strictly observed a prohibition on newspaper reporters attending meetings.

342. "Looking Backward; Women Clubs' Records." *Minneapolis Journal*, October 17, 1909, sec. 6, p. 4; October 24, 1909, sec. 6, p. 5.

Provides brief general history of study clubs and Minneapolis clubs in particular. Describes background to formation of General Federation of Women's Clubs in 1890.

343. Ludcke, Jeannette. *You've Come a Long Way Lady!: The Seventy-Five Year History of the Woman's Club of Minneapolis*. N.p.: The Organization, [1982]. 420 p. Appendix, illustrations.

The club was organized on March 23, 1907, to focus on citywide Minneapolis interests and originally included three departments: arts and letters, home and education, and social economics. Members worked for civic improvement, monitored the Minnesota legislature, and prepared surgical dressings for French relief during World War I. The study reveals many projects, social activities, financial struggles, and relationships with other clubs. It includes a thorough account of the 1970s restoration of the Ard Godfrey house in Minneapolis.

344. Lynnhurst Travel Club. *Yearbook*. Minneapolis: The Organization, 1916–29, 1942–44. (MHS).

Yearbooks for Minneapolis study club established in 1915 list annual program series organized around a country or region of the world—Scotland and Ireland, Italy, South America, and so on. Also includes names and addresses of active, associate, and honorary members. Yearbook for 1916–17 includes constitution and bylaws.

345. Macbride, Thomas H. *Culture and Women's Clubs*. University of Iowa Extension Bulletin no. 20. Iowa City: University of Iowa, 1916. 28 p.

Address to Minnesota Federation of Women's Clubs in Minneapolis on February 12, 1916. Compliments women's clubs and ties them to what he sees as the Lincoln tradition of humanitarianism and action. Challenges women to support minimum wage laws.

346. Merriam Park Study Class, St. Paul. *Yearbook*. St. Paul: The Organization, 1903/04–1925/26, 1927/28–1938/39, 1942/43–1945/46, 1947/48–1948/49, 1950/51–1954/55. (MHS).

Includes names of officers and program topics for club organized as part of the Federation of Women's Clubs in 1901. Names and addresses of members were included in the 1904/05 volume and in the editions after 1912/13. During the very early years members studied topics such as Germany or Shakespeare, and the yearbooks included historical outlines and lists of reference books. After 1910/11 the club brought in a number of outside speakers, and gradually the programs became lighter in nature. The 1919/20 volume includes the organization's constitution and bylaws.

347. Merriam Park Women's Club, St. Paul. *Yearbook*. St. Paul: The Organization, 1897/98–1917/18, 1953/54. (MHS).

Yearbooks include lists of officers and members' names and addresses. The group organized in 1895 to study literature, history, science, and current issues and became part of the Federation of Women's Clubs in 1906. The volume for 1897/98 contains a copy of the organization's constitution. The 1953/54 volume indicates that the club had become more social and less intellectual in nature.

348. Minneapolis Council of Woman's Organizations. *Woman's Council Magazine*. Minneapolis: The Organization, 1895–96.

Monthly publication of citywide association of clubs devoted to philanthropy, education, the arts, and social reform. Offers articles about local social-service projects, cultural activities, and national events.

349. Minneapolis Council of Woman's Organizations. *Yearbook.* Minneapolis: The Organization, 1897–99. 32 p. (MHS).

Lists officers, departments, standing committees, and member organizations for association founded to foster citywide communication among volunteer women's groups working in philanthropy, education, the arts, and social reform. Includes constitution and bylaws.

350. Minneapolis Federation of Delphians. *Yearbook.* Minneapolis: The Organization, 1934–37. (MHS).

Yearbooks give annual themes, calendar of events, and chapter directories for women's study club established in 1926. Also includes list of officers, committee rosters, constitution, and bylaws.

351. Minnesota Federation of Women's Clubs. *Annual Report.* Minneapolis: The Organization, 1896/97–1926/27, 1929/30–1932/33, 1933/34–1936/37, 1939. (MHS).

Features lists of state, district, and individual club members. After 1903/04 the publication included state committee reports and a roster of groups belonging to the General Federation of Women's Clubs. Also published under the titles *Yearbook, Minnesota Clubwoman* (or *Club Woman*), and *Minnesota Federation News.*

352. Minnesota Federation of Women's Clubs. *A Circular of Suggestions for Work and Study Along Educational Lines.* Washington, Minn.: The Organization, [1898?]. 8 p. (MHS).

Pamphlet outlines clubwomen's statewide program regarding school conditions. Focuses on public elementary and secondary school issues, such as the rationale for nonpartisan school boards, standards in teacher training, availability of library and art programs, and the adequacy and uniformity of teacher salaries. Considers some aspects of private and postsecondary education as well.

353. Minnesota Federation of Women's Clubs. *Directory, 1923–1924.* St. Paul: The Organization, 1923. [122 p.] (MHS).

Lists officers, departments, committees, and participating clubs statewide. Includes contact person(s) for each club and information about each group's focus. (Note: Minnesota Historical Society also holds the 1924–25 *Directory* and other ephemeral materials published by the federation and not annotated for this bibliography.)

354. Minnesota Federation of Women's Clubs. *Fifth District News Reel.* Minneapolis: The Organization, 1939–48. (MHS).

Newsletter, published monthly between October and April each year, discusses club activities, reports on work of federation departments, and announces coming events. The publication also contains program-planning hints and advertisements. (Note: Minnesota Historical Society holdings include April 1939, April 1940, January–February 1941, November 1941–January 1943, March–May 1943, January–April 1944, January 1945–October 1946, January 1947–April 1948.)

355. Minnesota Federation of Women's Clubs. *Midwinter Program.* Minneapolis/St. Paul: The Organization, 1902–03, 1908, 1910–14, 1916–17, 1920–26, 1929–42, 1946. (MHS).

Annual gathering held in Twin Cities in February featured reports of statewide department chairs and musical selections.

356. Minnesota Federation of Women's Clubs. *The President's Letter.* Minneapolis: The Organization, 1917–26.

Monthly newsletter focuses on civic improvements (parks and playgrounds), public welfare projects concerning child labor and migrant labor, and literary and cultural activities of members. Continued as *Minnesota Federation News* and *Minnesota Clubwoman.*

357. Minnesota Federation of Women's Clubs, Eighth District. *Program.* N.p.: The Organization, 1910, 1911, 1912, 1914, 1926. (MHS).

Annual meeting program includes order of business and presentations as well as names of district officers. The club districts followed contemporary congressional district lines, and the eighth district included northeastern Minnesota and cities such as Duluth, Cloquet, Eveleth, and Virginia.

358. Minnesota Federation of Women's Clubs, Fifth District. *Constitution and Bylaws.* Minneapolis: The Organization, 1913. (MHS).

Includes names and addresses of district officers, as well as names of members of standing committees.

359. Minnesota Federation of Women's Clubs, Fifth District. *The Market Basket.* Minneapolis: The Organization, May 15, 1913, October 1913, February 1914. (MHS).

Magazine contains committee reports as well as articles on topics of local and national interest, particularly those related to consumer issues. The publication includes advertisements and could be purchased at newsstands or by subscription.

360. Minnesota Federation of Women's Clubs, Fifth District. *Yearbook.* Minneapolis: The Organization, 1916/17–1954/55. (MHS).

Includes lists of names and addresses of state officers and district committee chairs as well as names of committee members. Yearbook also includes bylaws and a district club directory containing the names of each president and secretary and the subject of the annual course of study. After 1927/28 yearbook also features advertisements and a directory of the departments of work.

361. Minnesota Federation of Women's Clubs, First District. *Yearbook.* N.p.: The Organization, 1926/27–1927/28, 1929/30. (MHS).

Contains names and cities for district division chairs, county officers, and county division chairs. All volumes contain constitution and bylaws. Women's club districts followed contemporary congressional district lines, and the first district included southeastern Minnesota and cities such as Blooming Prairie, Stewartville, Lanesboro, and Albert Lea.

362. Minnesota Federation of Women's Clubs, First District Auxiliary. *Program.* N.p.: The Organization, 1909–14, 1918–19, 1921, 1926. (MHS).

Contains names of district officers as well as order of business and entertainment for annual meetings held in a number of cities, including Waseca, Albert Lea, Rochester, and Lake City. The club districts followed contemporary congressional district lines, and the first district included southeastern Minnesota. After 1926 the group omitted the word "Auxiliary" from its title and became known as the First District Minnesota Federation of Women's Clubs.

363. Minnesota Federation of Women's Clubs, Ninth District. *Program.* N.p.: The Organization, 1905, 1910, 1912, 1914, 1921, 1928, 1936. (MHS).

Includes names of district officers as well as order of business for annual meetings. The club districts followed contemporary congressional district lines, and the ninth district included northwestern Minnesota and cities such as Crookston, Fergus Falls, Ada, and Breckinridge.

364. Minnesota Federation of Women's Clubs, Second District. *Program.* N.p.: The Organization, 1911–12, 1914, 1918–19, 1922. (MHS).

Annual meeting program lists participants and order of business as well as entertainment. The club districts followed contemporary congressional district lines, and the second district included southwestern Minnesota and cities such as Worthington, New Ulm, Wells, and Redwood Falls.

365. Minnesota Federation of Women's Clubs, Seventh District. *Program.* N.p.: The Organization, 1909–11, 1912–13, 1918–22, 1936. (MHS).

Includes order of business, which features reports, lectures, and musical selections, and names of executive board members. The club districts followed contemporary congressional district lines, and the seventh district included west-central Minnesota and cities such as Granite Falls, Canby, Alexandria, and Tracy.

366. Minnesota Federation of Women's Clubs, Sixth District. *Program.* N.p.: The Organization, 1905, 1911, 1913, 1921, 1936.

Annual meeting program lists reports, talks, and musical selections as well as names of district officers. The club districts followed contemporary congressional district lines, and the sixth district included north-central Minnesota and such cities as Wadena, St. Cloud, Walker, and Brainerd.

367. Minnesota Federation of Women's Clubs, Tenth District. *Program.* N.p.: The Organization, 1922, 1926, 1936. (MHS).

Annual meeting program includes reports, entertainment, and addresses. The collection contains the 1921 *Directory,* which features the constitution and bylaws and names of district officers and chairs of departments as well as a list of the district's clubs and the names of the president and secretary of each club. The materials are cataloged with the 1943 state convention program, which contains the names of the Minnesota state federation officers and the district presidents. The club districts followed contemporary congressional district lines, and the tenth district included central Minnesota and cities such as Mora, Cambridge, Watkins, and Litchfield.

368. Minnesota Federation of Women's Clubs, Third District. *Program.* N.p.: The Organization, 1910, 1912, 1917, 1919–21.

Annual meeting program features reports, lectures, and musical selections. Volumes contain names of district officers. The club districts followed contemporary congressional district lines, and the third district included south-central Minnesota and cities such as Pine Island, Hastings, Northfield, and St. Peter.

369. *Minnesota Pine.* Duluth: Minnesota Division, American Association of University Women, 1971–. (U of M/Wal).

Quarterly newsletter of the state AAUW covers national policy concerning women's issues, projects of the state division and its branches, and members' activities. (Note: Limited retention, most recent two years only, at Walter Library, University of Minnesota.)

370. Monday Club, Minneapolis. *Yearbook.* Minneapolis: The Organization, 1890/91–1931/32. (MHS).

Although this group, organized in 1882, maintained a women's club format, it was made up primarily of married couples. They met in the evening to discuss varied topics, including literature, history, travel, current events, and art. They also enjoyed a social hour after each meeting and produced plays and games for their annual frolics. (Note: Yearbooks are bound along with a brief history of the club written in 1932; New Year's banquet programs from 1888, 1890–92, 1894, 1896–97, 1901–04; and miscellaneous items.)

371. Monday Literary Club, St. Paul. *Yearbook.* St. Paul: The Organization, 1916–55. (MHS).

Describes diverse, general interest annual program series for civic and cultural club organized in 1910 as an auxiliary to the East Side Commercial Club in St. Paul. Many, though not all of the yearbooks, include member and officer lists. (Note: Minnesota Historical Society holdings include 1914, 1923, and 1932 editions of the constitution and bylaws.)

372. National Council of Jewish Women, Minneapolis Section. *Yearbook and Directory.* Minneapolis: The Organization, 1961–66.

Biennial yearbooks for Jewish cultural and social welfare organization include descriptions of program activities, officer and committee lists, financial reports, and membership rosters. Extensive advertisements of possible use in researching social and economic networks.

373. National Society of New England Women, Puritan Colony No. 14, Minneapolis. *Constitution and Bylaws.* Minneapolis: The Organization, 1908. 19 p.

Provides membership standards and operating rules for Puritan Colony No. 14, a social and cultural organization celebrating New England ancestry in Minneapolis. Also lists charter members.

374. New Century Club, St. Paul. *Annual Report.* St. Paul: The Organization, 1888/89–1890/91, 1892/93–1904/05, 1906/07, 1908/09–1944/45, 1949/50, 1955/56, 1974/75, 1985/86–1987/88. (MHS).

Early volumes include presidential reports as well as names of officers, committee members, and club members. Treasurers' reports, the constitution, and the bylaws were also featured. Beginning with the 1890/91 volume each report also contains a directory of members' names and addresses and a schedule of presentation topics. The collection also includes programs printed separately for the years 1890/91–1900/01, 1902/03–1913/14, 1921/22. The title of the publication changed to *Program and Yearbook* in 1914/15.

375. New Century Club, St. Paul. *Articles of Incorporation and By-Laws.* St. Paul: The Organization, 1934. 10 p. (MHS).

The revision of the 1893 articles of incorporation reveals that membership was by election, and dues were five dollars per year but could be increased. The group held at least 12 meetings each year in an attempt to contribute to the intellectual development of its members.

376. *The New Century Club of Saint Paul, Minn.* St. Paul: The Organization, 1887/88. 14, [2] p. (MHS).

Contains names of officers, committee members, and club members as well as a brief history and a copy of the constitution and bylaws. The group held its first meeting in September 1887.

377. Oak Park Study Club, Minneapolis. *Yearbook.* Minneapolis: The Organization, 1917/18, 1921/22–1930/31, 1932/33–1951/52. (MHS).

Includes members' names and addresses and program topics on a great variety of literary and historical subjects as well as current events. The group organized in 1895 as the Oak Park Literary Club and changed its name in 1941.

378. *The Peripatetics of Minneapolis, 1890–1990.* [Minneapolis]: The Organization, [1990]. 103 p. (MHS).

A series of historical essays written by club members to celebrate the centennial of the organization. The papers, including one by Andrea Brainard, granddaughter of long-time member Clara H. Ueland, relate the work of outstanding members and highlight the major activities of the group, which focused on expanding the members' range of knowledge. There is a membership roster for the years 1890 to 1990.

379. Peterson, Garneth O. "Follies, 'Friendly Visiting,' and Women's Changing Roles: The Junior

League's First 75 Years." *Ramsey County History* 27, no. 2 (1992): 4–11. Illustrations.

Article summarizes organizational history of the Junior League of St. Paul from founding in 1917 by Elizabeth Ames Jackson, Elizabeth Skinner, and Anne White to 1992. Discusses volunteer work of members in city's social welfare organizations and on issues concerning the arts, education, and children. Analyzes how League membership, projects, and fund raising changed over 75 years. Focuses on long-term projects including Junior League Convalescent Home, Children's Hospital Association, St. Paul Community Service, Inc., St. Paul Rehabilitation Center, and Arts and Sciences Center; also looks at the "Follies" entertainments, Next-to-New shops, and other fund-raising efforts.

380. Railway Mail Association, Women's Auxiliary, St. Paul Branch. *Constitution and Bylaws.* N.p.: The Organization, 1925. 10 p. (MHS).

Provides mission statement, membership criteria, organizational structure, dues rates, and meeting schedule for benevolent group associated with railway postal clerks. Later editions published in 1932 and 1937.

381. Railway Mail Association, Women's Auxiliary, St. Paul Branch. *Yearbook.* St. Paul: The Organization, 1904/05–1917/18, 1919/20–1947/48, 1949/50. (MHS).

Relatives of employees and former employees of the United States Railway Mail Service organized in 1898 to seek social and literary advancement and to promote the employee interests of the Railway Mail Association. After 1905/06, yearbooks list members' names and addresses. Volume for 1904/05 contains constitution and bylaws. Meetings often included musical selections. The number of members increased significantly through the years to include more than 160 women in 1950.

382. The Ramblers, Minneapolis. *Yearbook.* Minneapolis: The Organization, 1897/98, 1905/06, 1907/08–1909/10, 1911/12–1925/26, 1927/28–1929/30, 1931/32–1933/34, 1936/37–1944/45. (MHS).

Study club organized in 1896 focused each year on the detailed history and background of one geographical area, such as England or Scandinavia. Yearbooks include lists of officers and committee members and after 1905/06 names of members. Issue for 1911/12 includes constitution and bylaws.

383. Saturday Club, Minneapolis. *Yearbook.* Minneapolis: The Organization, 1903/04, 1906/07–1945/46. (MHS).

Includes names of officers and program committee as well as names and addresses of members. The group, organized in 1899, studied a great variety of topics and often included musical selections in the programs. Volume for 1903/04 includes the constitution for the organization, which was called the Saturday Magazine Club through 1906/07.

384. Science, Literature and Arts Club, Minneapolis. *Yearbook.* Minneapolis: The Organization, 1932–54. (MHS).

Yearbooks for Minneapolis study club founded in 1932 provide schedules for annual program series organized around sociopolitical topics of local, national, and international interest. Includes names and addresses of members.

385. St. Cloud Reading Room Society. *Yearbook.* St. Cloud: The Organization, 1898/99–1905/06. (MHS).

Gives annual program schedule, calendar of events, and hostess assignments for study club organized in 1880. Also provides constitution, bylaws, and membership list.

386. Students Club, Morris, Minn. *Golden Anniversary.* Morris, Minn.: The Organization, 1945. 6 p. (MHS).

Souvenir program for 50th anniversary luncheon commemorating founding of social and cultural club in 1895. Includes menu, schedule of events, and a list of honored guests.

387. Thursday Club, St. Paul. *Yearbook.* St. Paul: The Organization, 1895/96–1924/25. (MHS).

Organized in May 1894 primarily for young single women. Provides lists of officers and committee members along with members' names and addresses. Includes constitution and bylaws and outline of program topics—primarily literary and historical. After 1910 topics became more concerned with current issues, and the number of married members increased.

388. Thursday Study Club, St. Paul. *Yearbook.* Minneapolis: The Organization, 1902/03–1917/18, 1919/20–1947/48, 1950/51–1954/55. (MHS).

Organized in 1899 as the Neighborhood Current Events Club, the group changed its name in 1906/07 and moved from a study of geographical regions to a greater variety of topics. Yearbooks include lists of officers and members' names and addresses.

389. Tourist Club, Minneapolis. *Yearbook.* Minneapolis: The Organization, 1903/04–1941/42. (MHS).

Yearbooks include names of officers and committees as well as members' names and addresses for club organized in 1891 to study background to travel. Topics include history, literature, art, and current issues. Some volumes, including 1911/12 and 1915/16, contain the club constitution. (Note: The end pocket of the second volume includes a two-page handwritten history of the club prepared by two long-time members.)

390. Violet Study Club, Minneapolis. *Yearbook*. Minneapolis: The Organization, 1913/14–1918/19. (MHS).

Includes lists of officers, committee members, and members of group organized in 1906 and federated in 1907. The club operated under the motto "Knowledge Is Power" and pursued topics on an annual theme, such as the 19th century or China, Japan, and the Philippines.

391. *Winter's Program, Woman's Club of Minneapolis*. N.p.: The Organization, 1918–20.

Describes fortnightly lecture series (national and local speakers) offered to members of social and cultural organizations.

392. *The Woman's Club, 1921–1922*. Fergus Falls, Minn.: The Organization, 1921. 5 p. (MHS).

Pamphlet provides 1921–22 calendar for Fergus Falls women's study club meetings organized around the theme "American Drama." Also identifies officers, program committee, and general members.

393. Woman's Club of Fergus Falls. *Constitution and By-Laws*. Fergus Falls, Minn.: The Organization, 1913. 5 p. (MHS).

Outlines organizational structure, meeting schedule, and dues for study club organized in 1913.

394. Woman's Club of Minneapolis. *Articles of Incorporation and Bylaws*. Minneapolis: The Organization, [1915?]. 8 p.

Describes membership procedures, governance, and "departments" of activity (arts and letters, home and education, and social economics) for cultural and public-service club.

395. Woman's Club of Minneapolis. *Bulletin*. Minneapolis: The Organization, 1913–71.

Published monthly, eight issues per year, October–May. Gives calendar of events, member news, officers and committees, and reports for ongoing projects of citywide cultural and public-service club founded in 1907.

396. Woman's Club of Minneapolis. *House Rules*. Minneapolis: The Organization, n.d. 8 p. (MHS).

Describes dining rooms, assembly rooms, library, ballroom, guest rooms, and other facilities maintained for members' convenience at the clubhouse on Oak Grove Street. Outlines procedures governing use.

397. Woman's Club of Minneapolis. *Program, Winter and Spring, 1946*. Minneapolis: The Organization, 1946. 4 p. (MHS).

Describes semimonthly programs offered by social and cultural club, January–April, 1946. Program series includes talks on local and international politics, the arts, and international travel. Also identifies ongoing study groups and classes.

398. Woman's Club of Minneapolis. *Yearbook*. Minneapolis: The Organization, 1914/15–1930/31.

Includes officer roster; annual program calendar; reports of the arts and letters, home and education, and social economics (later civic and social service) departments; president's report; and bylaws for social and cultural club founded in 1907. Also lists members and discusses operations of the organizations's clubhouse on Harmon Place.

399. Women's City Club of Saint Paul. *Constitution and Bylaws*. [St. Paul?]: The Organization, 1921. 8 p. (MHS).

Provides mission statement, membership criteria, organizational structure, dues, and meeting schedule for urban social and cultural club founded in 1921. Later edition published in 1930.

400. The Women's City Club of Saint Paul. *Finance Committee Annual Report*. St. Paul: The Organization, 1969. 2 p. (MHS).

Reflects optimism despite declining number of members and limited funds. Reports profits from cookbook sales, house tour, and style show as well as marked improvement in the management of the dining room.

401. Women's City Club of Saint Paul. *A History of the Women's City Club*. St. Paul: The Organization, 1948–49. 8 p.

Historical sketch describes origins and operations of social and cultural club in downtown St. Paul, 1920–48/49. Outlines initial cooperative arrangements with the Minnesota Club, decision to build separate facilities designed by architect Magnus Jemne, and musical galas produced to raise funds for the building. Also identifies active individuals, past presidents, and current officers.

402. Women's City Club of Saint Paul. *House Rules*. [St. Paul?]: The Organization, 1921. 7 p. (MHS).

Outlines terms of use for women's social and cultural club. The Women's City Club, located in the

Jemne Building in downtown St. Paul, maintained a dining room, assembly rooms, and dressing and bedrooms for its members and their guests.

403. Women's Federated Clubs, First District of Minnesota. *Proceedings [of the] District Convention, May 7–8, 1925.* Wabasha, Minn.: The Organization, 1925. 40 p. (MHS).

Reports on activities of federated women's clubs in southeastern counties—Dodge, Fillmore, Freeborn, Houston, Mower, Olmsted, Steele, Wabasha, Waseca, and Winona. Includes president's report and district reports for legislation, citizenship, Americanization, international affairs, conservation, public health, motion pictures, and other committees of the organization. Also features narrative descriptions of each member club and its activities over the preceding year.

404. *Yearbook [of] Woman's Literary Club, Litchfield, Minnesota.* N.p.: The Organization, 1901–16.

Annual programs for Meeker County organization include topics of discussion, lists of members and officers, constitution, and bylaws.

RELIGIOUS

405. American Lutheran Church Women. *Light in Dark Places: Third Triennial General Convention.* [Minneapolis?]: N.p., [1969?]. 120 p. Illustrations.

Program for national ALC women's general convention in Minneapolis, June 1969. Includes descriptions of conference events and profiles of presenters, delegate rosters, and committees involving many Minnesota women.

406. Bergstrom, Lillian. *A History and a Record of the Activities of the Walbo Ladies Aid.* N.p., 1983. 24 p. Illustrations.

Brief history of Swedish-American Lutheran women's organization in Walbo, Isanti County, 1883–1983. Contains précis of available minutes (including charitable gifts), plus more general community history. It appears the Ladies Aid disbanded about 1983.

407. Bishop, Mary A., and Mary Caroline Beaumont. *A History of the Guild of Catholic Women, 1906–1942.* St. Paul: The Guild, [1942?]. 62 p.

The St. Paul group organized to assist the poor, to care for church altars and vestments, and to present monthly evening entertainments. A sequel to 1913 pamphlet by Mrs. John Burke, it includes the original organizing letter circulated to the clergy,

a chronology of Guild activities, officer roster, and memoriam section.

408. Burke, Mrs. John. *Guild of Catholic Women, 1906–1913.* St. Paul: The Guild, [1913?]. 172 p.

Bylaws, organizational structure, membership list (including addresses and maiden names, if relevant), social-welfare activities, and narrative history of St. Paul club. Highly specific information concerning Guild members' activities and goals. (Note: Some annual reports also available in the Minnesota Historical Society collections.)

409. Evans, Margaret. "The Congregational Women of Minnesota." In *General Congregational Association of Minnesota Minutes of the Fifty-First Annual Meeting,* p. 42–46. Minneapolis: The Organization, 1906.

Author observes that church records kept since 1856 overlook role of women, particularly as fund raisers and Sunday school directors. Concludes that the church has not reached out enough to those in need.

410. Guild of Catholic Women, St. Paul. *Annual Report, Guild of Catholic Women.* St. Paul: The Guild, 1912. 56 p.

Lists officers, committees, general membership, and reports on the St. Paul Guild's relief department, employment bureau, juvenile court department, civic projects, and cultural programs.

411. Guild of Catholic Women, St. Paul. *Biennial Report, 1917–1919.* St. Paul: The Guild, 1919. 54 p.

Includes reports on the Catholic Infant Home, Guild Hall (a workingwomen's residence), the relief department, the needlework department, the juvenile court department, and other programs operated by the Guild in St. Paul. Also contains officer and committee lists, bylaws, articles of incorporation, and a complete membership list. (Note: Minnesota Historical Society copy bound with 1919–21 biennial report.)

412. *The Guild of Catholic Women, Inc., St. Paul.* St. Paul: The Guild, [1978?]. 2 p.

Brief history of the Guild's activities in St. Paul, 1906–78. Outlines changing strategies in fund raising and in charitable organizations supported.

413. Hadassah, St. Paul Chapter. *Bulletin.* St. Paul: The Organization, 1985–.

Monthly newsletter reports scheduled programs, membership news, notices, and fund-raising activities for Jewish women's organization. (Note: Description based on 1986–91 issues. Minnesota Historical Society holds additional runs under the following titles: *Kol Hadassah*, 1936; *Hadassah News Bulletin*, 1937–52; *Bulletin*, 1954–69.)

414. Hadassah, St. Paul Chapter. *Roster*. St. Paul: The Organization, 1975–.

Yearbooks provide officer lists, committees, membership roster, and descriptions of benevolent and social-welfare projects supported by this Jewish women's organization.

415. Hurley, Sister Helen Angela. *On Good Ground: The Story of the Sisters of St. Joseph in St. Paul*. Minneapolis: University of Minnesota Press, 1951. 312 p. Bibliographic notes, index.

Commemorative history covering the years 1851–1951. Includes institutional histories of several dozen schools established throughout Minnesota by the Sisters of St. Joseph of Carondelet with particular attention to St. Agatha's Conservatory, Derham Hall, and the College of St. Catherine in St. Paul. Other elements of interest include Sister Wilfrida Hogan's reminiscence of convent school at St. Joseph's Academy in the 1870s; a dual biographical sketch of Sisters Mary Seraphine (Ellen Ireland) and Mary Celeste (Ellen Howard), who were cousins and later administrators of the order; and a discussion of realities and stereotypes of convent life.

416. Jewish Educational Center Women. *Membership Year Book, 1938/39–1939/40*. St. Paul: The Organization, 1938/39. 23 p.

Membership lists for both the Jewish Educational Center Women and Jewish Educational Center Association (male) in St. Paul in the late 1930s. Both organizations focused on educational and social activities for the Jewish community of St. Paul. Includes board members and officer lists, plus names and addresses for general membership.

417. Kunz, Virginia Brainard. "The Guild of Catholic Women and Their 'Constant Effort to Brighten Lives . . .'." *Ramsey County History* 23, no. 1 (1988): 13–16.

Overview of the activities of the Guild in St. Paul, 1906–80s. Describes aid to Catholic immigrants and young working women, charitable and sewing projects, counseling for wayward young women, and residences and offices maintained by the Guild. Includes capsule biographies of Guild leaders, 1910–20s.

418. Minnesota Council of Federated Church Women. *Bulletin* 1 (September 1936): 1.

Describes founding meeting of the council, an interdenominational Protestant group dedicated to

the creation and maintenance of a Christian social order, at St. Mark's Episcopal Church in Minneapolis, 1936.

419. Minnesota Magdalen Society. *Report*. St. Paul: The Organization, 1875, 1890. (MHS).

Explains 1873 opening of the Women's Christian Home, established in St. Paul by a group of Protestant churches to assist women in leaving prostitution. Includes lists of officers, members, and cash donors; financial reports, including a legislative appropriation; constitution and bylaws; data on residents; and the rules of the house.

420. Sampson, Sister Ann Thomasine. *Care With Prayer: The History of St. Mary's Hospital and Rehabilitation Center, Minneapolis, Minnesota, 1887–1987*. [Minneapolis?]: St. Mary's Hospital and Rehabilitaion Center, 1987. 110 p. Bibliography, index, appendixes, illustrations.

Commemorative history is organized around the tenures of hospital administrators. Chronicles activities of Sisters of St. Joseph of Carondelet, medical staff, lay administrators, the nursing program, the auxiliary, and changes in health care delivery affecting the institution. Includes lists of religious and medical staff, chaplains, and auxiliary presidents.

421. Sampson, Sister Ann Thomasine. "St. Agatha's Conservatory and the Pursuit of Excellence." *Ramsey County History* 24, no. 1 (1989): 3–19.

Describes the music and arts program offered by the Sisters of St. Joseph of Carondelet at St. Agatha's Conservatory in St. Paul, 1884–1962. Places St. Agatha's in context of arts education locally and nationally and discusses clients and faculty. Includes considerable information about financial arrangements at the conservatory, its role in supporting other activities of the Province, and the daily routines of participating nuns.

422. Schloff, Linda Mack. *Our Story: A History of Hadassah, St. Paul Chapter, 1913–1988*. N.p., 1988. 27 p. Illustrations.

Commemorative history prepared for 75th anniversary of a local chapter of an international Jewish women's organization devoted to humanitarian and Zionist causes. Describes social, educational, and fund-raising activities.

423. Wandersee, Delores E. *History of the United Methodist Women, Mounds Park United Methodist Church, Saint Paul, Minnesota*. St. Paul: N.p., 1982. 21 p. References.

Historical sketches of Ladies Aid Society (1892–

ORGANIZATIONS AND CLUBS

1947), Women's Missionary Society (1902–47), Christian Service Guild (1945–60), church circles (1947–82), and United Methodist Women (1973–). Also includes information about women's organizations at Holman Church, which merged with Mounds Park United in 1978. Describes groups' activities and gives officer lists in many cases.

424. Woman's Missionary Society of the Presbytery of Minneapolis. *Program and Report of the Annual Meeting.* Minneapolis: The Organization, 1925–30. (MHS).

Provides annual meeting programs, officer rosters, treasurers' reports, and project listings for domestic and international missions. Also lists Minneapolis events for women's and young people's groups.

425. Womens American Baptist Mission Society. *Golden Jubilee Memorial.* N.p.: The Organization, 1921. 41 p. Illustrations.

Commemorates 50th anniversary of the organization's northwestern district, which included Minnesota, Wisconsin, North Dakota, and South Dakota. The group raised funds to support women missionaries in foreign countries, including Burma, Japan, India, and China. The publication contains records of contributions, reports of the mission activities, and individual photographs of the missionaries, the district officers, and the state secretaries of the society.

BENEVOLENT AND FRATERNAL

426. Daughters of Rebekah, Luella Lodge, No 5. *By-Laws of Luella Lodge, No. 5, Daughters of Rebekah, I.O.O.F.* St. Paul: D. E. Hardy Print., 1894. 16 p.

Describes meeting procedures, dues, and benefits for women's insurance society, affiliated with the International Order of Odd Fellows. Includes membership list.

427. *G.A.R. Roster.* Minneapolis: The Organization, 1903. 12 p. (MHS).

In addition to listing the officers for a number of GAR posts, the publication provides names of the officers for the Minnesota Department of the Woman's Relief Corps and for individual corps units in the state.

428. Masonic Women, St. Paul. *Yearbook.* St. Paul: The Organization, 1932/33–. (MHS).

Yearbooks of women's freemasonry group list officers, committees, social programs, and members over a 60-year period. (Note: Minnesota

Historical Society collection lacks 1933/34–1935/36.)

429. Minnesota Young Women's Christian Association. *Yearbook.* N.p.: The Organization, 1907–08. (MHS).

A state organization of local chapters located in Minneapolis, St. Paul, Albert Lea, Winona, Duluth, Moorhead, Windom, and other cities. Yearbooks contain the report of the state chair, statistics on members, and names and addresses of state executive committee members.

430. Woman's Christian Association of Minneapolis. *Report.* Minneapolis: The Organization, 1881–1948.

Reports on activities of benevolent organization founded in 1866. Describes residential facilities and educational and charitable endeavors managed by the group. Includes officers, participating churches, financial statement, constitution, and bylaws.

431. *Woman's Christian Association of Minneapolis, Minnesota, 1866–1942.* Minneapolis: The Organization, 1942. 63 p. Illustrations.

Sketches history of women's benevolent organization. Includes description of association programs for working women and aged couples, officers and membership lists, bylaws, and financial statement.

432. Woman's Relief Corps, Department of Minnesota. *General Orders No. 2.* Osseo, Minn.: The Organization, 1915. [4 p.] (MHS).

August 20, 1915, announcement of the national convention of the Woman's Relief Corps to be held in Washington, D.C., in conjunction with the 49th annual encampment of the GAR. The bulletin also contains reports on the work of corps units within the state.

433. Woman's Relief Corps, Department of Minnesota. *Proceedings of the . . . Annual Convention.* Minneapolis, 1884–1940.

Reports activities for women's auxiliaries to GAR posts statewide. Identifies officers and chapters. Describes assistance to Civil War veterans and their families and also Memorial Day commemorations.

434. Woman's Relief Corps, Department of Minnesota, Acker Relief Corps No. 7. *By-Laws.* St. Paul: The Organization, 1885. 8 p. (MHS).

Explains the rules and regulations of this St. Paul auxiliary to the GAR. In 1885 the admission fee was one dollar, and the dues were twenty-five cents, paid quarterly. A relief committee administered the requests for aid.

435. Woman's Relief Corps, Department of Minnesota, Garfield Corps No. 5. *History of Garfield Woman's Relief Corps No. 5.* [St. Paul]: The Organization, 1939. 32 p. (MHS).

Includes brief histories of the National Woman's Relief Corps, the Minnesota Department, and the Garfield Corps No. 5 of St. Paul. All were recognized auxiliaries of the GAR and dedicated their organizations to aiding widows and orphans of Civil War veterans. The volume also contains the Garfield Corps membership roster, brief messages from corps leaders, and advertisements.

436. Woman's Relief Corps, Department of Minnesota, George N. Morgan No. 4. *Program.* Minneapolis: The Organization, 1889. [8 p.] (MHS).

Program for a fund-raising benefit held at Harmonia Hall includes a brief report on relief work conducted in Minneapolis by this auxiliary to the GAR. Corps members had distributed gifts of cash and clothing to the needy families of Civil War veterans.

437. Woman's Relief Corps, Department of Minnesota, James Bryant Post No. 54. *Roster of the Officers and Members of James Bryant W.R.C. No. 54.* Minneapolis: The Organization, 1916. 10 p.

Lists members, officers, committees, and past presidents for GAR auxiliary organized in 1888. Bound with roster for James Bryant Post, No. 119. (Note: Minnesota Historical Society holds sundry issues, 1894–1948.)

438. Woman's Relief Corps, Department of Minnesota, Simon Mix Post No. 95. *Roster of Simon Mix Post, No. 95.* Pipestone, Minn.: The Organization, 1889. 24 p. Illustrations.

Includes objectives, eligibility criteria, and membership roster for Simon Mix Woman's Relief Corps No. 12, organized in 1885.

439. Woman's Relief Corps, Department of Minnesota, Southwestern Minnesota GAR Association and Auxiliary. *Organization, Time, and Place of Annual Reunions and Roster of Officers.* Pipestone, Minn.: The Organization, 1909. 63 p. Illustrations.

Provides brief sketch of regional GAR group, participating posts, past department commanders, and national encampments. Officers of the Woman's Relief Corps listed, 1892–1908.

440. Women's Christian Association of Saint Paul. *First Annual Report.* St. Paul: The Organization, 1874. [16 p.] (MHS).

Includes the organization's constitution, which indicates membership was open to any woman who held regular standing at an evangelical church. Members were to assess the needs of the poor in each ward and convey this information to the organization's city missionary. The report also contains the bylaws of the Helping Hand Society, which purchased goods for needy persons, and the industrial school, which made articles to be distributed to the poor. There is a treasurer's report and a membership list.

PROFESSIONAL

441. All the Good Old Girls, Inc. *Directory of Members.* Minneapolis: The Organization, 1979–81.

Lists members alphabetically and also by profession. Extensive advertisements by and for women throughout the directory. Continued by Minnesota Women's Network, 1982.

442. Business and Professional Women's Club. *St. Paul Business Woman.* St. Paul: The Organization, 1924–44. (MHS).

A monthly publication featuring news from chapters around the state as well as jokes, poetry, members' letters, and advertisements. The magazine also includes articles on state and national political issues related to women's lives, such as the controversy over the employment of married women.

443. *History of the Minnesota Association of Deans of Women from April 9, 1925, to March 27, 1943, Inclusive, by the Past President.* N.p.: The Organization, 1943. 57 p.

Provides brief précis of each president's administration, constitution and bylaws, list of charter members, and 1942–43 members list. Contains considerable information about the group's interests and presentations arranged for annual meetings. Membership includes college and high school administrators.

444. *The Minneapolis Business Woman.* Minneapolis: Business and Professional Women's Club, 1920–47.

Monthly journal of the Business and Professional Women's Club of Minneapolis (established in 1920 as the Business Women's Club). Includes club business, profiles of members, and social notes.

445. Minnesota Women's Network. *Directory.* Minneapolis: The Organization, 1982–.

Membership in this educational and service organization listed alphabetically and indexed by profession. Also includes board of directors and mission statement. Advertisements of interest in tracing

A delegation from the Women's International League for Peace and Freedom, seeking signatures on a national disarmament petition, received an official greeting from Mayor William A. Anderson of Minneapolis at city hall on August 1, 1931.

networks and in demonstrating approaches to women customers. Continues All the Good Old Girls, Inc., *Directory* (1979–81).

446. Minnesota Women's Network. *Networker.* Minneapolis: The Organization, 1982–.

Monthly newsletter of the Minnesota Women's Network. Features and profiles concerning career development and financial management for working women. Continues the *AGOG Newsletter* (1978–79) and *AGOG Networker* (1981–82).

447. Zonta Club, St Paul. *Roster.* St. Paul: The Organization, 1984–85. 61 p.

Lists officers, directors, members, and organizational code. Directory section includes business and home addresses, year joined Zonta, area of

business or professional activity, and birthdays (not year).

448. *The Zonta Paul.* St. Paul: The Organization, 1934–78.

Newsletter of the St. Paul Zonta Club, organized in 1926 by business and professional women concerned with civic issues, such as women's employment and urban development. Volumes include a calendar of events, news of members, and reports of conferences and meetings. During the 1950s, programs focused on concerns such as consumer affairs and the value of electricity for busy executives. By the 1970s interests returned to the civic arena when the organization vigorously supported passage of the Equal Rights Amendment to the U.S. Constitution.

REFORM AND ACTIVISM

449. Akre, Edna Honoria. "The League of Women Voters: Its Organization and Work." Master's thesis, University of Minnesota, 1926. 83 p. Bibliography, appendixes. (U of M/Wil).

Describes operations and early history of Minnesota branch in relation to the national organization. Written in an abstract, case-study style. While it lacks information on active individuals, it provides considerable detail about policy formation, recruitment, and fund-raising strategies.

450. American Association of University Women, Minnesota State Division. *Bloom Where You Are.* N.p.: The Organization, 1979. 58 p.

Program for 50th annual meeting of the Minnesota AAUW (St. Cloud, April 1979) contains branch highlights and reports of statewide committees in addition to convention events.

451. American Association of University Women, Minnesota State Division. *Yearbook.* N.p.: The Organization, 1960–75.

Yearbooks list state division officers and officers and committees for affiliate branches statewide and include constitution.

452. American Association of University Women, Minnesota State Division. *Yearbook and Directory.* N.p.: The Organization, 1976–79.

Yearbooks provide historical sketch; calendar of events; lists of officers, trustees, and committees; and membership rosters for statewide affiliate branches.

453. *Female Liberation Newsletter.* Minneapolis: Twin Cities Female Liberation Group, 1969–71.

Mimeographed monthly newsletter. Forum for articles and essays on sexual politics and gender policy issues. Coverage of other Minnesota communities. Continues as *Women's Liberation Newsletter,* 1971–?.

454. Fraser, Arvonne S. *Looking to the Future: Equal Partnership between Women and Men in the 21st Century.* Minneapolis: Women, Public Policy and Development Project, Humphrey Institute of Public Affairs, University of Minnesota, 1984. 45 p.

Provides overview of world conferences about women convened as part of the United Nations Decade for Women, 1976–85. Also discusses activities of women who work in nongovernmental associations to promote change on local, national, and international levels.

455. Gilman, Mrs. Robbins [Catheryne Cooke]. *Final Report of the Women's Co-operative Alliance, Inc.* Minneapolis: The Organization, 1932. 25 p.

Traces history of Minneapolis organization from December 2, 1915, when predecessor Women's Co-operative Committee first recorded minutes. Alliance involved many members and neighborhood mothers working to eliminate juvenile delinquency. Depression-era financial problems forced dissolution of the group.

456. Hargraves, Mildred Fearrington. *The First Fifty Years.* St. Paul: League of Women Voters of Minnesota, 1969. 40 p.

Commemorative history produced for 50th anniversary of the Minnesota League of Women Voters, 1919–69. Treats origins of woman suffrage movement, use of discussion method and other public education techniques, and participation in Minnesota, national, and international political matters. Includes lists of Minnesota League presidents, state delegates to the national League board, and recipients of the Hope Washburn award.

457. Hennepin County Farmer-Labor Women's Club. *Constitution and By-Laws.* Minneapolis: The Organization, 1938. 8 p. (MHS).

Adopted on June 3, 1938, by an organization that sought to unite all women to promote the welfare of the family and the community. Members had to be voted into the club, which was an affiliate of the Hennepin County Farmer-Labor Association.

458. Kroll, Becky Swanson. "Rhetoric and Organizing: The Twin Cities Women's Movement, 1969 to 1976." Ph.D. diss., University of Minnesota, 1981. 2 vols. 452 p. Footnotes, charts, appendixes, illustrations, bibliography.

Based on research in the Minnesota Women's Center Resource Collection at the University of Minnesota. Focused particularly on the newsletters of 32 women's organizations and interviews with key individuals. The author analyzed the rhetoric that mainstream, lesbian, and socialist groups used to describe their activities. Kroll attempted to examine the internal workings of the Twin Cities women's movement and studied participants as well as leaders in order to determine the content of small group communications. Appendix B contains a "Chronology of Key Events in the Twin Cities Women's Movement," which covers the years 1969 to 1976; the bibliography includes a section filled with a wealth of entries referring to journals, pamphlets, and other materials distributed by

Twin Cities women's organizations. Materials used in this study are now housed in the Social Welfare Archives at the university.

459. League of Women Voters of Minnesota. *The Articulate Voter*. Minneapolis: The League, 1945–55.

Newsletter directed to membership statewide. Discusses visiting nurse services and educational and political reform. Published under the title *Minnesota Woman Voter*, 1926–45, and *Minnesota Voter*, 1955–.

460. League of Women Voters of Minnesota. *Human Resources: Minnesota's Changing Patterns*. Minneapolis: State Organization Service, University of Minnesota, 1965. 72 p. Bibliography.

Study of inequality of opportunity in education and employment coproduced by the State of Minnesota, the University of Minnesota, and other public and private agencies. Documents pay inequities for women despite higher educational attainment than many men in the same positions.

461. League of Women Voters of Minnesota. *Minnesota Voter*. Minneapolis: The League, 1955–.

Newsletter directed to League of Women Voters membership statewide. Sample copies examined (1967–71) profile individual members, chapter activities, and political initiatives, such as reports on American Indians in Minnesota. Published under titles *Woman Voter*, 1921–25, *Minnesota Woman*, 1926–45, and *Articulate Voter*, 1945–55.

462. League of Women Voters of Minnesota. *The Woman Voter*. Minneapolis: The League, 1921–25. Illustrations.

Monthly newsletter for statewide membership, plus supplements during legislative sessions. Includes material on government structure; national, state, and local issues; election analysis; and League strategy and organization.

463. League of Women Voters of Ramsey County. *League Bulletin*. St. Paul: The Organization, 1934–49.

Normally published monthly, October through May, the newsletters included schedules of events, as well as reports on current legislation, the work of the organization's departments, and public education campaigns.

464. League of Women Voters of St. Paul. *Guide to the League, 1981–82*. St. Paul: The League, [1981?]. 13 p.

Brief history, statement of principles, board roster, calendar, and proposed activities for St. Paul League.

465. League of Women Voters of St. Paul. *St. Paul Voter*. Bulletins nos. 3–9. St. Paul: The League, November 1965–May 1966.

Monthly mimeographed newsletter describes activities of membership regarding legislative and civic questions.

466. League of Women Voters of the Greater Mankato Area. *The Mankato Voter*. Mankato: The Organization, 1966–84.

Newsletter includes a president's column, meeting notices, legislative information, and financial reports. The publication reflects the political issues of the times from a 1966 focus on antipoverty programs and the Vietnam War to 1984 concerns about family violence, water resources, and continued struggle over proposed ratification of the Equal Rights Amendment. (Note: A number of issues are missing from the Minnesota Historical Society holdings.)

467. McGuinness, Elizabeth Anne. *People Waging Peace*. San Pedro, Calif.: Alberti Press, 1988. 388 p. Epilogue, appendix, index, illustrations.

Survey of post-Vietnam peace movement nationally includes profile of Polly Mann, director of Women Against Military Madness (WAMM) in Minneapolis. Describes WAMM politics and strategies and also Mann's approach to public and family commitments. Activities of WAMM member Erica Bouza also noted.

468. Minnesota Governor's Commission on the Status of Women. *Minnesota Women*. St. Paul: The Organization, 1965. 82 p.

The commission's initial report on the status of women discusses education, employment, home and community, political and civil rights, and situation of minority women. Also includes membership of the commission, its contributing committees, and recommendation that the work of the group continue.

469. Minnesota NOW. *Equality in Minnesota*. St. Paul: The Organization, 1973–.

Monthly newsletter of the Minnesota chapter of the National Organization for Women provides news, book reviews, and announcements from chapters statewide, including the Twin Cities, Wayzata, Rochester, Austin, and St. Croix Valley.

470. Minnesota Woman Suffrage Association. *The Minnesota Bulletin*. Minneapolis: The Organization, 1901–08. (MHS).

This monthly newsletter began publication in September 1901. It contains news of suffrage meetings around the state and elsewhere, as well as reports of the executive board, news of legislative hearings, and notes on members. (Note: There are several issues missing from the Minnesota Historical Society holdings.)

471. Minnesota Woman Suffrage Association. *Yearbook*. Minnesota: The Organization, 1915–16. (MHS).

Yearbooks list officers, directors, committees, statewide affiliates, finances, and bylaws. The 1916 yearbook also contains brief descriptions of conferences and conventions held that year.

472. Minnesota Women for Agriculture, Inc. *Cook Around the Clock*. Lake Mills, Iowa: Graphic Pub. Co., [1986?]. 138 p. Illustrations.

Recipe collection published as a fund raiser by nonprofit, nonpartisan women's group committed to agriculture as a business and a way of life.

473. Minnesota Women's Consortium. *Capitol Bulletin*. St. Paul: The Organization, 1986–.

Weekly newsletter for umbrella organization, which serves 132 women's groups, includes news items on women's accomplishments, a calendar of events, legislative reports, and material on women's athletics. The publication also contains reprints of articles on current political issues, news of participating organizations, and statistical information on the status of women. The *Bulletin* includes a monthly edition focused on outstate Minnesota. After 1988 published as *Legislative Reporter*.

474. Owings, Chloe. *A Community Service Program in Parental Sex Education*. Minneapolis: University of Minnesota Press, 1931. 43 p. Appendix. (U of M/Wil).

Describes programs of the Women's Co-operative Alliance in Minneapolis, 1911–20s, including "parent education" projects in sex education. Paper II in a series of eight papers describing a joint project in family sex education undertaken by the Alliance and the Social Hygiene Research Program at the University of Minnesota, 1925–31.

475. Owings, Chloe. *A Social Hygiene Research Program*. Minneapolis: University of Minnesota Press, 1931. 12 p. (U of M/Wil).

Describes origins of collaboration on family sex education project undertaken by the Women's Co-operative Alliance of Minneapolis and the Social Hygiene Research Program at the University of Minnesota, 1925–31. Focuses on Alliance program and research expectations. Paper I in a series of eight about this project. (Note: Several of the series

bearing on women's experience were not available for review; interested researchers should pursue.)

476. Scovell, Bessie Lathe, comp. *Yesteryears: 62 Years with the Minnesota Woman's Christian Temperance Union, 1877–1939*. St. Paul: Minnesota Woman's Temperance Union, 1939. 264 p. Illustrations.

Documents officers, annual conventions, state districts, departments of work, life members, local unions, and Young Woman's Christian Temperance Union activities in the crusade against "beverage alcohol."

477. Starr, Karen. "Fighting for a Future: Farm Women of the Nonpartisan League." *Minnesota History* 48 (Summer 1983): 255–62.

Uses organizational materials to uncover hidden record of lives of farm women. Wives of Nonpartisan League members could vote and participate in the caucuses but primarily saw the organization as a social network through which they could work to save the farm family.

478. Taylor, Leslie A. "Femininity as Strategy: A Gendered Perspective on the Farmers' Holiday." *Annals of Iowa* 51 (Winter 1992): 252–77.

Assesses women's role in 1930s Depression-era farmers' organization. Increase in mortgage foreclosures in 1932 motivated Ladies Auxiliary to encourage and support husbands' withholding farm produce from the market. A few women worked within the rank and file. Discusses women's role in poultry and egg production. Raises important questions about the study of gender roles.

479. White, Mary S., and Dorothy Van Soest. *Empowerment of People for Peace*. Minneapolis: Women Against Military Madness, 1984. 37 p. Notes.

Pamphlet describes social action agenda for grassroots antimilitary protest and peace-making strategies. Uses female sources for policy and ethical statements throughout.

480. Woman's Christian Temperance Union. *Minnesota White Ribbon*. N.p., 1902–72.

Monthly newsletter reports state, regional, and national activities in the campaign against "beverage alcohol."

481. Woman's Christian Temperance Union. *Report, Twenty-Fifth Annual Convention, St. Paul, Minnesota, November 11–16, 1898*. Chicago: The Organization, 1898.

Reports program schedule for meeting, participating St. Paul institutions, and general business of organization devoted to the abolition of "beverage alcohol." The 1898 convention was dedicated to the memory of founder Emma Willard, who died early in that year. (Note: Minnesota Historical Society copy accompanied by pamphlet program.)

482. Woman's Christian Temperance Union, Blue Earth County. *Program, Second Annual Convention.* N.p., 1889. 4 p.

Lists activities and speakers for two-day meeting held in Methodist Episcopal Church, Amboy.

483. Woman's Christian Temperance Union, Hennepin County. *Annual Program.* [Minneapolis?]: The Organization, 1906/07–1953/54.

Names officers, presidents of local unions, and district superintendents for District No. 17. Gives program topics and calendar for monthly meetings devoted to the prohibition of "beverage alcohol."

484. Woman's Christian Temperance Union, Ramsey County. *Yearbook [of] Woman's Christian Temperance Union, District 23, Ramsey County, Minnesota.* N.p.: The Organization, 1915–17.

Provides membership information, directory to local unions and meeting times, and monthly institute programs for St. Paul and environs.

485. Woman's Christian Temperance Union of Minnesota. *Yearbook.* N.p., 1878–1940.

Provides addresses, reports, and constitutions of state organization and affiliates devoted to the prohibition of "beverage alcohol."

486. Woman's Civic League of St. Paul. *Civic League Program Calendar for 1902.* St. Paul: The Organization, 1901. 64 p. Illustrations.

Provides mission statement, officers, board of directors, and 1901–02 program descriptions for organization devoted to arts and crafts movement and civic reforms. Monthly calendar features satirical verse and pictures concerning political and environmental concerns in St. Paul.

487. Women Historians of the Midwest. *WHOM Newsletter.* St. Paul: The Organization, 1973–. (MHS).

Published five times each year until 1989, then four times each year, to serve midwestern women interested in the study of history. The newsletter includes announcements of meetings and conferences, news of members' activities, and minutes of steering committee meetings. Early editions contain lists of members' names and addresses. (Note: A number of issues are missing from the Minnesota Historical Society's microfilm collection, which contains January 1973 through December 1982.)

488. Women's Co-Operative Alliance, Inc. *Bulletin.* Minneapolis, 1921–31.

Monthly newsletter, printed in four-page format, features information about projects conducted through the Big Sister, education and publicity, and research and investigation departments of the organization. Issues from 1929–30 provide historical background on the organization, founded in Minneapolis in 1914 to protect children from victimization by adults. (Note: Minnesota Historical Society holdings missing some issues.)

489. Women's Co-Operative Alliance, Inc. *Organization Chart.* Minneapolis: The Organization, 1918. 15 p.

Series of charts illustrates relationships among board of managers, the executive committee, executive secretary, the three major departments of the organization—Big Sister, education and publicity, and research and investigation—and community conditions in the city of Minneapolis. Names women's organizations represented on the board of managers. Also includes mission statement for the better-movie movement.

490. Women's Co-Operative Alliance, Inc. *Publications.* Nos. 1–90. Minneapolis: The Organization, 1916–31.

Assorted reports and pamphlets include studies of community conditions in Minneapolis (1925–26), *Fifth Annual Report of the Big Sister Department* (1920), Alliance annual reports (1920, 1921–22, 1923), *Newer Aspects of the Citizens' Solution of the Motion Picture Problem* (1924), and various training programs for volunteers. All describe Alliance projects for improvement of family and civic conditions in Minneapolis. Also includes playbills for some cultural programs sponsored by the Alliance.

491. Women's International League for Peace and Freedom, Minnesota Branch. *The Peace Panorama.* Minneapolis: The Organization, 1936–37.

Monthly newsletter features articles on international and national politics, statewide meetings and rallies, and women's roles as community volunteers in the antiwar movement.

492. Women's Nonpartisan Clubs. *Minnesota: The Problems of Her People and Why the Farmers and the Workers Have Organized for Political Action.* Minneapolis: National Nonpartisan League, [1920?]. 16 p. Notes.

Describes programs of the Women's Nonpartisan

clubs in Minnesota about 1920. Directed at farm women and workingmen's wives. Essentially a critique of big government and big business practices as those impinge upon daily lives of ordinary people. Includes appeal to women as newly enfranchised voters.

493. YWCA of Minneapolis. *YWCA Leader Lunch VII.* Minneapolis: The Organization, 1984. 30 p.
Program for awards luncheon honoring arts administrator Mildred Friedman, businesswomen Karol D. Emmerich and Sharon Bredeson, community volunteer Mary Lee Dayton, educator Sunny Hansen, government planner and adminstrator Jan Hively, writer and community activist Carolyn Holbrook-Montgomery, attorney Susanne Sedgewick, and human services administrator Iris Freeman. Includes brief biographies of the honorees and keynote speaker, Janet O. Hagberg, list of luncheon sponsors and organizers, and YWCA mission statement concerning women's rights and the elimination of racism.

494. Zahniser, Jill D. "Feminist Collectives: The Transformation of Women's Businesses in the Counterculture of the 1970s and 1980s." Ph.D. diss., University of Iowa, 1985. 341 p. Notes, appendixes, bibliography, illustrations.
Analyzes the Amazon Bookstore and Red Star Herbs in Minneapolis along with the Women's Community Bakery and the *off our backs* publication in Washington, D.C. The study concluded that the late 20th-century collectives were more alienated from mainstream society than were earlier cooperatives and communes and that these feminist businesses served to strengthen the individuals who worked within them.

⫿⫿⫾ STATE and LOCAL HISTORY

TERRITORIAL PERIOD

495. Hollinshead, Ellen Rice. "A Sioux Medicine Dance and a Perilous Journey." *Ramsey County History* 3, no. 2 (Fall 1966): 12–16.

Reminiscences of Mendota in 1848 include a Dakota medicine dance, observations of daily life among diverse American Indians and early settlers of the area, and a difficult journey east to Michigan with U.S. Senator-elect Henry Sibley and his family. The author, a member of the Rice family prominent in early Minnesota affairs, later married and settled in St. Paul.

496. Peavy, Linda, and Ursula Smith. *The Gold Rush Widows of Little Falls: A Story Drawn from the Letters of Pamelia and James Fergus.* St. Paul: Minnesota Historical Society Press, 1990. 231 p. Index, illustrations.

Detailed historical study about public and private roles of frontier women. Issues explored through Pamelia (1824–87) and James (1813–1902) Fergus's family experiences of community building first in Little Falls and later in Montana Territory, 1850s–1910s. Based on correspondence during James Fergus's extended business absences, the study is particularly attentive to women's household and business management and to dynamics of reunion following independent living arrangements. Considerable comparative information concerning similarly situated friends, relatives, and business associates.

497. Upham, Warren. "The Women and Children of Fort Saint Anthony, Later Named Fort Snelling." *The Magazine of History* (New York) 21 (July 1915): 25–39.

Synopsis of women and families present at Fort Saint Anthony, 1819–25, prior to renaming as Fort Snelling. Based on genealogies and diaries. Most of individuals described were members of officers' families, but some were from the Selkirk settlement. Links these early European-American inhabitants to territorial place names in many cases.

STATE HISTORY

498. Bingham, Marjorie. "Keeping at It: Minnesota Women." In *Minnesota in a Century of Change: The State and Its People Since 1900,* edited by Clifford E. Clark, Jr., p. 433–71. St. Paul: Minnesota Historical Society Press, 1989. Notes, illustrations.

Survey article discusses women's history under sections titled Organizing for Change: 1900–17; World War I: 1914–1919; New Ideas, Old Problems: 1920s–30s; Watershed Era: World War II and the 1940s; The Rhetoric of Helpmate: 1950s; The New Woman's Movement: 1960s; Turnaround Decades: 1970s–80s. Focuses on contrast between successful group organizing among Minnesota women and the relative scarcity of well-known individuals. Includes African-American, American-Indian, and Hispanic women.

499. Sherr, Lynn, and Jurate Kazickas. *The American Woman's Gazetteer.* New York: Bantam Books, 1976. 271 p. Illustrations, bibliography, index.

Feminist travel guide, organized alphabetically by states and then cities. Section on Minnesota includes 27 entries for the Twin Cities and 15 other communities. Discussion of Dakota War of 1862 and archaeological sites reflects perspectives of the mid-1970s.

LOCAL HISTORY

500. Beito, Gretchen. *Women of Thief River Falls at the Turn of the Century: A Study of Life in a Boom Town, 1895–1905.* Thief River Falls, Minn.: Pennington County Historical Society, 1977. 40 p. Appendixes, illustrations.

Describes characteristics of women citizens and their principal occupations, community contributions, and leisure activities. Includes information about often overlooked groups—particularly American-Indian women and prostitutes. Based largely on written and taped reminiscences.

501. Fosburg, Catherine Haubrich. *Grandmother and Her Family*. [New Ulm, Minn.?]: Privately printed, n.d. 32 p. Illustrations.

Family reminiscence written about 1950 concerning emigration and settlement of a German family in New Ulm. Of particular interest in terms of emigration patterns and also numerous details of domestic and family life in late 19th and early 20th century.

502. *Women's Times*. Grand Marais, Minn.: N.p., 1978–84.

Forum created for women of Cook County included book reviews, interviews with local women, articles on current issues, discussion of the arts, recipes, letters, a "Mother's Corner," and advertisements. Beginning with the first issue, in February 1978, the journal was published monthly. In late 1979 issues began to combine months, and in 1981 it became a quarterly publication. After 1981 there was a break in publication, which ended with a 1984 annual edition.

TWIN CITIES METROPOLITAN AREA

503. Mason, Karen, and Carol Lacey. *Women's History Tour of the Twin Cities*. Minneapolis: Nodin Press, 1982. 91 p. Select bibliography, index, illustrations.

Provides nine tours entitled Minnesota Pioneers, Social Class-Social Service-Education, Ethnicity and Social Service, Downtown St. Paul Walking Tour, University Women, Working Women, Downtown Minneapolis Walking Tour, Health Care, Domesticity and the Nuclear Family: The Neighborhoods of Minneapolis. Focuses on economic and social diversity among Anglo women, with some attention to African-American and Jewish communities. Includes descriptions of each tour site listed and route maps. One of several public education projects undertaken by WHOM (Women Historians of the Midwest) in the 1970s and 1980s.

RURAL LIFE

504. *The Farm Woman Answers the Question: What Do Farm Women Want?* St. Paul: Farmer's Wife Magazine, 1926. 36 p. Illustrations.

Summary of national conference involving 20 invited participants convened in Chicago by the American Country Life Association and staff of *The Farmer's Wife* magazine, March 8–11, 1926. Provides background on conference organization and selected transcripts of discussions concerning education and the farm home, appreciations farm women seek, community development, and economic issues. Leonore Dunnigan, Dan A. Wallace, and Bess M. Rowe from *The Farmer's Wife Magazine* in St. Paul and Mrs. Robert C. Dahlberg from Springfield, Brown County, attended from Minnesota.

505. *The Farmer*. St. Paul: Webb Publishing Co., 1886–.

Weekly magazine that contains a wealth of information on rural life directed at Minnesota farm families over several generations. The first issue, published on May 13, 1886, initiated columns that focused on women's interests. By 1900 the magazine included articles on education, poultry, bee keeping, orchards, and gardens as well as mail-order services for household items, clothing patterns, and house plans. This format continued well into the mid-20th century along with pages of jokes and games for children. Since the 1960s the number of pages devoted specifically to women's issues has decreased. The January 1988 issues included inspirational columns and articles on day care and the dangers of pesticides.

506. *The Farmer's Wife*. St. Paul: Webb Publishing Co., 1897–39.

An extremely valuable social history source on rural life from the turn of the century until the publication was incorporated into the *Farm Journal* in 1939 and continued as *Farm Journal and Farmer's Wife* until 1945. Although the magazine achieved a national circulation, it always maintained a midwestern editorial focus. Issues included articles on world affairs, education, poultry and dairy production, and child rearing, along with a large selection of information on clothing patterns, fancy work, quilt designs, and recipes. There were songs, puzzles, and poems, as well as a number of letters from readers. After 1924 the publication focused more on organized movements, particularly the American Country Life Association.

507. Hampsten, Elizabeth. *Read This Only to Yourself: The Private Writings of Midwestern Women, 1880–1910*. Bloomington: Indiana University Press, 1982. 242 p. Reference notes.

Scholarly literary analysis of private writings by rural women at the turn of the century. The diaries, letters, and casual writings were collected in North Dakota in an attempt to document the lives of

A relaxed and companionable side of rural women's lives comes from Burnsville, about 1943, where Mrs. Frank Gerdermeir, Mrs. Mike Foley, Mrs. Tom O'Brien, Mrs. Martin Hayes, Mrs. Jim Keller, and Mrs. Eli Kearney gathered around a haystack, taking a break from farm work.

working women. The analysis reaches beyond North Dakota to involve much of the Upper Midwest.

508. Hargreaves, Mary W. M. "Women in the Agricultural Settlement of the Northern Plains." *Agricultural History* 50 (January 1976): 179–89.

Surveys women's experiences in the Dakotas, Montana, Kansas, and other Plains states, 1870s–1910s. Discusses "status role" when women were scarce, social isolation, medical concerns, rigors of homemaking in a semiarid climate, and frequently expressed appreciation for natural world.

509. Lindgren, H. Elaine. "Ethnic Women Homesteading on the Plains of North Dakota." *Great Plains Quarterly* 9 (Summer 1989): 157–73.

Examines homesteading records of Anglo-American, Scandinavian, and German women in three settlement periods in North Dakota, 1870s–1910. Documents completion rates on women's claims ranging from 5 to 20% throughout the state. Suggests varying cultural patterns associated with women's homesteading among ethnic groups studied.

510. McVoy, Edgar. "A Study of Wants and Their Satisfactions Among a Sample of Rural People in Minnesota." Ph.D. diss., University of Minnesota, 1941. 133 p. Appendixes.

Study of social and economic conditions on farms and in the village of Cambridge, Isanti County, in

the late 1930s. Largely a comparison of rural-farm and village perspectives. Principal finding is the dissatisfaction of farm women.

511. Neth, Mary. "Preserving the Family Farm: Farm Families and Communities in the Midwest, 1910–1940." Ph.D. diss., University of Wisconsin–Madison, 1987. 592 p. Footnotes, bibliography. (MHS).

Challenges urban-oriented assumptions that rural life was isolated and backward. The study, which focuses on the private world of family life and the informal community, concludes that many farm people actively participated in the changes that led to a centralized agricultural economy and modern agribusiness. The author includes a chapter on "Gender-Based Work and the Technology of the New Agriculture" in which she concludes that scientific experts attempted to redefine the work roles of rural women in order to turn them into middle-class consumers. The study focuses on the Upper Midwest, which includes Minnesota, Wisconsin, and the Dakotas.

512. Nickell, Paulena. "Rural Housing: A Study of 316 Master Farm Homemakers with Special Reference to Adequacy." Ph.D. diss., University of Minnesota, 1932. 185 p. Maps, appendixes, bibliography.

Based on nominations and questionnaires submitted for annual recognition of rural homemakers in the national magazine *The Farmer's Wife,* about 1927–31, this study offers a detailed view of homemaking activities, primarily on diversified farms of the Midwest and the Southeast. Self-descriptions of daily living conditions are presented alongside prescriptive literature from home economics and agricultural extension.

513. Nunnally, Patrick. "From Churns to 'Butter Factories': The Industrialization of Iowa's Dairying, 1860–1900." *Annals of Iowa* 49 (Winter 1989): 555–69.

Focuses on the butter trade in eastern Iowa as seen through the diary of Emily Hawley Gillespie, 1858–88. Associates modernization of the dairy industry with devaluation of women's traditional work.

514. "Oral History and Rural Women in the United States." *Oral History Review* 17 (Fall 1989): 1–23, 91–116.

Articles include a symposium, "The Representation of Women's Roles at the Oliver Kelley Farm" (Elk River, Sherburne County) by Amy Sheldon, Thomas A. Woods, and Joan M. Jensen; "If I must say so myself," a review essay on oral history collections with rural women nationally, by Nancy Grey Osterud and Lu Ann Jones; "Making the Personal Political: Women's History and Oral History," a review essay by Susan Armitage.

515. Ridgley, Donald. "History with a Heart—A Frontier Historian Looks at the 'Little House' Books of Laura Ingalls Wilder." *Heritage of the Great Plains* 20 (Winter 1987): 21–28.

Criticizes historians for ignoring what he sees as Wilder's valuable depiction of the American frontier experience, including the role of women.

516. Riley, Glenda. "In or Out of the Historical Kitchen: Interpretations of Minnesota Rural Women." *Minnesota History* 52 (Summer 1990): 61–71.

Historiographic essay explores roles of women before and after the "market economy" developed in various regions of the state. Quotes extensively from women's diaries, journals, and letters. Discusses difficulties of interpreting meaning of historical changes in women's lives for present-day audiences.

517. Thomas, Sherry. *We Didn't Have Much, But We Sure Had Plenty: Stories of Rural Women.* Garden City, N.Y.: Doubleday, Anchor Press, 1981. 185 p. Illustrations.

Selected and edited interviews with 12 middle-aged and elderly women representing rural areas nationally. Combines appreciation for historical experience of older informants with contemporary "back-to-land" perspectives of the 1970s. Alice Tripp of Belgrade, Stearns County—teacher, power line activist, protest candidate for governor in 1978—is one of the individuals profiled.

518. Wanless, Dorothy L., comp. and ed. *Century Farms of Minnesota: One Hundred Years of Changing Life Styles on the Farm.* Dallas: Taylor Publishing Co., 1985. 352 p. Illustrations.

Approximately one-third of more than 3,000 family-held century farms in Minnesota profiled by family members and friends. Organized alphabetically within counties. Includes contextual essay and complete list of century farm owners as of 1985. Considerable information about gender roles and family farming.

519. *Women for Agriculture Minnesota.* Warren, Minn.: The Organization, 1984–85.

Monthly newsletter reports statewide activities of women involved in production agriculture and in related public policy issues. Continues as *Minnesota Women for Agriculture* (1985).

ᴵᴵᴵᴵᴸ/ Regional Studies

GENERAL

520. Flora, Cornelia Butler, and Jan L. Flora. "Structure of Agriculture and Women's Culture in the Great Plains." *Great Plains Quarterly* 8 (Fall 1988): 195–205.

Study of men's and women's roles in agricultural production on family farms of Ellis County, Kans., from 1870s through 1930s. Compares activities of U.S.-born German and Russian-German family farm enterprises, looking at relationships among ethnicity, farming strategies, and women's and men's cultures.

521. *Plainswoman.* Grand Forks, N.Dak.: Plainswoman, Inc., 1977–89.

Monthly journal covers regional women's history in the Plains states and Upper Midwest and current women's concerns nationally. Individual issues organized thematically around topics such as childhood, Indian identity, friends and relations, agriculture, and art.

IOWA

522. Fink, Deborah. "Anna Oleson: Rural Family and Community in Iowa, 1880–1920." *Annals of Iowa* 48 (Summer–Fall 1987): 251–63. Notes.

Biographical essay concerning farming, community, and family activities of Anna Oleson (1832–1925), a Norwegian Quaker immigrant who settled in Marshall and later O'Brien counties in Iowa. The author documents extensive public activity on Oleson's part through research on family and kinship networks as distinct from "male" public records.

523. Fink, Deborah. *Open Country Iowa: Rural Women, Tradition and Change.* SUNY Series in the Anthropology of Work. Albany: State University of New York Press, 1986. 275 p. Notes, bibliography, index.

Anthropological study of rural women's activities in an unnamed northwest Iowa county, from 1910s to 1980s. Focuses on social process—patterns of interaction among women and between women and men in both public and private life. Considers work and social activities on and off farm, government policies, and the influence of World War II. Based on in-depth interviews, documentary research, and participation and observation in the community in 1982.

524. Riley, Glenda. *Cities on the Cedar: A Portrait of Cedar Falls, Waterloo and Black Hawk County.* Parkersburg, Iowa: Mid-Prairie Books, 1988. 79 p. Illustrations, index, sources, and suggested readings.

Community study of Black Hawk County, Iowa, from 1840s to 1980s. Combines women's and social history perspectives with local development or "booster" history.

525. Riley, Glenda. *Frontierswomen: The Iowa Experience.* Ames: Iowa State University Press, 1981. 211 p. Notes, bibliographic essay, index, illustrations.

Focuses on experience of white frontierswomen in Iowa, 1830–70. Some attention to African-American and foreign-born women as well. Based on close examination of primary sources. Divided into chapters concerning westward travel, urban and rural homes, women's work, diverse cultural heritages, the Civil War on Iowa's home front, "strong-minded women" myths, and realities concerning women's status.

WISCONSIN

526. Wisconsin Governor's Commission on the Status of Women. *Real Women, Real Lives: Marriage, Divorce, Widowhood.* [Madison]: The Commission, 1978. 96 p. Notes.

Overview of the legal status of women in Wisconsin in the 1970s. Largely concerned with situations of married women homemakers. Based on numerous case studies.

NORTH DAKOTA

527. Benson, Bjorn, et al. *Day In, Day Out: Women's Lives in North Dakota.* Grand Forks: University of North Dakota Press, 1988. 326 p. Index.

Thirty-seven multicultural essays, reminiscences, and analyses of women's lives in North Dakota, 19th century to 1980s. Inclusive of some often overlooked groups such as women religious, American Indians, and antisuffrage forces; African Americans, Hispanics, and lesbians are not as well represented. Conceived as a statehood centennial project, the collection is of interest for the ways it combines works by community historians, professional scholars, artists, and others.

528. *Women in Action: North Dakota Photographs.* East Grand Forks, Minn.: Plainswoman, Inc., 1982. Unpaginated. Illustrations.

Catalog for exhibition of same name. A project supported by the North Dakota Humanities Council, it features photographs of women at work and occasionally at play from the 19th century to the 1980s. Contains many classic views familiar to students of women's history and photography as well as some unusual historic images of rarely recorded everyday activities.

SOUTH DAKOTA

529. Alexander, Ruth Ann. "South Dakota Women Stake a Claim: A Feminist Memoir, 1964–1989." *South Dakota History* 19 (Winter 1989): 538–55. Illustrations, notes.

Chronicle of contemporary women's movement, 1960s–80s, incorporating considerable autobiographical perspective. Of comparative interest to Minnesota and other Upper Midwest states.

530. South Dakota Commission on the Status of Women. *South Dakota Women, 1850–1919: A Bibliography.* Pierre: The Commission, 1975. 24 p. Illustrations.

Pamphlet listing bibliographies, fiction, and nonfiction for South Dakota women, 1850–1919. Books and pamphlets only; excludes periodicals, county histories, and media presentations. Largely works of European-American settlement. Little

concerning American Indians, African Americans, or Hispanics, although a bibliography about Dakota women is described as being planned.

531. Stutenroth, Stella Marie. *Daughters of Dacotah.* Mitchell, S.Dak.: Educator Supply Co., 1942. 157 p. Illustrations.

Sketches of South Dakota governors' wives and other notable women active in philanthropy, the arts, education, church work, law, and landscape architecture. This work originated in the author's contributions, starting in 1908, to *Dacotah Magazine* and is of interest in terms of evolving attitudes toward women's roles and activities.

532. Williams, Elizabeth Evenson. *Reflections of a Prairie Daughter.* Brookings, S.Dak.: Prairie Daughter Publishing, 1989. 137 p. Illustrations.

Collection of columns written for the Brookings, S.Dak., *Daily Register,* 1985–89. Topics include local reminiscences, political figures, European travels, and national and state issues. The book includes a chapter on "Women's Roles and Issues."

PROVINCES OF CANADA

533. Kinnear, Mary, and Vera Fast, comps. *Planting the Garden: An Annotated Archival Bibliograpy of the History of Women in Manitoba.* Winnipeg: University of Manitoba Press, 1987. 314 p. Index, appendix, notes, and selected photographic collections.

Contains 1,446 entries organized alphabetically within categories entitled identity, work and activities, mentality, faith, and reform. Covers period pre-1867 to 1980.

534. Rasmussen, Linda, et al., comps. *A Harvest Yet to Reap: A History of Prairie Women.* Toronto: The Women's Press, 1976. 240 p. Bibliography, index, illustrations.

Profusely illustrated collective portrait of European-American women's lives in agricultural settlements of the Canadian prairies in the early 20th century. Information from diverse sources organized around topics of westward movement, daily life, reform politics, and suffrage. Includes biographical section and timeline.

⫿⫿⫿⫾/ Reliqion and Philosophy

RELIGION AND THEOLOGY
(including churches)

535. Bass, Dorothy C., and Sandra Hughes Boyd. *Women in Religious History: An Annotated Bibliography and Guide to Sources.* Boston: G. K. Hall & Co., 1986. 155 p. Index.

Bibliography of secondary literature considers women's history generally, as well as Protestant, Roman Catholic, Judaic, African-American, American-Indian, utopian, and various alternative religious movements. Numerous research strategies and specialized sources are noted throughout. (Note: Lutheran citations are largely Missouri Synod.)

536. Berg, Sister Carol. "Climbing Learners' Hill: Benedictines at White Earth, 1878–1945." Ph.D. diss., University of Minnesota, 1981. 214 p. Appendixes, bibliography.

Study of the Benedictine mission to the Ojibway in west-central Minnesota. Special attention to the boarding school as an instrument of cultural change and exchange and to missionaries' connections to St. John's Abbey, Collegeville, and St. Benedict's Convent, St. Joseph. Detailed bibliographic essay.

537. Boehlke, Catherine Gaines. *Profiles of Twenty-Five Episcopalian Women.* N.p., 1985. 52 p.

Contains biographical sketches of women active in church affairs statewide in the 19th and 20th centuries. Includes Sister Annette Relf (1840–1915), who founded Sheltering Arms, a Minneapolis orphanage; Jeannette Piccard (1895–1981), who was among the first women ordained as priests in 1974; Cornelia Whipple (1816–90), who helped to establish church schools; and recent presidents of Episcopal Church Women, Diocese of Minnesota.

538. Boyd, J. S. *How the Ladies Raised Their Money for Presbyterian Church Repairs.* N.p., 1902. 28 p.

Souvenir booklet containing humorous poetic tribute to women's fund-raising efforts on behalf of Greenleaf Presbyterian Church, summer 1902, in Greenleafton, Fillmore County. Describes specific strategies and sums raised by individuals. Poem composed by pastor and delivered in public meeting at church.

539. Congregational Conference of Minnesota. *Minutes of the . . . Annual Meeting of the Congregational Conference and the . . . Annual Meeting of the Congregational Women.* Minneapolis: Colwell Press, 1926–40.

Annual reports of the Minnesota Congregational Woman's Missionary Society bound with general conference minutes beginning in 1928. Woman's Society section documents budgets, activities, officers, and membership statewide. The Woman's Missionary Society formed in 1926, the result of a merger of the Minnesota Woman's Home Missionary Union and Minnesota Branch of the Women's Board of Missions of the Interior. Additional minutes for 1941–54 and 1955–66 bound with general conference proceedings for those years.

540. Gundersen, Joan R. "The Local Parish as a Female Institution: The Experience of All Saints Episcopal Church in Frontier Minnesota." *Church History* 55 (1986): 307–22.

Describes primary role of the Northfield Ladies Social Circle in founding, building, and financially supporting the operations of All Saints Episcopal Church, 1850s–1900. Discusses women's "shadow leadership" in the context of official, male hierarchies.

541. Gundersen, Joan R. "Parallel Churches?: Women and the Episcopal Church, 1850–1980." *Mid-America: An Historical Review* 69, no. 2 (1987): 87–97.

Analyzes changing roles of women in the Episcopal church as seen from "the pew up" and from "top down" national structures. Uses the Women's Auxiliary at All Saints Parish in Northfield, Rice County, to discuss parallel women's and men's organizations developed in the 19th century and the evolution of an "asymetrical" hybrid model in the 20th-

Thirteen-year-old Janet Pink prepared to read from the Torah in 1983 during her Bat Mitzvah at Adath Jeshurun, a Conservative Jewish synagogue in Minneapolis. At her side were her parents, Norman and Dorothy Pink.

century in which women participate in both women's organizations and an integrated governance and ministry for national and parish churches.

542. Hurley, Sister Helen Angela. "The Sisters of St. Joseph and the Minnesota Frontier." *Minnesota History* 30 (March 1949): 1–13.

Describes letters written in 1894 and 1895 by three members of the Sisters of St. Joseph of Carondelet who had taught in Minnesota Territory. After their arrival in St. Paul in 1851, members of this order proceeded to found schools in St. Paul, St. Anthony, and Long Prairie.

543. Ireland, John. "A Catholic Sisterhood and Education." In *The Church and Modern Society: Lectures and Addresses,* vol. 2, p. 303–25. St. Paul: Pioneer Press, 1904. (U of M/Wil).

Sermon delivered by Archbishop John Ireland at 50th anniversary celebration of St. Clara's College, founded by Sisters of St. Dominic at Sinsinawa, Wis., about 1854. Has some information about the order but focus is on Catholic education more generally and the role of sisters in furthering those aims.

544. Ireland, John. "A Catholic Sisterhood in the Northwest." In *The Church and Modern Society: Lec-*

tures and Addresses, vol. 2, p. 279–301. St. Paul: Pioneer Press, 1904. (U of M/Wil).

Sermon describing the work of the Sisters of St. Joseph of Carondelet in Minnesota, 1851–1902, delivered by Archbishop John Ireland at semicentennial celebration of St. Joseph's Academy in St. Paul. Chronicles activities of the order and also official position of the Roman Catholic church regarding women religious.

545. Lagerquist, L. DeAne. *From Our Mother's Arms: A History of Women in the American Lutheran Church.* Minneapolis: Augsburg Publishing House, 1987. 221 p. Notes, appendix, index.

Focus is on the women's societies, mid-19th century to 1980s, in those Lutheran churches that formed the American Lutheran Church in 1960. Discusses local societies of late 19th century and 20th-century history of increasing federation and consolidation.

546. Lindsay, Effie G. *Missionaries of the Minneapolis Branch of the Women's Foreign Missionary Society of the Methodist Episcopal Church.* Minneapolis: Murphy-Travis Co., 1904. 82 p. Illustrations.

Institutional history, 1883–1904. Includes profiles of women missionaries, many Minnesota born, supported by the society in India, China, and areas of Southeast Asia.

547. Lutheran Church in America, Minnesota Synod. *Convention Proceedings.* N.p.: The Organization, 1962–.

Minutes of the annual convention, Minnesota Synodical Unit, Lutheran Church Women (LCW), bound with general proceedings. LCW records include brief descriptions of convention program sessions, bylaws, officers, and financial report.

548. McDonald, Sister M. Grace. *With Lamps Burning.* St. Joseph, Minn.: Saint Benedict's Priory Press, 1957. 329 p. Appendixes, notes, bibliography, index, illustrations.

Centennial history of the Convent of St. Benedict in St. Joseph, 1857–1957. Focuses on congregational organization and on educational and social ministry to the immigrant Catholic community and to American Indians in central Minnesota.

549. Nevins, Katherine Juul. "Personality Correlates of Christian Feminists, Religious Fundamentalists and Feminists." Ph.D. diss., University of Minnesota, 1986. 210 p. References, appendixes.

Psychology study investigates similarities and differences among women professing religious and feminist values. Based on 1985 research with college students at public and private (including denominationally affiliated) campuses in the Twin Cities. Findings are that Christian feminists were more likely to affiliate with a church that ordained women and to describe themselves as politically independent. Otherwise, they share common expectations and experiences with both fundamentalists and feminists.

550. Order of St. Benedict. *Sponsa Regis.* Collegeville, Minn.: The Organization, 1929–65.

Monthly journal devoted to the Catholic sisterhoods offers homilies, a continuing forum concerning religious vocation, a question and answer column, and book notices. Continues under the title *Sisters Today,* 1965–.

551. Peterson, Susan Carol, and Courtney Ann Vaughn-Roberson. *Women with Vision: The Presentation Sisters of South Dakota, 1880–1985.* Urbana: University of Illinois Press, 1988. 332 p. Appendixes, notes, bibliography, glossary, index.

Critical history focuses on evolving roles within the Roman Catholic church and the order's work in education and health care. Especially attentive to issues of professionalism within the church and social services provided by the order.

552. Roman Catholic Bishops of Minnesota. *Woman: Pastoral Reflections.* St. Paul: Minnesota Catholic Conference, 1979. 20 p.

Pamphlet contains two papers on the subject of women and the church. The first paper, drafted by consultants to the Social Action/Social Welfare Department of the Minnesota Catholic Conference, affirms doctrines of equality and justice within and without the church for all women. The second paper, written by the bishops, characterizes family life and the example of the Virgin Mary as a model for all women in their public and private roles. Neither paper addresses the ordination of women.

553. Sampson, Sister Ann Thomasine. *The Ireland Connection.* St. Paul: St. Paul Province Sisters of St. Joseph of Carondelet, [1983?]. 72 p. Illustrations.

Collection of articles exploring influence of Mother Seraphine Ireland, Mother Celestine Howard, Sister Annetta Wheeler, and Archbishop John Ireland, all members of the same immigrant Irish family, upon the St. Joseph of Carondelet congregation. Articles include: "Richard and Judith Naughton Ireland and CSJ Root"; "Mother Seraphine Ireland and the Art of Persuasion"; "Sister Annetta Wheeler and Tradition"; "John Wheeler and CSJ Buildings." Period covered is mid-19th century through 1930s. A separately paginated pamphlet (8 p.) entitled "A Guide to Places of CSJ Historic Interest in Minnesota and North Dakota" is bound with *The Ireland Connection.*

554. *Women's Words: A Portfolio of Quotations from Selected Women of the Bible Calligraphed by Contemporary Women Artists.* Minneapolis: Martin Press, 1979. Unpaginated. (U of M/Wil-Rare books).

Selected passages attributed to Hannah, Ruth, Mary, Judith, Elizabeth, Susanna, and Mary Magdalene. Commentary by the Reverend Jeannette Piccard discusses the selections in context of 1970s feminist and religious concerns.

SPIRITUALITY

555. Kloberdanz, Timothy J. "The Daughters of Shiphrah: Folk Healers and Midwives of the Great Plains." *Great Plains Quarterly* 9 (Winter 1989): 3–12.

Ethnographic discussion of German-Russian folk healers and midwives in areas of North Dakota, Kansas, and Saskatchewan, 1870s–1970s, explores Christian and magic elements of their practices. Describes European customs, North American adaptations, and family specializations.

ılılı/ Visual, Literary, and Performing Arts

FOLK AND DOMESTIC ARTS

556. Burris, Evadene A. "Furnishing the Frontier Home." *Minnesota History* 15 (June 1934): 181–93.
Describes in detail a number of household items used in the 1850s, including beds, bedclothes, dishes, cooking utensils, pianos, linens, and carpets. The author also provides an analysis of furniture construction and cabin interiors.

557. Cerny, Catherine Anne. "Quilted Apparel: A Case Study of a Cultural Vehicle." Ph.D. diss., University of Minnesota, 1987. 302 p. References, illustrations.
Investigates the relationship of dress and identity among members of Minnesota Quilters, a predominately middle-class, married group of women who make and use quilted patchwork apparel, bedcovers, and wall hangings. Explores gendered, historical, social, expressive, and organizational dimensions of the organization. Based on mid-1980s research.

558. Goff, Lila J. "Byrdie Kraft and Her Furniture." *Minnesota History* 48 (Fall 1983): 303–8.
Describes Kraft family furniture items included in Minnesota Historical Society's museum holdings. The collection includes Mission-style pieces that Byrdie Kraft made in her shop class at Minneapolis North High School in the years before graduating in 1915.

559. Seidl, Joan M. "Consumers' Choices: A Study of Household Furnishing, 1880–1920." *Minnesota History* 48 (Spring 1983): 183–97.
Traces the development of home decoration styles as the consumer-oriented market increased the householder's appetite for possessions. The author focuses on the individual tastes of several Minnesota women, including Frances James, Helen Sommers, Stella Kincaid, and Ilma Cale.

560. Westbrook, Nicholas, and Carolyn Gilman. "Minnesota Patchwork." *Minnesota History* 46 (Summer 1979): 237–45.

In 1934 Dakota elder Isabel Roberts, Granite Falls, showed photographer Monroe Killy how women scraped a hide in the process of creating the supple material used for clothing or other articles often beautifully decorated with quillwork or beads.

Analyzes quilts as a form of female-created material culture. The article appeared in conjunction with a Minnesota Historical Society exhibit that interpreted quilts as a reflection of textile development and the presence of community bonds.

VISUAL, LITERARY, AND PERFORMING ARTS

THEATER AND MIME

561. Alive and Trucking Theater Company, Minneapolis. *Stage Left: 3 Plays from Alive and Trucking's First Year.* Minneapolis: The Company, 1973. 160 p. Illustrations.

Contains a brief history of the women's theater company, an essay on the political philosophy of the group, and biographical sketches of principal participants. Also contains texts for the three plays: *Pig in a Blanket, The People Are a River,* and *The Welfare Wizard of Ours.*

562. Flynn, Meredith. "The Feeling Circle, Company Collaboration, and Ritual Drama: Three Conventions Developed by the Women's Theater, At the Foot of the Mountain." Ph.D. diss., Bowling Green State University, 1984. 256 p. Bibliography, appendixes.

Analyzes contributions of At the Foot of the Mountain Theatre Company in Minneapolis to the national feminist theater movement, 1974–83. Discusses processes of company collaboration in the development of its plays, the use of the "feeling circle" as an acting exercise and personal "check-in" point for company members, and the group's use of ritual drama as a "healing" component of its productions. Also describes numerous productions, including *Ashes, Ashes, We All Fall Down,* about nuclear holocaust; *Rape; Junkie!; Moontree,* based on the Bluebeard story; *The Life,* an inquiry into prostitution; and *Clue in the Bird Bath,* a take-off on Nancy Drew mysteries.

563. Greeley, Lynne. "Spirals from the Matrix: The Feminist Plays of Martha Boesing, An Analysis." Ph.D. diss., University of Maryland, 1987. 329 p. Bibliography, appendixes.

Analyzes 22 plays written by Martha Boesing and produced by At the Foot of the Mountain Theatre Company in Minneapolis, 1974–84. Focuses on relationships between the personal and the political in Boesing's art. Contains considerable biographical data. Also provides extensive discussion of content and form in the playwright's work.

564. Lacy, Suzanne. *Whisper Minnesota: The Crystal Quilt/Older Women's Voices.* N.p., 1987. 24 p. Illustrations.

Pamphlet/program for the Crystal Quilt performance piece (1987) and larger Whisper Minnesota Project (1985–87). Both the Minneapolis performance and the overall project, which incorporated community organizing and leadership development in addition to art production, promoted active images of and opportunities for older women.

PAINTING, SCULPTURE, AND PHOTOGRAPHY

565. Baker, Tracey. "Nineteenth-Century Minnesota Women Photographers." *Journal of the West* 28 (January 1989): 15–23.

Traces women's contributions to photography beginning with Sarah Judd's daguerreotype business in Stillwater, 1848–50. Photography proved to be a popular and accepted business for women in several cities throughout Minnesota.

566. Cohen, Ronny. *Structure and Metaphor: Six Contemporary Visions.* Minneapolis: WARM Gallery, 1986. 22 p. Illustrations.

Catalog and checklist for 1986 Women's Art Registry of Minnesota (WARM), Minneapolis, exhibition featuring works by six contemporary Minnesota and New York artists: Harriet Bart, Elizabeth Erickson, Jeanette Fintz, Pat Hammerman, Judith Murray, and Jantje Visscher. Includes brief biography of each artist.

567. Cox, Richard W. "Wanda Gág: The Bite of the Picture Book." *Minnesota History* 44 (Fall 1975): 239–54.

Analyzes social concerns such as women's rights and the costs of modern industrial society in Wanda Gág's drawings, prints, and children's books, 1920–40. Discusses New Ulm and Twin Cities education, influences, and friendships, 1913–17, as preparation for Art Students League, Greenwich Village, and other New York City experiences in 1920s and 1930s.

568. Keim, Rebecca. *Three Women Artists: Gág, Greenman and Mairs.* Minneapolis: University of Minnesota, University Gallery, 1980. 34 p. Illustrations, notes, bibliography.

Catalog and checklist for 1980 exhibition featuring works by mid-20th-century Minnesota artists: printmaker and painter Wanda Gág (1893–1946), portraitist Frances Cranmer Greenman (1890–1981), and painter and printmaker Clara Mairs (1878–1963). Includes biographical essays and bibliographies for each.

569. Klammer, Paul W. *Wanda Gág: An Artist of Distinct Individuality.* New Ulm, Minn.: Brown County Historical Society, 1979. 18 p. Illustrations.

Profiles printmaker and children's book author and illustrator Wanda Gág (1893–1946), focusing on childhood in New Ulm and adult career in New York. Special attention to New Ulm sources for her art, especially Goosetown, an "Old World" section of the largely German community, and her maternal grandparents' farm outside town.

570. Scott, Alma, et al. "In Tribute to Wanda Gág." *The Horn Book Magazine* 23 (May–June 1947): 156–207. Illustrations.

Memorial issue of a specialty publication about children's literature, devoted to the life and work of Wanda Gág (1893–1946). Includes a series of tributes to the Minnesota-born author-illustrator: "Art for Life's Sake" by Anne Carroll Moore, "Wanda Gág" by childhood friend and fellow author Alma Scott, "Wanda Gág, Artist" by curator Carl Zigrosser, "Wanda Gág as Writer" by editor Ernestine Evans, "Wanda Gág, Fellow-Worker" by Rose Dobbs, "Wanda Gág, Fellow Artist" by Lynd Ward, and "Letters from Children to Wanda Gág" selected and edited by Gág's widowed husband Earle Humphreys.

571. *WARM Journal/Women's Art Registry of Minnesota.* Minneapolis: The Registry, 1980–89.

Illustrated quarterly journal focuses on activities and interests of contemporary women artists in Minnesota, 1980–89. Individual issues feature biographical profiles, exhibition and book reviews, and news and notes of national and regional women's art. Frequent thematic issues in 1983–84 organized around topics such as quality in women's art, the fashion magazine genre, eros, and success.

572. Women's Art Registry of Minnesota, Minneapolis. *WARM: A Landmark Exhibition.* Minneapolis: The Registry, 1984. 103 p. Illustrations.

Exhibition catalog and checklist for 12th-anniversary commemoration of the Women's Art Registry of Minnesota in Minneapolis. Includes biographical sketches for the 37 participating artists, plus administrative and membership data for WARM Collective Art Space, 1976–84.

573. Women's Art Registry of Minnesota, Minneapolis. *Private Collectors and Art by Women.* Minneapolis: The Registry, 1984. 40 p. Bibliography, illustrations.

Catalog for 1984 Women's Art Registry of Minnesota (WARM) exhibition featuring women artists' works held in private and corporate collections in the Twin Cities. Includes works by Wanda Gág, Alice Hugy, Frances Cranmer Greenman, Elsa Laubach Jemne, Clara Mairs, and Ada Wolfe—all Minnesotans active in the 20th century. Artists' biographies and exhibition checklist appended.

MUSIC AND DANCE

574. Burns, Inella. "Minnie Schoyen Hubbard." *Blue Earth County Historical Society Newsletter* 7, no. 2 (July 1978): 4–7.

Profile of Mankato violinist born in 1883. Includes European travel and study as a child and adult performance and musical promotion activities in southern Minnesota, Twin Cities, and nationally.

575. Dunn, James Taylor. "St. Paul's Schubert Club: Musical Mentor of the Northwest." *Minnesota History* 39 (Summer 1964): 51–64.

Traces the evolution of the club from musical matinees where local women performed. In 1882 the participants formed the Ladies Musicale, and in 1888 they changed their name to the Schubert Club after they began to admit as associate members women who were not trained musicians. The group remained a private club until 1958 when it became a nonprofit civic organization, sponsoring professional performance series.

576. Lamb, Barbara Sue. "Thursday Musical in the Musical Life of Minneapolis." Ph.D. diss., University of Minnesota, 1983. 266 p. Notes, bibliography, appendixes, illustrations.

Historical study of the Thursday Musical club of Minneapolis, 1892–1983, discusses the organization's origins in woman's club and music appreciation movements. Describes club structure and policies, services to members, sponsorship of various performance series, public education programs in schools and settlement houses, scholarship programs, and other philanthropic projects.

577. Parker, Linda Faye. "Women in Music in St. Paul from 1898 to 1957 with Emphasis on the St. Paul Public Schools." Ph.D. diss., University of Minnesota, 1983. 183 p. Notes, bibliography, appendixes.

Historical study surveys activities of women music teachers, music club members, and professional musicians in St. Paul, 1898–1957. Considers music education in public and parochial schools; collegiate programs at Hamline, Macalester, Concordia, and the Agriculture School of the University of Minnesota; the Schubert Club; and independent music schools. Elsie Shaw and Mathilda Heck of the St. Paul public schools, Katherine Hoffman, accompanist to Madame Schumann-Heink from 1906 to 1929, and Frances Boardman, music critic at the *St. Paul Pioneer Press,* 1922–47, are among the individuals documented.

ARCHITECTURE AND INTERIOR DESIGN

578. Cook, Christine, et al. *Expanding Opportunities for Single Parents Through Housing.* N.p.: Minneapolis/St. Paul Family Housing Fund, 1988. 105 p. Bibliography.

Analyzes housing needs of single-parent families (93% female-headed) in areas of design, financing mechanisms, management, neighborhood and location, and support services. Provides guidelines for new and existing housing and offers many illustrations for approaches suggested.

LITERATURE

579. Auchincloss, Louis. *Pioneers and Caretakers: A Study of 9 American Women Novelists.* Minneapolis: University of Minnesota Press, 1965. 202 p. Index.

Includes a chapter on novelist and memoirist Mary McCarthy, whose *Memories of a Catholic Girlhood* describes a harsh childhood in Minneapolis and St. Paul. Combines literary criticism with considerable biographical information. See also Auchincloss's introduction regarding roles of women writers in the United States.

580. *Hurricane Alice.* Minneapolis: Women's Learning Institute, 1983–.

Feminist review, published quarterly, featuring fiction, poetry, essays, and criticism. In recent years, individual issues such as adorning our bodies (spring 1989) and women and war (fall/winter 1988) organized around themes.

581. Kissane, Leedice McAnelly. "Ruth Suckow: Interpreter of the Mind of Mid-America (1900–1933)." Ph.D. diss., University of Minnesota, 1967. 374 p. Bibliography.

Analyzes the life and works of Iowa writer Ruth Suckow (1892–1960). Special attention to the roles of women in Suckow's realistic novels of the 1920s and 1930s and to the author's position as a prominent regionalist writer in the same period.

582. Schleuning, Neala. *America: Song We Sang Without Knowing: The Life and Ideas of Meridel Le Sueur.* Mankato: Little Red Hen Press, 1983. 171 p. Notes, bibliography, illustrations.

Book of essays exploring life and thought of Minnesota-based writer Meridel Le Sueur (1900–). Focuses on cultural, feminist, and political concerns. Based on interviews with Le Sueur, her family, and friends as well as published works and criticism.

583. Smith, Mary K. "Meridel Le Sueur: A Bio-Bibliograpy." Master's starred paper, University of Minnesota, 1973. 48 p. (MHS).

Bibliographical and biographical sketch of writer Meridel Le Sueur's career, 1924–73. Includes chronological listings for Le Sueur's published works plus critical writing about her.

584. Thorson, Gerald. "Tinsel and Dust: Disenchantment in Two Minneapolis Novels from the 1880s." *Minnesota History* 45 (Summer 1977): 211–22.

Analysis of the life and work of Drude Krog Janson and her husband, Kristofer, Norwegian immigrant writers who arrived in Minneapolis in the 1880s. Drude wrote *A Saloonkeeper's Daughter,* a novel of manners that takes place in Minneapolis and reveals the author's disenchantment with the city and her longing for Norway. Both Jansons returned to Europe in the 1890s.

585. Wilson, Louis B. "A Woman Pioneer in a New Profession, Medical Editing." *Mayo Alumnus* 18, no. 2 (April 1982): 20–23.

Biographical sketch of Maud Mellish Wilson (1862–1933), medical librarian and editor in Chicago and from 1907 to 1933 at the Mayo Clinic in Rochester. This appreciation, written by her widowed second husband, focuses on full-time editing activities (a rarity at the time) at Mayo.

FASHION DESIGN

586. Anderson, Marcia C., and Hilary Toren. "Wrapped in Style." *Minnesota History* 49 (Summer 1984): 57–64.

Describes a sampling of the Minnesota Historical Society's collection of capes, shawls, and mantles. Analysis of these artifacts provides insight into consumer tastes and reveals that the use of these garments cut across socioeconomic lines.

587. *Paris in the Cities: A Century of French Couture from the Wardrobes of Minnesota Women.* St. Paul: University of Minnesota, 1986. 16 p. Illustrations.

Catalog for tenth anniversary exhibit of Goldstein Gallery, University of Minnesota, features 39 day and evening costumes from couture and ready-to-wear collections. Includes information about use in the Twin Cities.

588. Rahm, Virginia L. "Human Hair Ornaments." *Minnesota History* 44 (Summer 1974): 70–73.

Describes the Minnesota Historical Society's collection of these Victorian fashion items popular in the state by the mid-1800s. Amateurs as well as professionals created jewelry, decorative wreaths, and mourning pieces from human hair.

MUSEUMS, GALLERIES, AND PERFORMANCE SPACES

589. Arradondo, Midge, and Sallie Lawrence. "What Women Can Do: The Story of W.A.R.M." *DeNovo,* Fall 1977, p. 22–31.

Feature article describes Women's Art Registry of Minnesota (WARM) members' activities to create Women's Collective Art Space in Minneapolis in 1976. Includes discussion of organizational mission and process.

590. Stevens, Mitchell L. "The Work of Art: A Case Study of a Women's Art Collective." Honors thesis, Macalester College, 1988. 69 p. References.

Ethnographic study based on interviews with 25 (anonymous) women involved with the Women's Art Registry of Minnesota (WARM). Discusses the origins of the collective as an informal support group for Twin Cities women artists in the early 1970s, formal opening of the WARM Gallery in 1976, and evolving operations and structures through 1988. Includes considerable discussion of personal and professional concerns in producing and exhibiting art. Also explores financial difficulties within the organization around 1987.

591. *When Two Worlds Meet: An Exhibition of Art by Icelandic and Minnesota Women Artists.* [Minneapolis?: WARM?], 1990. Unpaginated.

Catalog for exhibition at Women's Art Registry of Minnesota (WARM), Minneapolis, gallery produced in conjunction with the visit of Icelandic women politicians to Minnesota, Spring 1990. Discusses comparative cultural contexts and features works on themes of nature, history, and self by 22 contemporary artists from both countries. Cosponsored by Minnesota Worldwide Women, Second Wave, and WARM.

592. *Women's Sensibilities: A National Juried Exhibition.* Minneapolis: Women's Art Registry of Minnesota, 1986. 52 p. Illustrations.

Catalog for exhibit commemorating the tenth anniversary of the Women's Art Registry of Minnesota (WARM), Minneapolis, features works and statements by 94 artists; many are Minnesotans.

ⅠⅢ⅃⅃/ Education

593. Delta Kappa Gamma Society International, Minnesota. *Pioneer Women in Education of the State of Minnesota.* Winona, Minn.: The Organization, 1957. 16 p.

Pamphlet provides brief profiles of teachers active in Minneapolis, Austin, Mankato, Winona, Duluth, and St. Cloud in the late 19th and early 20th centuries.

594. [Minnesota] Commission on the Economic Status of Women. *Women in Minnesota.* St. Paul: The Commission, 1984. 45 p.

Joint publication of the commission with the Women, Public Policy, and Development Project, Hubert H. Humphrey Institute of Public Affairs, University of Minnesota, analyzes demographic characteristics, education, income, and occupational status of Minnesota women and girls. Based on 1980 census data.

595. Minnesota Council on the Economic Status of Women. *Minnesota Women and Education.* St. Paul: The Council, 1979. 28 p. Illustrations, note on sources.

Report documents differential treatment based on sex in public educational institutions throughout Minnesota in the 1970s. Special emphasis on relationship between schooling and economic status of women. Considers elementary and secondary education (including sports), vocational education, higher education, and older students. Includes a series of policy recommendations for each educational aspect examined.

PRIMARY AND SECONDARY SCHOOLS

596. *Ahead of Her Time: A Woman's History of Central.* St. Paul: Central High School History Project, 1975. 26 p. Illustrations.

Sketch of St. Paul Central High School (established in 1866) inspired by International Women's Year of 1975. Features profiles of locally and nationally notable women associated with the school: senior teacher May Newsom, suffragist Ida Lusk Holman, aviator Amelia Earhart, journalist Estyr Peake, and writer and editor Midge Decter.

597. Arnold, Richard Dean. "The Relationship of Teacher's Sex to Assigned Marks and Tested Achievement Among Upper Elementary Grade Boys and Girls." Ph.D. diss., University of Minnesota, 1966. 140 p. Bibliography, appendixes.

Education study investigates three factors: the generalization that girls are superior to boys in most school tasks; a change to more formal grading systems in elementary schools; the effect of increased percentage of male teachers in elementary schools. Based on 1965–66 research in a suburban St. Paul school district. Findings indicate that girls receive higher marks than boys do; marks assigned by female and male teachers are in general quite similar; male teachers tend to assign slightly higher marks.

598. Balcom, Tom. "Fraser School Celebrates Louise Whitbeck Fraser and 50 Years of Caring for Special Children." *Hennepin County History* 44, no. 4 (Winter 1985–86): 3–14.

Profile of Louise Whitbeck Fraser (1894–1976), teacher of children with mental handicaps, and Minneapolis (later Richfield) home-study school she founded in 1935. Includes overview of policies and theories regarding education of children with mental handicaps, 1930s–80s, and of Fraser's personal circumstances as a widowed and self-supporting single parent in mid-20th century.

599. Bullard, Polly. "Iron Range Schoolmarm." *Minnesota History* 32 (December 1951): 193–201.

Author recalls teaching school in Eveleth, St. Louis County, primary and secondary schools, 1908–11. Considerable information about her third-grade class, her approach to teaching English to children speaking diverse languages at home, treats, and Christmas celebration at school. Also describes liv-

W. Gertrude Brown, director of the Phyllis Wheatley Settlement House in Minneapolis, listened to some young participants in the agency's arts, education, and recreation programs about 1924.

ing and social arrangements for herself and other teachers.

600. Duncan, Kunigunde. *Blue Star: The Story of Corabelle Fellows, Teacher at Dakota Missions, 1884–1888.* Caldwell, Idaho: Caxton Printers, 1938; St. Paul: Minnesota Historical Society Press, Borealis Books, 1990. 216 p. Index, illustrations.

Memoir of Fellows's experiences teaching at Santee Mission in Nebraska and in several schools on the Cheyenne River Reservation in South Dakota as told to journalist Duncan in the 1930s. Extensive descriptions of her background and daily routines, school situations and students, and her courtship and marriage to a Dakota suitor. Unusually attentive to Dakota women's roles and activities.

601. Enger, Nancy R. "Priority-Performance Perceptions of the Women Public Secondary Principals in Minnesota in Eight Key Areas of Responsibility." Ph.D. diss., University of Minnesota, 1982. 194 p. Bibliography, appendixes.

Education administration study explores the perceptions of women principals and their superinten-

dents, secretaries, and teaching-counseling staffs regarding importance of selected instructional responsibilities and the principals' performances of those tasks. Based on 1981 research in 16 school districts statewide. Findings generally indicate strong correlations between all participants' expectations of the principals and performances by them, supporting women's competence in administrative positions.

602. Falk, R. Frank. "Self Concept and Mobility Aspiration: A Study of Changing Self Definitions of Teacher Aides." Ph.D. diss., University of Minnesota, 1969. 91 p. Bibliography, appendixes.

Sociological study of teacher-aides program in Minneapolis public schools in the mid-1960s. Focuses on self-concept of aides who are mostly women and members of minority group(s). (Note: Author uses "ghetto" as apparent euphemism for African-American identity throughout.)

603. Johnson, Richard Allen. "An Analysis of the Attitudes of Minnesota Secondary School Principals Toward the Issue of School Age Pregnant Girls Receiving Continuing Education in Their Own High School Throughout Their Pregnancy." Ph.D. diss., University of Minnesota, 1971. 121 p. Bibliography, appendixes.

Study assesses attitudes of Minnesota secondary school principals toward issue of allowing pregnant high school girls to remain in home schools. Context is widespread educational policy of suspension and dismissal. Findings include exclusionary attitudes toward pregnant school-age girls, among urban school administrators in particular, more widespread acceptance of continuing educational opportunities on the part of suburban and rural administrators.

604. Luetmer, Sister Nora. "The History of Catholic Education in the Present Diocese of St. Cloud, Minnesota, 1855–1965." Ph.D. diss., University of Minnesota, 1970. 555 p. Notes, references.

Historical study chronicles early years of public and parish or church-supported schools and evolving Catholic education system in the 20th century. Provides considerable information regarding religious sisterhoods that staffed the schools, including teacher education and organizational relationships within the church. Also includes ongoing discussion of church-state issues in education in an area of German settlement.

605. McCart, Patricia Ann. "Effects of an Independent School Merger on Boys' and Girls' Perceptions of Environmental Press [*sic*]." Ph.D. diss., University of Minnesota, 1971. 145 p. Bibliography, appendixes.

Education study explores female and male high school students' perception of institutional climate before and after the merger of two single sex schools. Based on research with students at St. Paul Academy (boys) and Summit School (girls) in St. Paul, 1968–70. Significant differences were found in the perception of female and male students before and after the merger. Author suggests the need for merged motivational systems for newly coed schools that incorporate elements of importance to each sex.

606. McDonald, Sister Grace. "A Finishing School of the 1880's: St. Benedict's Academy." *Minnesota History* 27 (June 1946): 96–106.

Describes secondary school established by the Sisters of St. Benedict at St. Joseph, Stearns County, in the early 1880s. The school attracted women students, primarily from business and professional families in the Midwest, Rocky Mountain states, and western Canada. It provided Christian education focused on academic, athletic, moral, and practical subjects.

607. McDonald, Sister Grace. "Pioneer Teachers: The Benedictine Sisters at St. Cloud." *Minnesota History* 35 (June 1957): 263–71.

Discusses the arrival in 1857 of six Benedictine sisters and their efforts to turn an entertainment hall in St. Cloud into the first Benedictine convent in Minnesota. They began by teaching six boarding students as well as non-Catholic piano students and found it necessary to adjust Benedictine life to frontier circumstances. They moved their school to St. Joseph, Stearns County, in 1863.

608. Olson, Alice. "And How a Frog in a Desk Drawer Became a Lesson in Biology." *Ramsey County History* 9, no. 1 (Spring 1972): 10–14.

Reminiscence of author's teaching and administrative work at School District 8 in Maplewood, 1929–39. Includes information about Parent Teacher Association, school discipline, student activities, and author's educational and administrative responsibilities in later life.

609. Olson, Alice. "50 Years a Teacher, She Looks Back at Her First School." *Ramsey County History* 8, no. 2 (Fall 1971): 3–9.

Memoir of author's first teaching position in District 12, rural Ramsey County, 1914–15. Includes descriptions of school routine, boarding arrangements with farm family, and an on-the-job accident.

610. Peterson, Carol Jean Willts. "Secondary School Counselors' and Nurse Educators' Perceptions of Trends in Nursing Education and Images of Nursing." Ph.D. diss., University of Minnesota, 1969. 350 p. Bibliography, appendixes.

Study explores Minnesota high school counselors' knowledge of nursing education and their images of nursing. Background for this study is declining enrollments and expanded need for graduate nurses in the 1960s. Provides wide-ranging discussion of nursing education and issues of the period. While counselors were found to be generally well informed, findings suggest that rapidly occurring changes in nursing curricula (four types of programs available in Minnesota during the research period) may contribute to uncertainty about the opportunities available in the field.

611. Rigg, Richard James. "The Relationship Between Female School Board Membership and the Achievement of Equality in Athletic Opportunities for Female Students in Fifty Small Minnesota Public School Districts." Ph.D. diss., University of Minnesota, 1984. 169 p. Footnotes, appendixes, bibliography.

Education administration study explores the influence of women school board members on equality issues, in this case, interscholastic athletics. Based on research in 50 school districts statewide, 1975–83. Findings report significant differences in the management styles and interests of female and male board members. However, the presence of women is not associated with greater athletic opportunities for female students.

612. Robertson, Sheila C., and Kathleen Ann O'Brien. *A Social History of Women: Primary and Intermediate Social Studies.* N.p.: Women Historians of the Midwest, 1981. 29 p.

Introductory packet for teachers integrating women's history into the elementary school curriculum. Focus is on women's work; includes brief biographies of women of Minnesota. One in a series of curriculum packets develped by WHOM (Women Historians of the Midwest) in 1981–82; an accompanying time-line poster also produced.

613. Wood, Frank Henderson. "Differences in the Attainment Value Placed on Achievement in School Activities by First- and Third-Grade Boys and Girls of High and Low Socioeconomic Background." Ph.D. diss., University of Minnesota, 1965. 170 p. Bibliography, appendixes.

Education study investigates the existence of "feminine and middle class biases" in the elementary school curriculum. Based on 1960s research in the Minneapolis public school system. Findings suggest that boys place less value on achievement in school tasks generally; girls and boys value different activities among the choices offered; socioeconomic background was not associated with the variations reported within the study.

VOCATIONAL, PROFESSIONAL, AND RELIGIOUS EDUCATION

614. [Minnesota] Council on the Economic Status of Women. *Vocational Education.* St. Paul: The Council, 1979. 3 vols. [33, 10, 43 p.]

Series of reports evaluates sex equity in vocational education in Minnesota, 1978–79. Volume one discusses programs and staff for area vocational-technical institutes (AVTIs). Volume two provides comparative statistics for all 33 AVTIs statewide. Volume three surveys female students in nontraditional courses (for example, auto mechanics, welding, agricultural production). Findings suggest that AVTIs reflect sex segregation found in the labor market generally.

615. [Minnesota] Council on the Economic Status of Women. *Vocational Education Sex Equity Report: Post-Secondary 1981.* St. Paul: The Council, 1981. 40 p.

Analyzes sex bias and stereotyping in area vocational-technical institutes (AVTIs) statewide. Reports on enrollment trends, budgets, and staff patterns, 1979–81. Documents increased and more equitable participation by women in almost every area studied.

616. [Minnesota] Council on the Economic Status of Women. *Vocational Education Sex Equity Report: Post-Secondary, 1982.* St. Paul: The Council, 1982. 40 p.

An analysis of women's participation in the vocational education system statewide. Discusses enrollment, program types, curriculum areas, budgets, staffing patterns, and student income following graduation. While finding some improvement in discriminatory patterns reported in the 1970s, it also documents continuing significant differences in funds allotted for women's and men's education and differences in occupations and earnings of women and men graduates.

617. [Minnesota] Council on the Economic Status of Women. *Vocational Education Sex Equity Report: Secondary 1981.* St. Paul: The Council, 1981. 32 p.

Analyzes female students' participation in vocational education at the high school level by curriculum areas such as agriculture, health occupations, and home economics and by program type (sex segregated or integrated). Also gives follow-up figures on further education and employment of vocational students. Principal finding is that female graduates have lower earnings than males regardless of high school curriculum area.

COLLEGES AND UNIVERSITIES

618. Augsburg College, Ad Hoc Committee on the Status of Women. *Final Report.* Minneapolis: The College, 1972. 49 p.

In-house study reports on personnel policies and employment patterns affecting faculty women at Minneapolis liberal arts college associated with the Evangelical Lutheran Church in America, 1960–72. Documents discrimination in recruitment, salaries and fringe benefits, promotion and tenure, faculty committee assignments, and administrative opportunities. Recommends procedures to ensure equitable participation of women in teaching and governance.

619. Ayers, Edel Ytterboe. *The Old Main.* Anniston, Ala.: Higginbotham and Sawyer, 1969. 123 p. Illustrations.

Reminiscences about St. Olaf College staff and students written by the daughter of a staff member. Ayers's father was a professor at the Northfield college from the 1880s to 1904; her widowed mother worked at various jobs in the college dining halls. Of special interest in terms of domestic and financial provisions for a widow with children.

620. Carlson, Margaret Sughrue. "The Relationship Between Organizational Factors and Perceived Power: A Study of Female Administrators in Minnesota Institutions of Higher Education." Ph.D. diss., University of Minnesota, 1983. 266 p. References, appendixes.

Study explores concept of power held by female administrators and its exercise within academe. Based on 1981 research with 30 female administrators at the University of Minnesota and in the Minnesota State University system. Principal findings include: systemic factors are more important than positional factors in academic settings; empowerment of female administrators is linked to historic equity patterns within the institution; leadership opportunities are linked to academic preparation and expertise, not administrative skills; participating administrators described themselves as reluctant to engage in organizational politics.

621. Davis, Sandra Lee Ottsen. "Factors Related to the Persistence of Women in a Four-Year Institute of Technology." Ph.D. diss., University of Minnesota, 1973. 527 p. References, appendixes.

Counseling study investigates the interests, personalities, backgrounds, experiences, and "persistence" of women entering science and engineering fields. Based on comparative research with female and male students at the Institute of Technology, University of Minnesota, 1960–71. Documents significant differences between female and male students regarding existence of mentors, importance of the school's reputation, attitudes toward social relationships, and relative breadth of interests.

622. Duffey, Margery Ann. "Personal and Situational Factors Relating to the Career Development of Persons Completing Masters Programs in Nursing." Ph.D. diss., University of Minnesota, 1967. 155 p. Appendixes, bibliography.

Study explores applications of graduate school training made by nurses returning to positions in teaching and administration. Based on research with graduates of University of Minnesota master's program, 1951–62. Findings suggest that vocational development is a continuous process characterized by alternating periods of formal education and practice; curriculum offerings emphasizing evaluative techniques may be needed; nursing educators appear to be more motivated to seek additional education than are administrators.

623. Fitzgerald, Sheila Mary. "A Career Development Study of Elementary School Teachers." Ph.D. diss., University of Minnesota, 1972. 196 p. Bibliography, appendixes.

Study investigates pursuit of graduate education as an element of professional growth among primary teachers. Pays particular attention to differences in female and male career patterns. Based on 1971–72 research with students enrolled in the Master of Arts program for elementary education, University of Minnesota–Twin Cities. Although six times as many women as men participated in the study, men were more likely to complete graduate training. Also, 45% of project participants expected to leave teaching within five to ten years.

624. Gallucci, Jo Anne Marie. "A Study of the Effects of a Deliberate Curriculum Intervention on the Change in Cognitive Factors Influencing Women's Achievement Orientation." Ph.D. diss., University of Minnesota, 1982. 660 p. References notes, references, appendixes.

Experimental study examines ways in which inter-

vention, in this case a specially designed course, may increase women's achievements in academic, work, and social relations. Based on 1981 research at Mankato State University, Metropolitan State University, and Anoka-Ramsey Community College. Reports positive results in attitudes concerning success-failure, success-reality, and student-defined goals for the course work.

625. Hanson, Marcia E. "Women in Leadership Roles at the University of Minnesota." Typescript, 1972. 74 p. Bibliography, appendixes.

Graduate student research paper produced at University of Minnesota examines role of women faculty and students in university governance. Analyzes representation, advancement, and salaries (if appropriate) in terms of early 1970s feminist concerns. Suggests changes in curriculum, pay scales, financial aid, and hiring that would increase women's participation.

626. Harris, Martha Isabel. "A Study of Conceptions of the Head Nurse Role Held by Students in Selected Nursing Programs." Ph.D. diss., University of Minnesota, 1962. 142 p. Notes, bibliography, appendixes.

Results of 1958 study focusing on nursing programs and anticipated student career choices at ten Minneapolis–St. Paul hospitals and colleges. Discusses student backgrounds, attitudes concerning nursing and marriage as vocations, and administrative and care-giving roles in nursing.

627. Hauser, Kathleen Rock. *Eighty Years of University of Minnesota Doctorates, 1887–1967.* [Minneapolis?]: Women Historians of the Midwest, 1973. 5 p.

Brief analysis of doctorates in all fields awarded to women at the University of Minnesota. Includes list of 22 history dissertations and authors.

628. Hilleboe, Gertrude M. *Manitou Analecta.* Northfield, Minn.: St. Olaf College, 1968. 126 p. Illustrations.

Reminiscences of 20th-century staff and students at St. Olaf College, a coeducational institution affiliated with the United Norwegian Lutheran Church, in Northfield. Hilleboe knew the school as an undergraduate student, a teacher of Latin, and as a dean of women, 1915–58. Considerable attention to experiences of women students and staff.

629. Layton, Patricia Lynn. "Self-Efficacy, Locus of Control, Career Salience and Women's Career Choice." Ph.D..diss., University of Minnesota, 1984. 247 p. Notes, references, appendixes.

Psychology study of women's career development choices based on 1983 research with women students at the University of Minnesota and Iowa State University. Variables examined included high school grades, nontraditional interests, family socioeconomic status, parents' education, mother's choice of career, and personal locus of control. Study found significant differences between Iowa and Minnesota samples, possibly due to demographic differences in the two student bodies.

630. Marquis, Mary L. *The Higher Education of Women.* Albert Lea, Minn.: Simonson and Whitcomb, 1907. 15 p.

Address in favor of higher education for women delivered before Presbyterian Synod of Minnesota by president of Albert Lea College, a church-affiliated school, in October 1906. Places Albert Lea College in tradition of Smith, Wellesley, Vassar, and other schools for women "in the older states."

631. Melbo, Mary Margaret. "Stressors, and Their Relationship to Selected Psychological, Situational, and Demographic Variables for Veterinary Medical Students." Ph.D. diss., University of Minnesota, 1981. 269 p. References, appendixes.

Educational psychology study conducted in 1980 explores stress factors in the professional education of veterinarians. Its secondary purpose is to establish a data base describing students (40% female and 60% male) in the College of Veterinary Medicine at the University of Minnesota, including their attitudes toward women in the profession. Findings report agreement by female and male students regarding presence of obstacles to women in the field. However, female and male respondents differed significantly in their descriptions of the obstacles, females identifying external factors such as sex-role stereotypes and the scarcity of women in positions of power and males focusing on physical and emotional traits specific to women and on family and home responsibilities.

632. Merrill, Ruth Atherton. "An Evaluation of Criteria for the Selection of Students in the School of Nursing of [the] University of Minnesota." Ph.D. diss., University of Minnesota, 1937. 297 p. Bibliography, appendixes.

Study inspired by high drop-out rates in nursing schools nationally. Based on research with students in University of Minnesota nursing program during the 1930s. Considerable information about background and interests of nursing students.

633. Morgan, Rebecca Susan Wilmoth. "Sex Differences in Factors Related to Achievement in College

Students." Ph.D. diss., University of Minnesota, 1975. 116 p. References, appendixes.

Study explores patterns of personality characteristics related to female and male college achievement through standard testing instruments and peer evaluation ratings. Based on research with students at Bethel College in St. Paul, 1969–71. Findings were that for both female and male students the most significant measures were peer ratings concerning "achievement orientation" and intellectual curiosity.

634. Morgan, Sylvia. "Intersection: Personal and Professional—A Women's Studies Administrator in a Rural Setting." *Women's Studies International Forum* 9, no. 2 (1986): 163–70.

Autobiographical essay explores interconnections between personal life and professional work as coordinator of women's studies program at Moorhead State University, 1970s–80s. Discusses distinctive qualities of regional society in northwestern Minnesota, students' perceptions of women's roles, author's experience of job discrimination, and university politics and economics, among other topics.

635. Nahm, Helen. "An Evaluation of Selected Schools of Nursing with Respect to Certain Educational Objectives." Ph.D. diss., University of Minnesota, 1946. 527 p. Bibliography, appendixes.

Examines social and intellectual background of 428 students at 12 schools of nursing in Minnesota in 1944. Contains considerable information about students' families, cultural resources, and educational experiences. Recommends a series of changes to broaden and democratize nursing education.

636. Nelson, Helen Young. "Factors Related to the Extent of Mortality among Home Economics Students in Certain Colleges of Minnesota, Wisconsin and Iowa, 1943–50." Ph.D. diss., University of Minnesota, 1952. 131 p. Notes, bibliography, appendix.

Study explores voluntary drop-out rate among home economics students at 14 colleges and universities in Minnesota, Iowa, and Wisconsin, 1943–50. The work is based on college records and mail-out questionnaire sent to 2,263 former students. Context is drop-out rate in higher education nationally. Extensive quotations from former students regarding marriage, finances, curriculum organization, and illness as factors in voluntary withdrawal.

637. Park, Georgia Korner. "The Mixed Dorm: Its Effect on Student Personality, Social Life, and Sex Attitudes and Behavior." Ph.D. diss., University of Minnesota, 1972. 290 p. Bibliography, appendixes.

Field study describes experimental institution of "mixed" (room-by-room female and male accommodations) dormitory at Macalester College, St. Paul, 1969–70. Author reports that the mixed dorm attracted relatively shy students looking to increase informal contacts and ease with opposite sex. Further, an "incest taboo" appeared to operate in-house regarding sexual activity among housemates. Also suggests that students choosing various dorm options—single-sex, coed (segregated), and mixed—have different characteristics and needs; colleges should provide multiple options.

638. *The Planner.* Minneapolis: Minnesota Planning and Counseling Center for Women, University of Minnesota, [1969–70?].

Newsletter published by University of Minnesota counseling center. Coverage focuses on educational opportunities and social support, such as child-care services for women students at the Twin Cities campus of the university. Of interest for discussion of women's liberation movement.

639. *Sanford Hall: Residence Hall for Women.* Minneapolis: University of Minnesota, 1934. 8 p. Illustrations.

Describes facilities, social programs, services, and fees at women's dormitory named for Maria L. Sanford, a well-known professor at the University of Minnesota.

640. Schletzer, Vera M., et al. *Continuing Education for Women: A Five-Year Report of the Minnesota Plan.* Minneapolis: University of Minnesota, 1967. 78 p.

Describes University of Minnesota program designed in the 1960s to return educated women to the work force and to assist women in developing new interests and objectives. Discusses coordination of university-wide resources for the program, characteristics of participating students, the counseling program developed to accompany academic offerings, the curriculum, job placement, and supporting services, including scholarships and child care.

641. Siegel, Hildegarde Julia. "A Study of Professional Socialization in Two Baccalaurate Nursing Education Programs." Ph.D. diss., University of Minnesota, 1967. 224 p. Bibliography, appendixes.

Comparative study investigates the development of professional views and related personal values among students in the University of Minnesota and Marquette University (Milwaukee) nursing pro-

grams, 1966–67. Provides considerable information about students' backgrounds and career expectations.

642. Stecklein, John E., and Gail E. Lorenz. "Academic Woman: Twenty-Four Years of Progress?" *Liberal Education* 72, no. 1 (1986): 63–67.

Compares authors' 1980 research on academic women in Minnesota with earlier studies conducted in 1968 and 1956. Reports little change in overall statistics: 28% of teaching faculty were women in 1956, 27% were in 1980. In the 1980 study, a smaller proportion of women than men held doctorates and tenure; women derived more of their total income solely from institutional salaries. Men published more, requested more research grants, and served as consultants more often.

643. Vega, Flavio. "The Effect of Human and Intergroup Relations Education on the Race/Sex Attitudes of Education Majors." Ph.D. diss., University of Minnesota, 1978. 191 p. Appendixes, bibliography.

Study evaluates effects of human relations course on education students' attitudes concerning sex and race. Based on 1970s research at St. Cloud State University. Provides considerable information about public discussion of these issues at the time. Results show that educational programming can lessen racist and sexist attitudes.

COMMUNITY EDUCATION

644. Ebersole, J. F., ed. *Women and the State.* Minneapolis: Minnesota Academy of Social Sciences, 1915. 203 p. Appendix, index.

Papers and proceedings of the eighth annual meeting of the academy focus on minimum wage laws, mothers' pensions, provision for women in the correctional system, and suffrage. Includes Mrs. Andreas (Clara) Ueland and Josephine Schain on the advantages of woman suffrage and Lavinia Coppock Gilfillan and Mrs. Elbert L. (Florence Welles) Carpenter on disadvantages.

645. Hattendorf, Katharine Wood. "A Study of a Home Program for Mothers in Sex Education." Ph.D diss., University of Iowa, 1930. 420 p. References, tables.

Author on leave from Women's Co-operative Alliance to study sex education program developed in Minneapolis by Catheryne Cooke Gilman. Based on interviews with and data collected from mothers in Iowa City and Cedar Rapids, Iowa.

Libraries

646. Clift, Robert Benjamin. "The Personality and Occupational Stereotype of Public Librarians." Ph.D. diss., University of Minnesota, 1976. 172 p. Reference notes, references, appendixes.

Study explores stereotypes of librarians as an occupational group from points of view of librarians and their patrons. Includes consideration of "old maid" stereotype for women, "effeminate" for men, and high ratio of women to men in the field. Based on 1970s research in Duluth and the Twin Cities.

647. Ostendorf, Paul John. "The History of the Public Library Movement in Minnesota from 1849 to 1916." Ph.D. diss., University of Minnesota, 1984. 587 p. Notes, bibliography, appendixes.

Encylopedic study explores "leadership role of women" played by individuals such as Gratia Countryman and Clara Baldwin and groups such as the Minnesota Federation of Women's Clubs. Includes chapters on the women's roles, Minnesota librarians and other leaders, and a collective profile of persons working in the library profession. Extensive bibliographic essay.

Adult Education

648. *Compleat Scholar*. Minneapolis: Continuing Education and Extension, University of Minnesota, [1986?]–.

Quarterly newsletter describes noncredit classes, lectures, and travel, published by the office of extension and continuing education for women, University of Minnesota–Twin Cities.

649. Flashman, Sharon Leslie. "The Women's Learning Institute: A Case Study in Alternative Feminist Education." Ph.D. diss., University of Massachusetts, 1979. 349 p. Bibliography, appendixes.

Education study explores differences between feminist education and "traditional male-dominated" education. Based on 1970s research at Maiden Rock, a noncredit, nondegree, community-based project in Minneapolis. Describes alternative education model, including personal and subjective elements of curriculum and nonhierarchical social relations in courses and bureaucratic structures. Also discusses gradually emerging lesbian identity of the organization.

Ⅲⅼⅼⅼ/ Economics and Employment

WORK

650. Bowman, Kathleen. *Minnesota Women: State Government Employment.* St. Paul: Minnesota Council on the Economic Status of Women, 1977. 24 p.

Report on equal access to jobs and economic security for women employed throughout Minnesota state government in 1977. Council documents lower pay scales and widespread discriminatory practices. Includes recommendations for change.

651. Braun, Dennis Duane. *An Occupational Profile of Minnesota Women.* Mankato, Minn.: Department of Sociology, Mankato State University, 1975. 27 p.

Documents high proportion of part-time work, sex segregation within occupations, underrepresentation in professional categories, and substantial pay inequities for women workers statewide.

652. Brodie, Jane Silon. "The Effect of Selected Family Variables on the Achievement Motivation of Employed Married Women." Ph.D. diss., University of Minnesota, 1981. 209 p. References, appendixes.

Psychology study explores multiple roles of wife, mother, homemaker, volunteer, and employee among three occupational groups: professional/managerial, crafts/operatives/technicians, clerical/service/labor. Based on 1980 research with women employees of the state of Minnesota. The intent was to investigate the links, if any, among family life-cycle stage, sex role attitudes, women's and spouses' responsibility for household tasks, and occupational achievement. Findings suggest that there are links among family variables and achievements for women and, further, that many of these questions should be applied to male career development as well.

653. Gyorky, Zsuzsanna Klara. "The Influence of Selected Individual and Situational Variables on the Career Patterns of Women." Ph.D. diss., University of Minnesota, 1982. 180 p.

Psychology study investigates women's decision making regarding career and family. Based on research with clients of the Vocational Assessment and Counseling Program, University of Minnesota, 1974–78. Describes three work patterns—homemaking, intermediate, and career. Suggests that the career is strongly associated with a particular age cohort, the post-World War II baby boom, as well as education levels.

654. League of Women Voters of Minnesota. *Women in the Labor Force.* Minneapolis: The League, 1962. 12 p. Bibliography.

Pamphlet based on 1960s state and national statistics describes characteristics of working women. Includes jobs held, wages, existence of discrimination, policy concerns, and proposed legislation.

655. League of Women Voters of Minnesota. *Women in the Minnesota Labor Force Or Is the Status Still Quo?* St. Paul: The League, 1971. 8 p.

Pamphlet provides summary of League issues, 1949–71. Outlines state and national statistics, plus League positions concerning women in the workplace. Asks readers whether renewed initiatives concerning sex discrimination in housing, education, and other public arenas should be undertaken.

656. Minnesota Council on the Economic Status of Women. *Minnesota Women: A Profile.* St. Paul: The Council, 1977. 57 p. Illustrations, references, appendixes.

Report gives overview of women's status in Minnesota in area of general characteristics, education, marital and family status, income, employment, and state service, 1900–75. Based on federal, state, and private data sources.

657. [Minnesota] Council on the Economic Status of Women. *Minnesota Women: City and County Employment.* St. Paul: The Council, 1980. 26 p. Appendix.

Analyzes local government's performance as a "model employer" of women. Demonstrates that women are concentrated in traditionally female fields such as health and welfare and in clerical jobs. Also reports that women's salaries reflect the pattern of lower earnings compared to men in the labor market as a whole; this is true regardless of occupational group, jurisdiction, or geographic location.

658. Minnesota Council on the Economic Status of Women. *Newsletter.* 1976–83.

Monthly newsletter provides news of council activities, summaries of its research projects, notes from other state commissions, and announcements of events sponsored by women's organizations.

659. [Minnesota] Council on the Economic Status of Women. *Women in Minnesota.* St. Paul: The Council, 1980. 40 p.

Describes social and economic characteristics of Minnesota women. Publication of official state commission is based on 1977 data gathered by the Office of the State Demographer.

660. Minnesota State Planning Agency, Office of State Demographer. *Characteristics of Women in Minnesota, 1977.* St. Paul: The Office, 1980. 35 p. Appendixes.

Report based on findings from the Minnesota Household Survey conducted in 1977. Documents gains in educational attainment and labor force participation among women while their occupational conditions and earnings relative to men remain unchanged.

661. Minnesota State Planning Agency, Office of State Demographer. *Minnesota Labor Force, 1977.* St. Paul: The Agency, 1979. 37 p. Appendixes.

Describes broad range of characteristics for employed women and men. Focuses on various aspects of women's increased participation in the labor force, the single biggest change documented in this report.

662. Seaburg, Deborah Jean. "Gender, Ability Level and Work Experiences as Factors in the Self-Assessment of Work Abilities." Ph.D. diss., University of Minnesota, 1983. 185 p. References, appendixes.

Psychology study investigates self-estimates of intellectual, cognitive, and motor abilities. Based on 1975–79 research with clients of the career counseling service at the University of Minnesota. Findings indicate that clients generally tend to underestimate their intellectual and perceptual capacities; further, women clients underestimated to a greater extent than men. Suggests importance of career counselor's role in assisting clients in developing more accurate self-perceptions and, ultimately, career choices.

663. Thoni, Richard J., et al. *Women and the World of Work: A Career Education Resource Guide.* St. Paul: Minnesota Department of Education, 1972. 40 p.

Career planning exercises designed for use in high school classes explore widely held social attitudes concerning women's work opportunities and describe women's employment options about 1970.

664. Woman's Occupational Bureau, Minneapolis. *War-Time Replacement in the City of Minneapolis.* Occupational Bulletin, no. 2. Minneapolis: Vocational Information Service, 1919. 19 p. Illustrations.

Survey conducted in 1918 documents replacement of men by women in Minneapolis industry during World War I. A collaborative project of the State Department of Labor, Council of National Defense, and the Woman's Occupation Bureau, the study analyzes 647 replacement employments. Includes discussion of types of businesses making replacements, kinds of work performed, and comparative wage and hour figures.

Paid Work

665. Engel, John William. "Changing Attitudes Toward the Dual Work/Home Roles of Women: University of Minnesota Freshmen, 1959–1974." Ph.D. diss., University of Minnesota, 1978. 204 p. References, reference notes, appendixes.

Study documents increased acceptance of women's work outside the home. Context is the effects of the "second women's movement" of the 1960s on popular attitudes and beliefs. Based on comparative research with College of Liberal Arts freshmen (female and male) at the University of Minnesota in 1959 and 1974.

666. Minnesota Department of Economic Security. *Minnesota Female Employment: Nonagricultural Industries, 1940–1979.* [St. Paul?]: The Department, 1980. 20 p.

Study shows increase in women's employment in nonagricultural sectors of the Minnesota economy, 1940–79. Based on federal census figures, 1940–70, and U.S. Department of Labor Current Employment Statistics, 1970–79. Provides information for female employment in all categories of: manufacturing, nonmanufacturing—mining, construction, transportation, communications and public utilities, retail trade, wholesale trade, finance/insurance/real estate, services, government.

667. Minnesota Public Interest Research Group. *Sexual Discrimination in Employment Agencies.* Minneapolis: The Organization, 1972. 38 p. Appendixes, footnotes.

Report documents gender-based discrimination in counseling and referrals for female and male job seekers at several dozen Twin Cities employment agencies. Based on telephone and field surveys about 1970.

668. Sorensen, Glorian Christine. "Gender Differences in the Effects of Employment on Health." Ph.D. diss., University of Minnesota, 1983. 323 p. References, appendix.

Comparative sociology study investigates relationships among gender, work experience, and cardiovascular disease. Based on data collected by the Minnesota Heart Study, University of Minnesota School of Public Health, 1980–82. Findings suggest gender-specific differences in some areas; for example, men's occupational attainment tends to rise more as a consequence of education than is true for women. Also, marriage restricts women's occupation development while it supports men's. However, in terms of health status, similar jobs tend to have similar consequences for individual women and men.

669. Taylor, Etta M. *How: A Practical Business Guide for American Women of All Conditions and Ages Who Want to Make Money But Do Not Know How.* Minneapolis: The Author, 1893. 79 p. (MHS).

Describes a wide variety of business, professional, domestic, industrial, and sales work available to women. Examples (Minnesota and national) occasionally include names and addresses. Offers suggestions concerning thrift and financial planning.

670. Treece, Eleanor Mae Walters. "Vocational Choice and Satisfactions of Licensed Practical Nurses." Ph.D. diss., University of Minnesota, 1967. 233 p. References, appendixes.

Study explores family background, educational interests, and levels of job satisfaction reported by licensed practical nurses (LPN). Based on research with selected graduates of 12 LPN programs in Minnesota, 1955–64. All respondents, save one, were female. Principal findings are that prospects for advancement were an important factor in retaining LPN practitioners; greatest vocational problem seemed to be ill-defined role *vis-à-vis* other health care workers.

Labor

671. Aronovici, Carol. *Women in Industry in Minnesota in 1918.* St. Paul: Minnesota Department of Labor and Industries, 1920. 35 p.

Reports on survey conducted in 1918–19. Describes industries and wages, marital status and family support, hours of labor, and social characteristics of women workers in metropolitan and rural areas of the state. Documents large numbers of women receiving wages below minimum subsistence established by law and "excessive proportion" of women workers employed over sixty hours per week.

672. Berger, Fred E., and Joseph S. Smolen, eds. *Conference on the Status of Working Women in Minnesota, May 17–18, 1963.* Minneapolis: General Extension Division, University of Minnesota, 1963. 44 p.

Edited proceedings of a conference sponsored by the Women's Bureau of the U.S. Department of Labor, the Minnesota Industrial Commission, and the University of Minnesota provides schedule of events, faculty list, and registrants list (with addresses). Also includes texts of speeches entitled "Women Who Work" by Esther Peterson, "Legal Aspects of Concern to Women Workers" by June Cedarleaf, "The Economic Situation of Women Workers" by Ray Solem, "Education and Training" by Vera M. Schletzer, "Attitudes in Relation to Women Workers—An Employer Viewpoint" by Mrs. Darcy Truax, and "Attitudes in Relation to Women Workers—A Labor Viewpoint" by Bea Kersten.

673. Bloodsworth, Jessie. *Women's Work in Minnesota Under CWA and ERA.* [St. Paul?]: Minnesota Emergency Relief Administration, 1935. 9 p.

Pamphlet describes employment programs involving 9,000 needy women at 600 Civil Works Administration (CWA) and Emergency Relief Administration (ERA) sites statewide. Gives overview of federal program structure, participating institutions in Minnesota, and specifics of nursing, library, and education positions, social surveys, office work, and janitorial and cleaning projects undertaken.

674. Elmer, Manuel Conrad. *A Cooperative Study of Women in Industry in Saint Paul, Minnesota.* St. Paul: St. Paul Association of Public and Business Affairs, [1924?]. 47 p.

Reports study undertaken by Saint Paul Association of Public and Business Affairs, the Young Women's Christian Association, the State Industrial Commission, and the University of Minnesota. Describes work in retail sales, manufacturing, offices, food preparation and distribution, hotels and restaurants, and laundries. Discusses demographic characteristics of employed women, training and education, turnover, labor unions, employment bureaus, and employers' attitudes toward women, wages, and housing.

675. Faue, Elizabeth. *Community of Suffering and Struggle: Women, Men, and the Labor Movement in Minneapolis, 1915–1945.* Chapel Hill: University of North Carolina Press, 1991. 295 p. Appendix, notes, bibliography, index, illustrations.

Study argues that the late 20th-century decline of organized labor has its roots in the failure to recognize and include gender issues in the great organizing drives of the 1930s. Focuses on community and workplaces in Minneapolis.

676. Faue, Elizabeth Victoria. "Women, Work and Community, Minneapolis, 1929–1946." Ph.D. diss., University of Minnesota, 1987. 349 p. Notes, bibliography.

Historical case study uses Minneapolis data to argue that the 20th-century labor movement has ignored and alienated working-class women. The author locates the causes for this situation in the economic and cultural crises of the 1930s Depression. Offers a close analysis of how gender shapes historical experience.

677. Kellett, Suzy. "In Trouble." *People,* November 27, 1978, p. 107–10.

Coverage of only bank strike in Minnesota history after one year of picketing. The story of eight women bank tellers who struck at Citizens National Bank in Willmar over equal compensation. (Note: Also subject of documentary film *The Willmar Eight.*)

678. Minneapolis-Moline Power Implement Co. *Special Regulations for Women Production Workers.* Minneapolis: The Company, [194–?]. 6 p.

Special regulations for women production workers at Minneapolis-Moline's Hopkins plant during World War II. Pamphlet addresses payroll deductions, sickness and absence policies, war-bond deductions, and the union shop agreement with Local No. 1138, United Electrical, Radio and Machine Workers of America (CIO).

679. Minneapolis-Moline Power Implement Co. *Welcome to Our Women Production Workers.* Minneapolis: The Company, [194–?]. 10 p.

Introductory handout for World War II women production workers at Minneapolis-Moline. Pamphlet addresses payroll, safety, and security. Also describes some negative stereotypes about women's participation in industrial production as "imaginary."

680. [Minnesota] Council on the Economic Status of Women. *Women in the Trades: A Study of Apprenticeship in Minnesota.* St. Paul: The Council, 1979. 24 p. Appendixes.

Analyzes women's participation in training for skilled trades, such as carpentry, auto mechanics, pipefitting, and plumbing—rapidly growing and well-paying occupational opportunities in the late 1970s. Findings report that women apprentices (1.2% of total in Minnesota) are more likely than men to have college educations and to report barriers to entering and remaining in the trades; they also are more likely than men to have positive attitudes toward unions and to anticipate participation in union activities. Recommends a series of measures to increase awareness among women of apprenticeship opportunities.

681. Starkweather, M. L. *First Biennial Report of the Woman's Department, Bureau of Labor, Commerce and Industry of the State of Minnesota, 1907–1908.* St. Paul: The Department, 1909. 29 p.

Reports on the number and condition of employed women statewide. Includes sections on boarding practices, workplace cleanliness and ventilation, inspection of food establishments, and wages and hours. Discusses the problem of the "child-woman," girls 16–18 years of age, old enough to leave school and parental guidance for the work force but not necessarily well equipped to negotiate the difficulties of independent living on low pay. Also includes rationale for an expanded women's bureau in Minnesota and comparative legislation from other states.

682. *Tradeswomen Today.* New Brighton, Minn.: Tradeswomen Today, 1986–87.

Newsletter aimed at uniting and supporting women in the building trades. The publication includes information on apprenticeships, health issues, emergency shelters, and employment opportunities. Distributed in conjunction with the newsletter of the Twin Cities Coalition of Labor Union Women.

683. Union Victory Girls. *From U.V.G. to G.I. Joe.* Minneapolis: Union Victory Girls, 1945. 4 p. Illustrated.

(Monthly?) newsletter for labor union members in service during World War II. News of women and men in uniform and home-front notes from Minneapolis. Provides information about women's roles in area AFL, CIO, and Railroad Brotherhood locals during wartime. (Note: Description based on February 1945 issue.)

Rose Halleck Boosalis (Mrs. Peter) counted money next to the safe, probably in the back room of the Greek-American family business, The Olympia Fruit and Confectionery, Minneapolis, about 1903. City directories gave separate listings to Peter as proprietor and Rose as manager of the store.

684. Young Women's Christian Association [Duluth]. *Women at Work: A Survey of Industrial Women Workers in Duluth.* Duluth: The Association, 1945. 30 p. Bibliography, appendix.

Pamphlet produced by the YWCA Industrial Committee explores women workers' plans for post-World War II employment. Includes discussion of wartime jobs and performance, working and home conditions, and attitudes concerning unions and interracial work force.

Business and Professional

685. Best, Joel. "Careers in Brothel Prostitution: St. Paul, 1865–1883." *Journal of Interdisciplinary History* 12 (Spring 1982): 597–619.

Analyzes social characteristics of St. Paul madams and "inmates" of their houses. Describes *de facto* taxation of brothels by St. Paul city government. Discusses prostitution both as a "deviant" career and as a chosen profession that offered the possibility of a comfortable life. Also discusses reentry into "respectable" life through marriage, domestic service, and independent investments.

686. Best, Joel E. "Long Kate, Dutch Henriette and Mother Robinson: Three Madams in Post-Civil War St. Paul." *Ramsey County History* 15, no. 1 (1979): 3–12.

Profiles three women—Kate Hutton, Henrietta Charles, and Mary E. Robinson—who operated houses of prostitution in St. Paul during the 1860s and 1870s. Discusses the structure of the brothel business of the period, the difficulties, and the spectacular successes—in this case, Robinson's—that were possible.

687. Blade, Timothy Trent. "Olson's Dry Goods: A Family History." *Hennepin County History* 45, no. 1 (Spring 1986): 4–17.

Describes dry goods store operated by the author's grandmother, Agnes Olson, in Minneapolis, 1922–32. Focuses on retail goods and services offered, plus social role of the store in its neighborhood.

688. Borst, Charlotte G. "The Training and Practice of Midwives: A Wisconsin Study." *Bulletin of the History of Medicine* 62 (Winter 1988): 606–27.

Statistical study of Wisconsin midwifery in late 19th and early 20th centuries analyzes the occupation in terms of age, class, marital status, ethnic background, geography, and training. Author concludes that the practice of midwifery died out in the early 20th century because midwives were too varied to develop leaders within their group, and as a result physicians made the crucial decisions for training and licensing.

689. Crawford, Jacquelyn S. *Women in Middle Management: Selection, Training, Advancement, Performance.* Ridgewood, N.J.: Forkner Publishing Corp., 1977. 156 p. References, appendixes.

Study explores work histories of women managers in Minneapolis and St. Paul companies in the 1970s. Based on research with 91 companies. Provides considerable information about private and professional activities of participating managers. Highlights role of women's colleges—the College of St. Catherine, in particular—in offering educational and counseling support.

690. Cunningham, Gary L. *People of Color and Women in Real Estate: A Special Focus on Hennepin,*

Ramsey and Dakota Counties. Minneapolis: Metropolitan Community Housing Resource Boards, 1985. 62 p. Footnotes, appendixes.

Documents underrepresentation, pay inequities, and occupational segregation among women and persons of color (primarily African Americans) working in Twin Cities real estate agencies about 1980. Provides good overview of real estate procedures and commission structures.

691. Davis, Julia. "The Early Work Adjustment of Women Engineers." Ph.D. diss., University of Minnesota, 1984. 292 p. References, appendixes.

Study documents first-year-on-the-job experiences reported by a group of women engineers. Based on 1982 research with members of the Minnesota chapter of the Society of Women Engineers. Context is increasing entry of women into nontraditional fields and conservative attitudes of male engineers regarding women's roles.

692. Elmer, Manuel Conrad. *A Study of Women in Clerical and Secretarial Work in Minneapolis, Minn.* Minneapolis: Woman's Occupational Bureau, 1925. 42 p.

Reports findings from 1924 study of 276 establishments employing five or more women clerical employees. Discusses employment opportunities, employment classifications, general duties of clerical workers, age distribution, length of service, labor turnover, salaries, education of workers, experience, training programs (when available), promotions, living arrangements, and employer preferences regarding single women, and racial and national groups. First in a series of studies on women's work planned by the bureau.

693. Flint, Peter Lee. "Sex Differences in Perceptions of Occupational Reinforcers." Ph.D. diss., University of Minnesota, 1980. 211 p. References, appendixes.

Study explores existence of sex differences in occupational-reinforcement factors among female and male respondents in 12 professional groups. Based on 1970s research with selected participants throughout Minnesota. Results show that job satisfaction is a consistent predictor of an individual's perceptions, while providing little support for sex-related analysis of participants' responses.

694. Flint, Robert Thomas. "The Relationship of Women's Tenure in Occupational Therapy to Strong Vocational Interest Blank and Demographic Variables." Ph.D. diss., University of Minnesota, 1970. 121 p. Appendixes, bibliography.

Study of shortages among licensed occupational therapists (OTs), a predominately female profession, and possible remedies through recruitment of trained, but not currently practicing, women explores decision to leave profession and factors that might induce return to practice. Based on 1960s research with registered OTs throughout Minnesota. Findings suggest that marriage and child rearing are important, but inadequately studied, factors in women's work patterns and that the "vague" and "low status" nature of OT work is responsible in part for attrition.

695. Goering, Lois A. "An Examination of Selected Factors Associated with Attitudes of Extension Professionals Toward Women in Management in the Minnesota Agricultural Extension Service." Ph.D. diss., North Carolina State University, 1986. 165 p. References, appendixes.

Provides history of Minnesota Extension Service with regard to women's employment and of 1978 consent decree ordering full representation of women in faculty employment at the University of Minnesota. Results of 1985 research concerning employee attitudes regarding women managers at the extension service indicate that gender is the primary factor influencing an individual's attitude. Women are more favorable toward women as managers regardless of other characterisitics; men are less so. Among men respondents, married men with agricultural backgrounds tend to be more negative than single men from other educational fields. Both women and men who have worked with women supervisors are more positive toward women entering management.

696. *Gopher Tidings*. Hibbing: Minnesota Press Women, 1943–69(?).

Newsletter of Minnesota Press Women. Mix of professional and social notes. Extensive information regarding individual members, journalistic activities statewide, annual meetings, and other projects of the MPW. Generally a monthly publication in period 1943–57. Publication site shifts around the state. Description based on 1948 issues.

697. Hamerston, Peg, comp. *WICI Reunion '87: Where We've Been; Where We're Going*. N.p.: Twin Cities Chapter, Women in Communications, Inc., [1987?]. 47 p. Illustrations.

Commemorative pamphlet produced for 70th anniversary of Theta Sigma Phi journalism sorority at the University of Minnesota. Features reminiscences by alumnae from the 1920s through the 1970s, registrants list for 1987 reunion, and 1987–88 board of directors.

698. Henderlite, Marilou Prow Glasrud. "A Study of Licensed Women School Administrators." Ph.D. diss., University of Minnesota, 1987. 229 p. Bibliography, appendixes.

Education study explores personality traits and background factors of two groups—women who earn school administration licenses, but do not ever occupy administrative positions, and licensed women who choose to leave administrative work. Based on research with graduates of the Education Administration Program, University of Minnesota, 1973–85. No clues explaining these differences in career paths are evident from standardized test results. Author suggests that the answers lie in respondents' biographical comments concerning sex discrimination, absence of mentors, and lack of opportunity.

699. Higley, Merle. *Women in Banking in the City of Minneapolis.* Minneapolis: Vocational Information Service of the Woman's Occupational Bureau, 1919. 23 p.

Pamphlet describes organization of work and opportunities for advancement in banking, 1917–19. This was the local business whose work force was most affected by World War I enlistments and draft and subsequent replacement (up to 40%) by women employees. This analysis assumes that the field will continue to be open to women.

700. Jerde, Judith. "Mary Molloy: St. Paul's Extraordinary Dressmaker." *Minnesota History* 47 (Fall 1980): 93–99.

Profiles Mary O'Keefe Molloy (1862–1924), an Irish American who operated a fine dressmaking establishment, 1879–1912. Discusses the exceptional artisanry of Molloy gowns, the dressmaker's annual trips to Paris, and the structure of the women's clothing industry during Molloy's years of activity. Also describes home and family life with husband Herbert N. Molloy and their children.

701. Meriwether, Crystal K. "Women in Educational Administration in Israel and the United States." Ph.D. diss., University of Minnesota, 1984. 382 p. Notes, bibliography, appendixes.

Comparative study of women secondary school principals in Israel and Minnesota explores demographic characteristics, experiences in seeking employment, job satisfaction, and career aspirations. Based on 1982–83 survey research and interviews. Findings suggest that obstacles to career advancement for women were more likely to be external—negative attitude of employer, lack of mentor, and

lack of networks. In this study, sex discrimination was found to be more common in Minnesota.

702. Mills-Novoa, Beverly Ann. "A Study of Selected Variables Affecting the Career Progression of Women in Higher Education Administration." Ph.D. diss., University of Minnesota, 1980. 304 p. Bibliography, appendixes.

Explores background factors, institutional influence, career expectations, and job satisfaction among women administrators in higher education. Based on 1979 survey research in private and public institutions throughout Minnesota. Provides good description of women administrators as a group. Identifies highest educational degree, shared responsibility for household and/or children, and influence within the institution as among the most important variables for participants.

703. Minnesota Center for Women in Government, Hamline University. *Women Breaking and Entering: Minnesota Women in Nontraditional Careers in Government Share Their Experiences.* St. Paul: The Center, 1990. 26 p. Illustrations.

Features the observations of seven women: historian Sara Evans, city administrator Sharon Klumpp, police sergeant Lora Setter, scientist Helen Boyer, Department of Natural Resources official Karen Bowen, farmer Kris Sanda, and Golden Valley mayor Mary Anderson. Focus is on diverse management styles among professional women in the 1980s.

704. Minnesota Governor's Council on Rural Development. *Rural Women: An Untapped Resource.* N.p.: The Council, 1984. 75 p. Footnotes, illustrations.

Proceedings of conference on women in business held in Willmar in 1983. Includes presentations on women's ethics and values, management, and practical observations from women business owners.

705. Monnig, Sister Gretta. "Professional Territoriality: A Study of the Expanded Role of the Nurse." Ph.D. diss., University of Minnesota, 1975. 142 p. References, appendixes, tables.

Study based on a 1974 survey of Minnesota physicians and nurses (random sample of 300 nurses and 300 physicians) explores attitudes toward expanded role of nurses that developed out of 1960s changes to the health care delivery system. Participants' responses analyzed for differences in attitudes toward autonomy, accountability, and identity of the nurse practitioner. Context is professional territoriality within health care field and competitive and cooperative models for behavior.

706. Murphy, Lucy Eldersveld. "Her Own Boss: Businesswomen and Separate Spheres in the Midwest, 1850–1880." *Illinois Historical Journal* 80 (Autumn 1987): 155–76.

Examines 19th-century census and business directory data regarding self-employed women in the Midwest. Discusses business activity in four areas: artisans (including needle trades), merchants, professionals, and providers of accommodations. Reports that business activity was more common than is recognized and suggests ways that the "true cult of womanhood" supported these activities.

707. Nolting, Earl, Jr. "A Study of Female Vocational Interests: Pre-College to Post-Graduation." Ph.D. diss., University of Minnesota, 1967. 220 p. References, appendixes.

Educational psychology study investigates women's vocational interests prior to college studies and following graduation and employment. Based on research with selected alumnae of the University of Minnesota, 1958–65, active in fields of elementary education, home economics, occupational therapy, medicine, social work, art, and library science. Findings show a strong relationship between academic major and employment in some of the occupations tested. Also suggests need for additional work exploring influences of maturation and vocational experiences on self-reported interests.

708. Penn, Margaret Helen. "The Relationship of Job Involvement and Sex-Role Identity to Women's Job Stress and Job Satisfaction." Ph.D. diss., University of Minnesota, 1987. 108 p. Reference notes, bibliography, appendixes.

Psychology study explores work-related stress among women. Based on 1980s research conducted with administrative, professional, and clerical staff at the Minneapolis locations of Honeywell, Inc. Findings suggest that competitiveness may be a more important motivator for women than has been previously recognized; high job involvement does not necessarily lead to strain; the personality attributes masculinity and androgyny are central to understanding work-related issues; job satisfaction in women is complex and cannot be assessed by a single instrument.

709. Pfleger, Helen Warren, as told to George A. Rea. "Volstead and Prohibition: A Roaring '20's Memoir." *Ramsey County History* 12, no. 1 (Spring–Summer 1975): 19–22.

Memoir of Civil Service clerk/receptionist's work with the St. Paul Prohibition Office, 1925–54, provides information about Andrew J. Volstead's tenure as consultant and office reorganization following repeal of Prohibition Amendment in 1933. Also describes earlier work experiences, 1915–25.

710. Pickering, Glenn Scott. "An Empirical Study of a Sample of Re-entry Women." Ph.D. diss., University of Minnesota, 1985. 190 p. References, appendix.

Comparative study of demographics and personality attributes of women reentering the labor market. Based on 1985 research with students enrolled in Re-entry Adult Program (REAP) at the College of St. Catherine, St. Paul, and with continuously employed career women at Twin Cities firms. Findings suggest that personality characterisitics of the two groups are similar, but demographics differ. Continuously employed career women tend to be younger (30s) and to have lower family incomes and higher aspirations. Reentry women tend to be older (40s) and to have higher family incomes, low level jobs, and relatively low aspirations.

711. "Remembering Maud Mellish Wilson." *Mayo Alumnus* 18, no. 2 (April 1982): 18–20.

Outlines Wilson's activities as founder of the Mayo Clinic Library and Mayo's Section of Publications in Rochester, 1907–33.

712. Rife, Gladys Talcott. "Personal Perspectives on the 1950s: Iowa's Rural Women Newspaper Columnists." *Annals of Iowa* 49 (Spring 1989): 661–82.

Discusses personal or opinion columns written by rural women for post-World War II newspapers. Analyzes columnists' subject matter—daily family life, landscape, rural community, and national policy questions—and their roles as working women.

713. Roberts, Nancy C. *Transforming Leadership: A Process of Collective Action.* Strategic Management Research Center, Discussion Paper no. 43. Minneapolis: University of Minnesota, 1985. 44 p. References, notes.

Case study analyzes leadership offered by female superintendent of a suburban Twin Cities school district in the early 1980s. Describes participatory management style, which included board, staff, students, and parents, and successful resolution of a financial and planning crisis. Pays considerable attention to "charisma" as a factor in the superintendent's leadership, locating this characteristic in her handling of the crisis rather than her personality.

714. Rowe, Laura M. *Executive and Buying Positions for Women in Department Stores.* Minneapolis: Woman's Occupational Bureau, 1923. 12 p.

Discusses opportunities in financial, operating, personnel, merchandise, and publicity divisions about 1920.

715. Seder, Margaret Aline. "Vocational Interest Patterns of Professional Women." Ph.D. diss., University of Minnesota, 1938. 72 p. Bibliography, appendixes.

Analysis of women's and men's responses to Strong Vocational Interest Blank, a popular guidance counseling tool. Specific elements studied include gender as a factor in occupational interests and femininity-masculinity. Women's sample includes physicians and life insurance agents from Twin Cities and other midwestern cities in the 1930s. Concludes that interests of men and women following the same occupations appear to be substantially the same; gender differences are relatively unimportant.

716. Setter, Gerald Leonard. "The Hours of Work Supply Decision: A Study of Metropolitan and Rural Minnesota Nurses." Ph.D. diss., University of Minnesota, 1974. 166 p. Appendixes, bibliography.

Economic study of the market for nurses in Minnesota with particular attention to the delivery of health care in nonmetropolitan areas. Based on research with general duty nurses (registered and licensed practical) in Twin Cities, Duluth, Rochester, and outstate in 1970. Findings include significant differences in RN and LPN behavior based on registered nurses' position as secondary contributors to household income and licensed practical nurses' situation as equal or primary wage earners in their households. Also suggests importance of fringe benefits as factor in nurses' economic decisions.

717. Stead, William H. *Opportunities for Women Trained in Home Economics.* Minneapolis: Woman's Occupational Bureau, 1928. 62 p. Appendix.

Prepared for schools and agencies offering vocational guidance and placement services to women in the 1920s. Describes teaching opportunities, dietetics in hospitals, and positions in foods, textiles, and clothing businesses. Based on Twin Cities research.

718. Steinmetz, Cheryl Fales. *Business Women of Minneapolis, 1870–1880.* Minneapolis: Privately published, 1989. 40 p. Bibliography.

Based on city directory and census sources, this study describes businesswomen active in Minneapolis and St. Anthony during the 1870s. Prin-cipal occupations include dressmaking, millinery, clerking, textile work, boardinghouse and hotel keeping, food and catering businesses, artistic and musical employment, and medicine.

719. *A Study of Job Motivations, Activities, and Satisfactions of Present and Prospective Women College Faculty Members.* Minneapolis: University of Minnesota, 1960. 100 p. Bibliography.

Summarizes an uncompleted research project investigating the status of women college teachers in Twin Cities area institutions in 1959. Although fragmentary, provides extensive and varied testimony concerning women's perceptions of the presence of sexual discrimination in employment.

720. Sylvester, Stephen G. "Avenues for Ladies Only: The Soiled Doves of East Grand Forks, 1887–1915." *Minnesota History* 51 (Winter 1989): 291–300.

Analyzes the success and subsequent decline of houses of prostitution. The city's saloons flourished after nearby North Dakota adopted a prohibition amendment in 1890. Several women entrepreneurs, including Chloe Mulnix, competed as hotel operators, and the city of East Grand Forks collected considerable revenue from monthly fines imposed upon prostitutes and madams. After 1913 the Wallace-Fossum Abatement Act closed all houses of prostitution in Minnesota.

721. Tinsley, Diane Johnson. "Characteristics of Women with Different Patterns of Career Orientation." Ph.D. diss., University of Minnesota, 1972. 361 p. Appendixes, references.

Pyschology study compares characteristics of homemaker and career-oriented women. Based on 1950s data collected from University of Minnesota students and 1970s follow-up study. Findings report differences in personal interests, family backgrounds, high school and college activities, reasons for attending college and selecting a major, self-ratings of personal traits, marriage and family situations, and community settings.

722. Tracy, Jane. "A Study of Minneapolis Dressmakers at the Turn of the Century." Typescript, 1980. 83 p. Illustrations, appendix, bibliography. (MHS).

Brief analysis of census and city directory information about women dressmakers in Minneapolis, 1880–1920, accompanied by maps and original data sheets.

723. *Vocations Open to College Women.* Bulletin of the University of Minnesota, Extra Series no. 1. Minneapolis: The University, 1913. 39 p.

Suggests lines of work in addition to teaching open to women graduates who intend to be self-supporting. Contains 16 essays on social service work, photography, domestic arts and sciences, libraries, journalism, nursing, and clerical jobs. Written by women practitioners in Minnesota. Many of the essays include reading references.

724. Wolfson, Karen Thelma Peyser. "Career Development of College Women." Ph.D. diss., University of Minnesota, 1972. 141 p. References, appendix.

Educational psychology study investigates vocational and homemaking roles. Based on 1930s research with University of Minnesota students and 1960s follow-up with same group in midlife. Findings suggest that college major, matriculation, and graduate school plans are strongest indicators of vocational commitments.

725. Women and Minority Business Enterprise Program. *W/MBE Directory.* Minneapolis: The Organization, 1988. 19 p. Index.

Lists professional services and businesses, giving firm name and address, services offered, contact person, year started, and women or minority status. While focusing on the Twin Cities metropolitan area, this directory also includes some outstate Minnesota listings.

726. Women's Counseling Service. *The Document: A Declaration of Feminism.* Minneapolis: The Organization, 1971. 35 p. (MHS).

Explains collective views of women active in counseling field. Announces goal of a feminist socialist revolution.

727. *Women's Directory.* St. Paul: FH Publications, 1986–.

A Twin Cities sourcebook features the women's yellow pages, local and national women's organizations, and products and services for women.

728. Women's Industrial Exchange. *The Women's Industrial Exchange of Minneapolis.* Minneapolis: The Exchange, 1886. 4 p.

Pamphlet describes sales program for handmade articles and lunches offered at the Minneapolis Exchange in 1886.

729. Woog, Alice Bechik. "Attitudes of Teachers Toward Female Administrators." Master's thesis, College of St. Thomas, 1985. 88 p. Bibliography, appendixes.

Education administration study explores attitudes of female and male teachers toward females in school administration. Context is 12–13% participation of women in administrative positions, 1950–80. Based on survey research with teachers (K-12) throughout Minnesota, 1983–84. Findings report no significant differences in attitudes on part of female and male respondents concerning women administrators. Recommends a series of measures in education programs for teachers, networking among women administrators, and individual career paths to increase women's participation in administration.

730. Wright, Barbara H. *Business Openings for Women in Minneapolis.* Minneapolis: Woman's Occupational Bureau, 1921. 8 p.

Pamphlet describes employment opportunities in stocks and bonds, real estate, public accounting, insurance, and banking.

Unpaid Work

Homemaking

731. Burris, Evadene A. "Keeping House on the Minnesota Frontier." *Minnesota History* 14 (September 1933): 263–82.

Explains late 19th-century household concerns, such as use of kerosene lamps, cellar drainage, soapmaking, mosquito protection, sturdy fences, and free-flowing wells.

732. Dresselhuis, Ellen. *The Legal Status of Homemakers in Minnesota.* Washington, D.C.: Homemaker's Committee, National Commission on the Observance of International Women's Year, 1977. 37 p. Notes, bibliography.

Analyzes laws and judicial precedents affecting situations of homemakers not employed outside the home. Primarily concerned with issues of economic inequality. Considers real property, child custody, divorce, physical abuse, inheritance, and social security.

733. Ellis, Bonnie. "Wife, Mother—Doing the Work of Six 'For the Sake of Being Supported'." *Ramsey County History* 8, no. 1 (Spring 1971): 3–7. Bibliography.

Description of late 19th- and early 20th-century women's domestic labor in Minnesota households. Based on diary of Polly Caroline Bullard and manuals of housewifery, notably Estelle Woods Wilcox's *The New Buckeye Cookbook,* published in St. Paul (1904), and Catharine E. Beecher and Harriet Beecher Stowe's *The American Woman's Home* (1869), distributed nationally. Counter-nostalgic in tone.

734. Hoover, Helen. *A Place in the Woods.* New York: Alfred A. Knopf, 1969. 292 p. Illustrations.

Memoir describes 1950s relocation from professional life in Chicago to year-round residence in a wilderness cabin in northeastern Minnesota. Focuses on establishment of home, development of coping skills in "tenderfoot" years, and shared responsibilities with husband Adrian Hoover. Also describes origins of author's career as a free-lance nature writer and husband's design and illustration activities.

735. Inman, Lydia Lucille. "Exploratory Study of Household Equipment Subject Matter for Secondary School Home Economics Curricula." Ph.D. diss., University of Minnesota, 1963. 189 p. Bibliography, appendixes.

Study of the use and operation of common kitchen equipment in 270 young-married households in Minnesota and Iowa about 1963. Focus is on high school home economics curriculum as a source of knowledge for practical operation and consumer decision making for household appliances. Considerable information about nature and extent of homemaking skills.

736. Jellison, Katherine. "Let Your Corn Stalks Buy a Maytag." *Palimpsest* 69 (Fall 1988): 132–39. Note on sources.

Analysis of home-appliance advertising and farm-life literature concerning modern improvements to rural Iowa homes, 1929–39. Discusses frequent gap between farm and home improvements, also the effects of New Deal programs, especially "high-line" power from the Rural Electrification Administration and crop reduction checks from Agricultural Adjustment Administration, in supporting new domestic technology and consumption patterns.

737. Lever Brothers Co. *Modern Home Laundering: A Book of Practical Information Based on Tested Methods, Dedicated to the Modern Woman.* N.p.: The Company, 1933. 34 p. Illustrations, index.

Pamphlet distributed with Zenith washing machines (Duluth agency) in the 1930s. Directed to middle-income housewives. Detailed description of home laundering procedures. Includes information about fabrics, clothing items, and household linens likely to be used. Compares modern machine techniques to earlier washday practices.

738. Minneapolis Tribune and Minneapolis Star, Research Department. *Retail Revolution, 1955–1965.* Minneapolis: The Company, 1965. 62 p. Appendix.

Surveys shopping habits of women in Minneapolis and suburbs. Documents increasingly mobile shoppers who regularly use suburban centers, city shopping districts (for example, Uptown or Chicago-Lake), and the downtown central business district. Also notes relative decrease in downtown shopping. Prepared for circulation to newspaper advertisers.

739. Minnesota Displaced Homemaker Program. *From Surviving to Thriving: Displaced Homemakers Do Start Over.* [St. Paul?]: Minnesota Department of Jobs and Training, 1990. 25 p.

Describes statewide Displaced Homemaker Program. Mostly first-person accounts by women who have used program services.

740. Nelson, James Earle. "An Empirical Investigation of the Nature and Incidence of Ecologically Responsible Consumption of Housewives." Ph.D. diss., University of Minnesota, 1974. 276 p. Bibliography, appendixes, tables.

Marketing study attempts to define characteristics of ecologically aware housewives. Based on 1970s research in Twin Cities metropolitan area. Study documents concerns about laundry detergents and soft drinks in particular and suggests a link between relative affluence and ecological concern. Emphasizes methodology rather than interpretation.

741. Sundberg, Sara Brooks. "A Female Frontier: Manitoba Farm Women in 1922." *Prairie Forum* 16 (Fall 1991): 185–204. Graphs.

Analysis of United Farm Women of Manitoba's 1922 Rural Home Survey. Assessment found living and working conditions much the same as in 1890s. Male farmers eager to adopt technological advances in field equipment and livestock care often were not interested in investing in labor-saving devices for their wives. Provides model for study of farm women.

Volunteerism

742. Kreidberg, Marjorie. "An Unembarrassed Patriot: Lucy Wilder Morris." *Minnesota History* 47 (Summer 1981): 215–26.

Profiles Morris (1864–1935), a Minneapolis author and community volunteer active in historic preservation. Describes her roles as founder and organizer of the Old Trails Chapter of the Daughters of the American Revolution in 1913; coordinator of *Old Rail Fence Corners,* a book of reminiscences by Minnesota pioneers; and organizer of numerous military memorials in Minnesota and elsewhere. Morris was among the first women elected to the Minnesota Historical Society Executive Council in 1921.

743. Stuhler, Barbara Jeanne. "The Administration of a Volunteer Civic Organization: The League of Women Voters of Minnesota." Master's thesis, University of Minnesota, 1951. 151 p. Appendix, bibliography.

Analyzes history and administrative patterns of a statewide citizen agency conceived as an experiment in adult education, 1919–50. Describes structure, board of directors, staff, finance, office management, and reporting system. Also offers comparisons to other volunteer civic organizations. Pays considerable attention to differences between voluntary and more formal organizations.

WORKPLACE
(including home and agriculture)

744. Brandt, Gail Cuthbert. "Postmodern Patchwork: Some Recent Trends in the Writing of Women's History in Canada." *Canadian Historical Review* 72 (December 1991): 441–70.

Traces recurring patterns and designs in the study of women's lives with a particular focus on gender in the work place. Challenges historians to consider gender issues and raises questions applicable to the study of Minnesota women.

745. Danes, Sharon. *Minnesota Farm Women: Who Are They and What Do They Do?* [St. Paul?]: Minnesota Extension Service, University of Minnesota, 1988. 8 p.

Research report summarizing 1988 farm women survey. Focuses on women's work on and off the farm, plus participation in family farm management decisions.

746. Fink, Deborah, and Dorothy Schwieder. "Iowa Farm Women in the 1930s: A Reassessment." *Annals of Iowa* 49 (Winter 1989): 570–90. Notes.

Survey article, based on 1930s documentary sources coupled with 1980s anthropological fieldwork, reconstructs farm women's contributions to the household and farm economies through poultry-keeping and dairy enterprises, gardening, food preservation, and other home-produced goods. Also discusses the advent of electricity and other improvements in daily life in 1930s.

747. Haney, Wava G., and Jane B. Knowles, eds. *Women and Farming: Changing Roles, Changing Structures.* Boulder, Colo.: Westview Press, 1988. 390 p. Notes, bibliography, index.

Papers from the Second National Conference on American Farm Women in Historical Perspective held in Madison, Wis., October 1986. Papers of interest to Minnesota and Upper Midwest researchers include "Building the Base: Farm Women, the Rural Community, and Farm Organizations in the Midwest, 1900–1940" by Mary Neth, "Sidelines and Moral Capital: Women on Nebraska Farms in the 1930s" by Deborah Fink, and "Off-Farm Labor Allocation by Married Farm Women: Research Review and New Evidence from Wisconsin" by Mary R. McCarthy, et al.

748. Hunter, Dianna. *Breaking Hard Ground: Stories of the Minnesota Farm Advocates.* Duluth: Holy Cow! Press, 1990. 196 p. Resource list, glossary, illustrations.

Includes 31 oral histories with couples and individuals active in Minnesota's Farm Advocate Program during the 1980s. Detailed discussions of financial aspects of contemporary farming. Considerable attention to women's roles in farm activities and reform movements.

749. Iverson, Joanne M. "Rural Farm Wives in Minnesota, 1900–1917." N.p., [1978?]. [16 p.] Typescript. (MHS).

Unpublished manuscript discusses women's roles in farm chores, housework, child rearing, and community volunteerism. Based on the *Farmer's Wife* magazine and other sources.

750. Kohl, Edith Eudora. *Land of the Burnt Thigh.* New York: Funk & Wagnalls, Inc., 1938; St. Paul: Minnesota Historical Society Press, Borealis Books, 1986. 296 p.

Experiences of two sisters from St. Louis who homesteaded in south-central South Dakota about 1907. Good descriptions of homestead conditions and community, experiences of other homesteading women, job opportunities, interactions with American-Indian neighbors, and economic development of the prairie.

751. Minnesota Agri-Women. *Ag News: The Newsletter of Minnesota Agri-Women.* [Warren, Minn.?]: The Organization, 1988–.

Eight-page newsletter published by women working in agriculture. Topics covered in sample 1990 issue include pesticide use, treatment of farm animals, and organizational matters.

752. Neth, Mary. "Gender and the Family Labor System: Defining Work in the Rural Midwest." Paper

93

presented at the annual meeting of the Social Science History Association, Blacksburg, Va., October 1990. 26 p. (MHS).

Evaluation of approximately 30 Wisconsin, North Dakota, and Iowa oral histories reveals that the gender-related labor patterns in midwestern agriculture varied according to ethnic background, crop specializations, and family composition. Study uncovers a variety of male and female attitudes toward gender roles.

753. Rathge, Richard W. "Women's Contribution to the Family Farm." *Great Plains Quarterly* 9 (Winter 1989): 36–47.

Sociological essay reevaluates "work" in family economy and suggests an alternative definition that acknowledges women's role in home and farm maintenance and other "hidden" activities. Based on 1983 research with North Dakota families.

754. Webb, Anne B. "Forgotten Persephones: Women Farmers on the Frontier." *Minnesota History* 50 (Winter 1986): 134–48. Notes, illustrations.

Profiles four women who homesteaded in the Midwest of 1850s–80s: Harriet Griswold of Isanti County, Pauline Auzjon and Emma Setterlund who tended claims in western Minnesota, and Emeline Guernsey of Mitchell County, Iowa. Explores social characteristics of the women, including marital status, parenthood, and native-born and immigrant status, in addition to decision making and physical work on respective farms.

755. Wilson, Gilbert. *Buffalo Bird Woman's Garden: Agriculture of the Hidatsa Indians.* Minneapolis: University of Minnesota, 1917; St. Paul: Minnesota Historical Society Press, Borealis Books, 1987. 127 p. Illustrations.

Detailed account of 19th-century village agriculture from the Hidatsa informant Buffalo Bird Woman (b. 1839) as told to anthropologist Gilbert Wilson in 1912. Locale is Missouri River valley in present-day North Dakota. Describes traditional agricultural practices and recipes for corn, sunflowers, squashes, beans, and tobacco. Comments on white men's farming and on women's roles in Hidatsa agriculture.

INCOME/PAY EQUITY

756. Daines, Jeanette Kleven. "The Conception of Comparable Worth: Examining a Policy Issue." Ph.D. diss., University of Minnesota, 1986. 233 p. References, appendixes.

Study of comparable worth as a policy concept;

analyzes multiple assignment of meanings through anthropological, economic, psychological, philosophical, labor relations, and legislative perspectives. Provides legislative, judicial, and social history of concept. Based on 1980s research with Minnesota scholars (University of Minnesota) and situations. Primary finding is deep tension among definitions offered, reflecting broader social uncertainties and disagreements about this policy.

757. Evans, Sara M., and Barbara J. Nelson. "The Impact of Pay Equity on Public Employees: State of Minnesota Employees' Attitudes Toward Wage Policy Innovation." In *Pay Equity: Empirical Inquiries,* edited by Robert T. Michael, Heidi I. Hartman, and Brigid O'Farrell, p. 200–221. Washington: National Academy Press, 1989. Tables, graph.

Article analyzes the effect of Minnesota's 1982 State Employees Pay Equity Act, the nation's first state attempt to implement a complete comparable worth policy. The study, a part of the University of Minnesota's Comparable Worth Research Project, examines the effect of the law on employees and focuses on attitudes toward pay equity, perceived impact of the policy, and job satisfaction.

758. Evans, Sara M., and Barbara J. Nelson. *Wage Justice: Comparable Worth and the Paradox of Technocratic Reform.* Chicago: University of Chicago Press, 1989. 244 p. Appendixes, notes, index.

Case study of comparable worth or pay equity implementation for public employees in Minnesota, 1983–87. The focus is on consequences of pay equity for women and minorities in a state that has been a leader in this field. The authors provide detailed analyses of policy initiation, political decision making, and institutional governance.

759. Minnesota Commission on the Economic Status of Women. *Minnesota Women and Poverty.* St. Paul: The Commission, 1985. 15 p. Charts, graphs, map.

This statistical study reveals that 41% of Minnesotans living below the poverty level in 1979 were women. Further analysis assesses Minnesota poverty according to family type, age, region, and income level.

760. Minnesota Council on the Economic Status of Women. *Minnesota Women: Income and Poverty.* St. Paul: The Council, 1978. 38 p. Illustrations.

Documents high incidence of poverty among women. Discusses contributing factors—training, part-time work, low wages, inflation, and single-parent households. Also describes conditions of older women and role of public assistance. Includes excerpts from testimony taken in public hearings throughout Minnesota.

761. Minnesota Council on the Economic Status of Women. *Minnesota Women: Work & Training.* St. Paul: The Council, 1977. 25 p. Illustrations.

Report documents discrepancy between expected and actual needs for economic self-sufficiency among Minnesota women during the 1970s. Recommends a series of changes in job training, education, employment, and social services to meet increased participation of women in paid labor force, especially those who are displaced homemakers.

762. National Organization for Women, Twin Cities Chapter, Employment Task Force. *The Position of Women as a Disadvantaged Group in Minnesota State Government.* Minneapolis: The Organization, 1976. 27 p. Appendix, references.

Describes status of women in state government employment relative to white men and "disadvantaged" workers of African-American, Hispanic, and American-Indian descent. Based on analysis of 1976 state payroll. Principal finding is that disadvantages due to gender are greater than those due to race and ethnicity. Suggests that affirmative action for women and for minorities should be separated.

763. Roberg, Janice Elizabeth. "Occupational Segregation and Comparable Worth in the Public Sector of Suburban St. Paul." Honors thesis, Macalester College, 1981. 21 p. Bibliography, appendixes.

Business and economics study analyzes gender equity in the salary system in Arden Hills, Inver Grove Heights, Lake Elmo, Mounds View, Rosemount, Roseville, South St. Paul, Stillwater, and White Bear Lake. Considers administrative and nonadminstrative occupations. Findings document a tendency to pay women's occupations less than men's occupations identified as comparable. Based on 1981 research with suburban jobholders, a volunteer panel of personnel professionals, and economic statistics.

764. Taylor, Susan Hartman. "Conceptual and Methodological Issues in the Assessment of Sex-Related Pay Discrimination." Ph.D. diss., University of Minnesota, 1988. 364 p. References.

Explores three definitions of comparable worth: an administrative view based on job worth assessed by job evaluation ratings and organizational pay structures; an academic model explaining pay differentials in terms of race, sex, and productivity; legal precedent based on varying ratios of intent, productivity, and job worth. Also assesses the effects when these definitions are applied in selected everyday situations. Based on 1980s research using data from the Department of Employee Relations, State of Minnesota. Findings show systematic inequities favoring "male" jobs using all three definitions of comparable worth.

FINANCE (including pensions, insurance, business, and industry)

765. Groth, Kay A. "Woman's Fraternalism with a Focus on Two Minnesota Women's Fraternal Benefit Societies." Unpublished paper, Macalester College, 1989. 10 p. Notes, list of sources.

Student paper describes the Order of Hermann Sisters, 1890–1988, organized by German women in New Ulm, and the Degree of Honor, 1910–, affiliated with the Ancient Order of United Workingmen in St. Paul. Outlines insurance benefits, social activities, and other services offered.

766. [Minnesota] Council on the Economic Status of Women. *Minnesota Women and Money: A Study of Insurance, Retirement Income, Credit, and Taxes.* St. Paul: The Council, 1979. 44 p. Sources.

Discusses myths and realities regarding earned and inherited income. Describes effects of public and private financial systems—including insurance, social security, pensions, investments, credit, and taxes—on women's economic security. Recommends specific measures that would end discrimination in economic practices.

IIII/ LAW AND GOVERNMENT

LAW AND LEGISLATION

General—Law and Legislation

767. Minnesota Commission on the Economic Status of Women. *Legislative Program.* St. Paul: The Commission, 1987, 1988, 1991. (U of M/Law Library).

Pamphlets outline commission's agenda concerning women's programs, family support, economic development, health, and a women's history center in Minnesota. (Note: Established as an advisory council to the governor and the legislature in 1976, the organization became a joint legislative commission in 1983.)

Suffrage

768. Hurd, Ethel Edgerton. *Woman Suffrage in Minnesota: A Record of the Activities in Its Behalf Since 1847.* Minneapolis: Minnesota Woman Suffrage Association, 1916. 52 p. Index.

Chronicles activities of pioneer suffragists, 1847–1915, local and statewide organizations, 1866–1915, and officers and officials, 1881–1915. Also describes the *Minnesota Bulletin,* a statewide newsletter published 1899–1909, annual state fair activities, public relations with area newspapers, lectures sponsored, links to the Minneapolis School and Library Association, and Minnesotans' participation in the suffrage parades produced nationwide, May 2, 1914. The author, a principal in state suffrage politics, supplies considerable detail about early arrangements and alliances.

769. Jones, Tessie. *The Philosophy of Anti-Suffrage.* Minneapolis: Minneapolis Association Opposed to the Further Extension of Suffrage to Women, [1915?]. 6 p.

Pamphlet describes suffrage as "external" remedy for social ills that require "internal" or spiritual commitment to family and "laws of nature."

770. Koupal, Nancy Tystad. "The Wonderful Wizard of the West: L. Frank Baum in South Dakota, 1888–91." *Great Plains Quarterly* 9 (Fall 1989): 203–15.

The only two women in the Minnesota House of Representatives in 1943 were Mabeth Hurd Paige, who entered the legislature in 1923, and Gladys Joe Brown, a page.

Thought-provoking comparison of L. Frank Baum's treatment of women's culture and suffrage issues in his roles as a newspaper editor and later as author of the Oz books.

771. League of Women Voters of Minnesota. *Institute of Government and Politics.* [Minneapolis and St. Paul]: The Organization, 1923–29.

Programs for annual institutes on national and international policy cosponsored by the League and the University of Minnesota. The institutes were held in conjunction with League annual meetings focusing on that organization's public education goals in the first decade following woman suffrage.

772. Stanton, Elizabeth Cady, et al. *History of Woman Suffrage.* Rochester, N.Y.: Susan B. Anthony, 1902. 4 vols.

Sarah Burger Stearns describes suffrage work in Minnesota during the 1860s and 1870s (3:649–61).

Julia B. Nelson discusses suffrage activity in the 1880s (4:772–82).

773. Subialka, Carol A. "The Ideology of Minnesota's Woman Suffrage Movement: 1910–1920." Senior thesis, History Department, University of Minnesota, 1987. 39 p. Notes, bibliography.

Discusses the operations of the Minnesota Woman Suffrage Association in relation to the National American Woman Suffrage Association and to local antisuffrage forces. Includes considerable data from pro- and antisuffrage speeches and tracts. While recognizing the fundamentally moderate agenda of Minnesota suffragists, the author suggests that their ideas concerning women's roles were "more varied" than is commonly recognized.

774. Ueland, Mrs. Andreas [Clara H.] *The Advantages of Equal Suffrage*. Minneapolis: Minnesota Academy of Social Sciences, 1914. 16 p.

A leader of the Minnesota suffrage movement, Ueland (1860–1927) delivered this speech concerning women's participation in civic life in 1914. It is a classic statement of the gender-equality argument at that time.

775. Ziebarth, Marilyn. "Woman's Rights Movement." *Minnesota History* 42 (Summer 1971): 225–30.

Overview of woman suffrage activity in Minnesota, 1857–1919, provides national context in addition to personalities, organizations, and circumstances specific to this state.

Protective

776. Deming, Eliza Evans. *Second Biennial Report of the Minnesota Minimum Wage Commission to the Governor and Legislature of the State of Minnesota, April 1, 1918, to January 15, 1921*. Minneapolis: The Commission, 1921. 95 p.

Analyzes wages and hours for women workers generally and for some specific occupations, such as those in telephone-telegraph establishments and restaurants. Compares women's and men's earnings. Provides history of minimum wage commission.

777. *Employment Discrimination Law*. Advanced Legal Education no. 261. St. Paul: Hamline University, 1985. 173 p.

Discusses federal and Minnesota laws regarding proof of discrimination, procedures in filing judicial and administrative claims, compensation discrimination, age discrimination, disability discrimination, and sexual harassment. Sponsored by Hamline School of Law educational service to practicing attorneys.

778. Minnesota Department of Labor and Industries. *Laws Regulating the Employment of Children, Prescribing the Hours of Labor for Women, and Creating Minimum Wage Commission*. St. Paul: The Department, 1913. 19 p.

Sets forth regulations governing hours of labor, meals, work breaks, and sanitary conditions for women employed in retail trade, factories, restaurants and kitchens, and telephone-telegraph establishments. Also outlines procedures to be followed in determining state minimum wage for women and minors.

779. Minnesota Department of Labor and Industry. *Employment of Women, Minors and Children*. St. Paul: The Department, 1949. 19 p.

Outlines laws on hours and minimum wages. Also describes duties of Minnesota Industrial Commission relative to employed women and minors.

780. Minnesota Institute of Legal Education (MILE). *Sexual Harassment Discrimination*. Minneapolis: The Organization, 1985. 182 p.

Provides overview of discrimination cases relating to comparable worth, disability, religious freedom, age discrimination, and marital status. Notes current procedural precedents. Also discusses distinctions between public and private sector claims, dispute resolution techniques, and employment law considerations.

781. [Minnesota Minimum Wage Commission.] *First Biennial Report of the Minnesota Minimum Wage Commission to the Governor and Legislature of the State of Minnesota, August 1, 1913, to December 31, 1914*. Minneapolis: The Commission, 1914. 55 p.

Summarizes history of the commission; specific wage laws applicable to women, children, and male minors under 21 years; and actual wages reported by employers and employees. Provides extensive discussion of the cost of living for women workers in various Minnesota communities and the legal history of the minimum wage commission.

782. Minnesota Minimum Wage Commission. *Supplement to First Biennial Report of the Minnesota Minimum Wage Commission to the Governor and Legislature of the State of Minnesota, March 1st, 1918, to March 1st, 1919*. St. Paul: The Commission, 1919. 30 p.

Gives a brief history of the commission and the institution of minimum wages for women and minors. Discusses an unsuccessful legal challenge to the Minnesota law and also application of minimum wage provisions to apprenticeship situations.

783. Minnesota Wage Commission. *The Minnesota Minimum Wage Law.* Bulletin nos. 1 and 2. St. Paul: The Commission, 1914, 1918. 32, [17] p.

Bulletin no. 1 includes the attorney general's opinion of 1913 upholding the law that established a minimum wage in Minnesota, questions raised by Twin Cities employers, and a relevant Oregon Supreme Court opinion of 1914. Bulletin no. 2, which carries the title *Minimum Wage Commission,* contains court documents related to a challenge of the 1913 statute. In December 1917 the Minnesota Supreme Court unanimously overturned a lower court ruling that had declared the law unconstitutional. Includes wage commission orders.

SOCIAL WELFARE

784. *Social Welfare History Group Newsletter.* Minneapolis: Department of History, University of Minnesota, 1956–. (U of M/Wal).

News and notes concerning social welfare history regionally and nationally. Publication somewhat irregular. Starting in the 1950s, three issues produced annually; summer-fall issue devoted to bibliography. (Note: Complete run available at Social Welfare History Archives.)

785. Wattenberg, Esther, ed. *Room at the Top: Moving Women Into Administrative Positions in Social Welfare.* Minneapolis: Center for Urban and Regional Affairs, University of Minnesota, 1978. 28 p.

Proceedings of a conference organized by the National Association of Social Workers and Center for Urban and Regional Affairs to examine high participation of women as social-welfare clients and social workers and their low participation as policymakers and administrators. Includes essays on Minnesota social welfare, women in managerial positions, administrative styles, and an exercise in administrative decision making.

Public

786. Hertz, Susan H. "The Politics of the Welfare Mothers Movement: A Case Study." *Signs: Journal of*

Women in Culture and Society 2 (Spring 1977): 600–611.

Discusses the activities of three welfare mothers' organizations active in Minneapolis in the 1960s and 1970s—AFDC League, Direct Action Recipients of Welfare, and Minnesota Welfare Rights Organization. Pays particular attention to role of these organizations in redefining welfare recipients as citizens, rather than as clients.

787. League of Women Voters of Minneapolis. *More About Welfare.* Minneapolis: The League, 1978. 12 p. Appendixes.

Analysis of welfare reforms proposed by President Jimmy Carter in 1978. Includes explicit discussion of women with children, displaced homemakers, and other gender-specific aspects of welfare policy. Appendixes include selected testimony before Ad Hoc Welfare subcommittee hearing on H.R. 9030 in Minneapolis, November 16, 1977; interview with director of AFDC program; National Association of Social Workers statement.

788. League of Women Voters of St. Paul. *League of Women Voters Welfare Position.* St. Paul: The League, 1972. 8 p. Appendix.

Analysis of federal and state welfare policies of the early 1970s. Includes discussion of gender distinctions in household assistance plans and day care. Appendix describes particulars of the Minnesota system.

789. Women's Professional and Service Projects. *Newsletter.* [St. Paul?]: Minnesota Works Progress Administration, 1936.

Monthly newsletter reports on state and federal programs in the arts, historical research, nursing, handicrafts, sewing, and other fields. Includes considerable detail and evaluative comments about featured activities. (Note: Minnesota Historical Society holds three issues from 1936.)

Private

790. Balcom, Tom. "An Orphan Remembers." *Hennepin County History* 42, no. 3 (Fall 1983): 16–18.

Reminiscence of Swedish immigrant girl's stay at Washburn Memorial Orphan Asylum in Minneapolis, 1897–1907. The anonymous informant's recollections include comments on selected staff, layout, and routines at the asylum, plus circumstances that led both to her placement in the institution and to a reunion with her family at age 13.

791. Hobbie, Ann S. " 'Much Good Work Must Here Be Done,' The Neighborhood House and Eastern European Jews." Honors thesis, Macalester College, 1988. 108 p. Bibliography.

Describes operations and activities of Neighborhood House, a settlement house on the West Side of St. Paul, 1897–1957. Founded to serve the Jewish community, it became a nonsectarian center, aiding a diverse immigrant community within a decade. Pays particular attention to the roles of Jewish women as volunteers and as neighborhood residents. Also analyzes administrations and activities of social workers Margaret Pentland, 1903–08(?), and Constance Currie, 1918–57.

792. McClure, Ethel. "The Protestant Home of St. Paul: A Pioneer Venture in Caring for the Aged." *Minnesota History* 38 (June 1962): 74–85.

Organized on May 4, 1867, as the Ladies Christian Union at a meeting where pioneer teacher Harriet Bishop recorded the minutes. The institution, which represented a number of Protestant denominations, originally focused on aiding the homeless —particularly women and children. In 1883 the organization opened a residence for the aged, which in 1935 became the Protestant Home. The group was also known by several other names, including the Ladies Relief Association and the Home of the Friendless Association.

793. Shoemaker, Nancy. "Urban Indians and Ethnic Choices: American Indian Organizations in Minneapolis, 1920–50." *Western Historical Quarterly* 19 (November 1988): 431–47.

Analyzes the conflict between loyalty to the reservation and the reality of life in the city, a dilemma many Indians faced in the 20th century. Article includes discussion of Amabel Bulin, a Dakota woman married to a Scandinavian, who became a volunteer social worker in the 1920s and developed a number of informal programs to assist Indians moving from reservations to Minneapolis. She also served as director of the Minnesota General Federation of Women's Clubs, Indian Division, during the late 1930s and early 1940s.

794. Stadum, Beverly Ann. " 'Maybe They Will Appreciate What I Done and Struggled': Poor Women and Their Families—Charity Cases in Minneapolis, 1900–1930." Ph.D. diss., University of Minnesota, 1987. 462 p. Bibliographic essay.

Explores the experiences of poor families in Minneapolis in the early 20th century through records of Associated Charities (later the Family Welfare Association). Focuses on the interactions of two groups of women: female clients representing their families and social workers representing the agency. Provides voluminous information about living conditions and the developing social work profession. Emphasizes initiative and internal decision making of client families.

795. Stadum, Beverly. " 'Says There's Nothing Like Home': Family Casework with the Minneapolis Poor, 1900–30." *Minnesota History* 51 (Summer 1988): 43–54.

Utilizes Associated Charities case records at University of Minnesota's Social Welfare History Archives to explain origins of social work in the city. Women carried many of the family burdens caused by the large number of underpaid and underemployed workers. Living conditions, health concerns, broken families, and absent fathers are among the issues discussed.

LEGAL RIGHTS

796. Christopherson, David N., comp. *Minnesota Marriage and Divorce Laws.* Minneapolis: U.S. Divorce Reform Inc., 1972. 65 p.

Compilation of Minnesota statutes on marriage, divorce, child custody, and related matters about 1971–72. The publisher is described as a nonprofit organization promoting "equalization" changes in divorce laws.

797. *Economic Problems of Families in Transition.* Advanced Legal Education no. 30. St. Paul: Hamline University, 1978. 17 p.

Reprints three lectures describing legal and financial issues of spousal support: Joline Gitis, "Background Information on Displaced Homemakers"; Charles C. Schultz, "Child Support Enforcement"; and Bonnie Watkins, "Council on the Economic Status of Women." Sponsored by Hamline School of Law educational service to practicing attorneys.

798. Ericson, Kathryn. "Triple Jeopardy: The Muus vs. Muus Case in Three Forums." *Minnesota History* 50 (Winter 1987): 298–308.

Focuses on Oline Pind Muus's 1879 lawsuit against her husband Bernt Muus requesting control of her inheritance and alleging neglect and cruelty. Describes the Muuses' shared backgrounds in genteel Norwegian society, marriage and immigration to Minnesota in 1859, Bernt's ministry to Norwegian Lutheran congregations throughout the state, and Oline's housekeeping at their home in Holden, Goodhue County. Discusses the civil court case, church discipline proceedings arising from the civil suit in the 1880s, and newspaper coverage of all aspects of these cases, including perceptions that the Norwegian community chose to remain "isolated" from mainline American culture. Also gives follow-up information about Oline's (1838–1922) later years in Minneapolis and Alabama and Bernt's (1832–1900) in Holden and Norway.

799. [Minnesota] Commission on the Economic Status of Women. *A Woman's Place: A Guide to Women's Legal and Economic Rights in Minnesota.* 3d ed. St. Paul: The Commission, 1985. 43 p. Illustrations.

Pamphlet discusses women's legal rights in areas of consumer practices, education, employment, finances, family, and domestic violence. Includes statewide resource list.

800. Minnesota Continuing Legal Education. *Sexual Harassment: Avoiding, Establishing and Defending Liability.* St. Paul: Minnesota State Bar Association, 1989. [150 + p.]

Contains articles analyzing sexual harassment law, the "hostile work environment problem," preventive tactics, complaint handling, and litigation strategies. Authors are Minnesota attorneys specializing in these issues. Produced as a service to practicing lawyers.

801. Minnesota Council on the Economic Status of Women. *Sexual Harassment Task Force Report.* St. Paul: The Council, 1982. 20 p. Bibliography.

Summarizes local and national studies of sexual harassment. Describes relevant legal definitions and court precedents. Suggests resources, including sample policy statements, a list of organizations that enforce sex discrimination laws, and selected readings. Recommends addition of sexual harassment to state Human Rights Act, inclusion of sexual harassment among other "good causes" for leaving a job, and continued development of preventive measures among employers and labor unions and of referral resources for persons who have been harassed.

802. Minnesota Governor's Commission on the Status of Women. *Interim Report.* St. Paul: The Commission, 1964. 73 p. Tables, graphs.

Prepared in response to Governor Karl F. Rolvaag's executive order of November 13, 1963. The report includes a list of commission members; the names of committee members are given along with committee reports and recommendations. The commission focused primarily on employment conditions, civil and political rights, education, and home and community services. Members recommended that the commission continue under an executive order, seek a legislative appropriation, and expand to include members representing business, industry, and agriculture.

803. Minnesota Governor's Commission on the Status of Women. *Minnesota Women: Final Report, July 1, 1965–July 1, 1967.* St. Paul: The Commission, [1967?]. 27 p.

Report on activities of commission in areas of education, employment, family life, legal rights, public relations, and appointive posts. Also includes overview of commission activities for entire span of existence, 1963–67, and membership roster. The Division of Women's Affairs in the newly created Department of Human Rights assumed the Commission's responsibilities in 1967.

804. Minnesota Governor's Commission on the Status of Women. *Progress Report.* [St. Paul?]: The Commission, 1966. 7 p.

Describes work in progress by education, employment, citizen volunteer, legal rights, "strengthening" family life, and roster (of qualified women for elective and appointive office) committees of the commission. Lists commission members, 1965–67.

805. Minnesota Supreme Court. *Minnesota Supreme Court Task Force for Gender Fairness in the Courts: A Final Report.* St. Paul: The Court, 1989. 226 p. Appendix.

Final report on an internal evaluation (1987–89) to determine whether gender bias affects the fairness of Minnesota courts. Report documents extensive bias in conduct of cases involving family law, domestic violence, criminal enforcement, and sexual violence. Task force members also identified areas of administrative concern in courtroom environments, the proportion of women judges appointed, and court employment.

806. Minnesota Women's Consortium. *1987 Minnesota Women's Economic Action Plan.* St. Paul: The Consortium, 1988. 8 p. Illustrations.

Pamphlet describes a women's agenda developed by members of the consortium, public officials, and others during a series of weekly meetings about 1987. Topics considered include equality, human rights, education, and health and family issues.

807. Minnesota Women's Consortium. *1989 Minnesota Women's Economic Action Plan.* St. Paul: The Consortium, 1989. 8 p.

Sequel to 1987 plan developed by same group. Considers issues of physical danger, adolescent women, women with children, women in school, housing, work, child health, justice, and retirement.

808. Motl, Jonathan R., and Katherine Berkvam. *Minnesota Women's Legal Rights Handbook.* Rev. ed. Minneapolis: Minnesota Public Interest Research Group, 1981. 64 p.

Handbook discusses legal rights of women in areas of employment, family law, education, health, finance, and sexual violence. Text is based on state and applicable federal law in 1981. (Attorneys Michele Morley and Mary Mahoney edited and revised the 1976 edition of the work.)

809. Pruitt, Mary Christine. " 'Women Unite!' The Modern Women's Movement in Minnesota." Ph.D. diss., University of Minnesota, 1987. 324 p. Bibliography.

Analyzes feminist activity in 20th century through discussion of suffragists, the 1950s peace movement, African Americans' social justice organizations, DFL politics, and 1970s women's rights and liberation. Considers a broad spectrum of cultural and political action groups while documenting many links among individuals and institutions.

810. Schain, Josephine, comp. *Laws of Minnesota Relating to Women and Children.* Minneapolis: Minneapolis Civic Improvement League, 1908. 91 p. Glossary, index.

Handbook prepared for clubwomen of Minnesota lists laws relating to women in personal relations, property rights, personal property, contract rights, and penal statutes. Accompanying section describes laws relating to children.

811. Tyler, Leona Elizabeth. "Factors Conditioning the Development of Interest in Adolescent Girls." Ph.D. diss., University of Minnesota, 1940. 190 p. Bibliography, appendixes.

Psychological study of feminist interests and attitudes conducted among students of public and private high schools in Minneapolis and St. Paul during the 1930s. Findings include widespread acceptance of feminist ideals concerning domestic and legal rights coupled with expression of antifeminist social attitudes concerning conduct of daily activities.

812. University of Minnesota Law School. *Faces of Struggle: Midwest Regional Conference, Women and the Law.* Minneapolis: The Law School, 1985. 104 p. Bibliography.

Conference addresses diverse aspects of women's legal status, rights, and opportunities. Also contains biographical notes for dozens of participating professional women from Minnesota and the region.

813. Williams, Essie W. *Legal Status of Women and Children in Minnesota.* St. Paul: Minnesota Woman Suffrage Association, 1911. 32 p.

Pamphlet written on behalf of the Minnesota Woman Suffrage Association in reply to questions circulated to each state by the National American Woman Suffrage Association. Discusses property rights of married women, spousal responsibilities, marriage and divorce, protective legislation (civil and criminal) concerning women and girls, labor laws, franchise rights, and educational and business opportunities open to women.

814. Zachary, Louis L. "The Attitudes of Minnesota Community College Personnel Concerning Affirmative Action in Minnesota State Supported Community Colleges." Ph.D. diss., University of Minnesota, 1980. 226 p. Bibliography, appendixes.

Study designed to assess the affirmative action program within Minnesota's 18 state-supported community colleges. Based on 1976–79 research surveying personal beliefs of full-time college staff members and examination of institutional employment records. Findings include a strong record in hiring white females and a poor one for minorities. Also evidence of job-related sex stereotyping among men and women respondents.

CRIME, PRISONS, AND PUNISHMENT

815. Barden, Donna Marie Farrell. "A Comparison of the Histories of Delinquent Boys and Girls." Ph.D. diss., University of Minnesota, 1969. 102 p. Appendixes, bibliography.

Psychology study explores personal characteristics of female and male delinquent teenagers. Based on 1960s research with young people held at Lino Lakes diagnostic facility. Findings report high levels of family disunity, conflict with parents, school problems, and self-labeling as "social misfits" among all participating juveniles. Also reports generally more intense negative responses among female respondents.

816. Colaiuta, Victoria B. *Genesis II: A Two-Year Evaluation Report.* St. Paul: Evaluation Unit, Minnesota Crime Control Planning Board, 1978. 208 p. Notes, graphs.

Evaluation of the largest nonresidential, community-based corrections program for adult women in Hennepin County, 1977–78. Describes clients, criminal behaviors, treatment program, goals, and cost-effectiveness.

817. Frederiksen, Sharon Jenine. "A Comparison of Selected Personality and History Variables in Highly Violent, Mildly Violent, and Non-Violent Female Offenders." Ph.D. diss., University of Minnesota, 1975. 232 p. Appendixes, bibliography.

Study of personalities and experiences of women who commit physical aggression against other adults. Based on 1973–74 research with subjects located through Hennepin and Ramsey county court records. Compares personality characteristics of females and males charged with assault. Suggests link between experience as victim of assault and likelihood of later commission of assault.

818. Knudson, Barbara Lagerstedt. "Career Patterns of Female Misdemeanant Offenders." Ph.D. diss., University of Minnesota, 1968. 187 p. Bibliography, appendix, tables.

Sociological study of personal histories and criminal patterns of female petty criminals. Based on 1954 commitments to the Minneapolis Women's Detention Home. Basic finding that misdemeanor offenders are not likely to become felons but will probably require social-service assistance in future.

819. Minnesota Department of Corrections. *The Future of Women Offenders in the Minnesota Correctional System.* St. Paul: The Department, 1978. 40 p. Appendixes.

Describes the "women offender" population and correctional facilities located in Shakopee, Stillwater, and Sauk Centre. Notes relative decline in services available to incarcerated women in the 1970s. Recommends comprehensive planning, a permanent advisory board on women's concerns, strict enforcement of humane care in all detention and incarceration facilities, and creation of community-based programs. Also suggests follow-up studies in areas of sentencing guidelines, employment, services for women who are mentally retarded or mentally ill, and juvenile services.

820. Minnesota Department of Corrections. *Institutional Placement of the Woman Offender.* St. Paul: The Department, 1979. 70 p.

Report prepared for state legislature. Context is inadequate facilities at Shakopee, the only Minnesota prison for women offenders, and general neglect in area of female corrections nationally. Includes basic research on women offenders in Minnesota and explores options for additional facilities

through new construction and/or adaptation of existing male and juvenile offender institutions.

821. Minnesota Department of Corrections. *Women Offenders at Minnesota Correctional Institution for Women, 1976.* [St. Paul?]: The Department, 1976. 38 p.

Describes social characteristics and correctional histories of individuals incarcerated at the Minnesota Correctional Institution for Women in Shakopee. Discusses inmate programs and security and also provides follow-up on recently released prisoners. Addresses parenting concerns of inmates, among other topics.

822. *The Reflector.* Shakopee, Minn.: Minnesota State Reformatory for Women, November 1935–June 1939. (U of M/Wal).

Monthly newsletter produced by inmates describes daily life in the institution and circumstances that led to individuals' imprisonments. Created as a part of the reformatory's English program. Also contains considerable information about corrections policy and rehabilitation techniques.

823. Sadacca, Mark. *Newgate for Women: An Evaluation of a Community Corrections Program for Women Offenders.* St. Paul: Evaluation Unit, Minnesota Crime Control Planning Board, 1977. 69 p.

Evaluates residential program in St. Paul serving women offenders on probation or parole, 1974–77. Describes clients, educational and employment assistance, recidivism rates, and costs of services.

824. Saibel, Laura F. "A Project to Study the Institutional Adjustment of the Inmates of the Minnesota Reformatory for Women, As Reflected by Their Scores on a Standardized Opinions Scale, and by Matrons' Ratings." Plan B research project, University of Minnesota, 1941. 77 p. Bibliography, appendixes.

The standardized test measurements ventured in this project proved inconclusive. The paper provides individual case histories for selected prisoners and considerable description of day-to-day conditions at the women's reformatory near Shakopee about 1940.

MILITARY AND DEFENSE

825. Kaiser, Gregory P. "World War II Women's Civil Defense: Winona, Minnesota." Unpublished paper, St. Mary's College, Winona, 1986. 23 p. Notes, bibliography.

During World War I Red Cross workers made bandages at Welcome Hall, a center of many activities in St. Paul's African-American community.

Student history paper chronicles the activities of volunteer Victory Aides in civil defense and benevolent work and Red Cross workers in health.

826. Minnesota Office of Civilian Defense, Welfare Division. *A Handbook for Victory Aides.* St. Paul: The Organization, [1942?]. 69 p.

Reference manual for women volunteers in state civilian defense program during World War II. Describes structure of Victory Aides program and aides' duties in public information, salvage, Red Cross, rationing, and related activities.

827. Woman's Liberty Loan Committee. *Report of the Federal Chairman, Ninth Federal Reserve District, Woman's Liberty Loan Committee.* Minneapolis: Victory Liberty Loan, 1919. 22 p.

Describes organization of women's volunteer efforts (parallel to men's) to sell war bonds during World War I. Includes state reports for Minnesota, Wisconsin, and other states in the district. Identifies county chairs.

POLITICS

828. American Anti-Socialist League. *What Socialists Say About Marriage.* Passaic, N.J.: The League, n.d. 1 p.

Anti-Socialist pamphlet quotes Frederick Engels, Mrs. Ethel Snowdon, George Bernard Shaw, and others on the subject of marriage. Equates socialism and free love.

829. Beito, Gretchen. "Coya Come Home." *Plainswoman* 6, no. 3 (November 1982): 8–10.

Brief analysis of news coverage and popular attitudes concerning the balance between domestic and civic responsibilities in Democratic-Farmer-Labor party legislator Coya Knutson's career, 1950–58. Discusses Knutson's active representation of northwestern Minnesota constituents in the state legislature and the U.S. Congress. Also describes political infighting, involving Knutson's alcoholic husband, that ended her political career.

830. Buell, C. J. *The Minnesota Legislature of 1923.* St. Paul: Privately published, 1923. 109 p. Illustrations.

Contains profiles of the first four women to be elected to the House of Representatives: Myrtle A. Cain of Minneapolis, Sue M. Dickey Hough of Minneapolis, Hannah J. Kempfer of Otter Tail County, and Mabeth Hurd Paige of Minneapolis. Includes each woman's assessment of her first legislative session.

831. Center for the American Woman and Politics. *Women in Public Office: A Biographical Directory and Statistical Analysis.* New York: R. R. Bowker Co., 1976. 455 p. Appendix, index.

National directory, organized by state, lists women officeholders, including U.S. Congressional delegation; state, county, and city officials; judges; and state boards and commissions.

832. Clarke, Harold D., and Allan Kornberg. "Moving Up the Political Escalator: Women Party Officials in the United States and Canada." *Journal of Politics* 41 (May 1979): 442–77.

Comparative study of women's and men's participation in political party organizations is based on

1970s research in Seattle, Minneapolis, Vancouver, and Winnipeg. Principal finding is that women devote more time to party work and generally achieve less "career success" in these voluntary associations than do men.

833. Drazen, Kathy H., et al. *Celebrating 10, 1973–1983.* N.p.: DFL Feminist Caucus, 1983. 42 p. Illustrations.

Commemorative pamphlet includes reminiscences of caucus founders, timeline noting important events in the organization's history, list of supported candidates, and statement of principles.

834. Farmer-Labor Women's Federation of Minnesota. *The Women's Political Primer.* [Minneapolis?]: The Federation, [1934?]. 6 p.

Farmer-Labor appeal to women voters discusses health, homemaking, education, employment, and civic "housekeeping."

835. Groeneman, Sid. "Candidate Sex and Delegate Voting in a Pre-Primary Party Endorsement Election." *Women & Politics* 3 (Spring 1983): 39–56.

Political science study assesses the impact of candidates' gender on party delegates' voting decisions. Based on 1977 research concerning the contest between JoAnne Thorbeck and Bob Burck for the DFL endorsement, Minneapolis seventh ward city council seat. Author reports that the female candidate won due to party delegates' desire to increase the ranks of elected women.

836. Illinois Association Opposed to Woman Suffrage. *Socialism vs. Legal Marriage.* Chicago: The Association, 1910. 4 p. (MHS).

Antisuffrage and anti-Socialist pamphlet describing women's maternal responsiblities as reasons for exemption from politics and public life. (Note: Cataloged with Minnesota Nonpartisan League materials at the Minnesota Historical Society.)

837. League of Minnesota Municipalities Information Service. *Female Judges in Minnesota, 1975.* St. Paul: The Service, 1975. 8 p.

Lists of female judges, mayors, legislators, constitutional officers and executives, and city council members in Minnesota in 1975. Includes business addresses and districts as appropriate.

838. League of Women Voters of Minneapolis. *What the Candidates Tell You: Election Handbook, November 4th, 1924.* Minneapolis: The League, 1924. 22 p.

Pamphlet produced for 1924 election contains candidate biographies and position statements. Includes Susie W. Stageberg, Farmer-Labor candidate

for secretary of state, and Mabeth Hurd Paige, Myra Griswold, Sue M. Dickey Hough, and Mrs. G. A. Petri, all candidates for the state legislature.

839. League of Women Voters of Minnesota. *Positions for Action.* St. Paul: The League, 1970. 12 p.

Pamphlet outlines 1969–71 state program of the League. Major positions include support of legislative reform, property tax reform, equality of opportunity for all citizens including women, party designation of legislative candidates, and associated election law reform.

840. Minnesota Center for Women in Government. *Women Making a Difference: Minnesota Women Talk about Women's Impact on Government and the Political Process.* St. Paul: The Center, 1988. 22 p. Illustrations.

Features five published speeches from the center's 1987–88 breakfast meeting series, "Women Making a Difference." Speakers include Dr. Reatha Clark King, president of Metropolitan State University, "Working to Change the System"; Representative Ann Wynia, Minnesota House Majority Leader, "Women's Skills in the Political Process"; Metropolitan Council member Josephine Nunn, "Tapping the Values of the Community"; Diane Ahrens, commissioner and chairperson of Ramsey County Board, "Government Women's Response to Women"; and Nina Rothchild, commissioner of Minnesota Department of Employee Relations, "Leading the Way for Pay Equity."

841. Minnesota Historical Society. *Hubert H. Humphrey Papers, Including the Papers of Muriel Buck Humphrey Brown: A Summary Guide.* St. Paul: Division of Archives and Manuscripts, Minnesota Historical Society, 1983. 35 p. Illustrations.

Muriel Buck Humphrey, wife of Hubert Humphrey, was an active partner in her husband's political career and a U.S. Senator. Her papers, 1950–78, include family correspondence and scrapbooks, materials relating to her work on the problems of persons with mental handicaps, legislative record files, and senatorial files dating to her service as U.S. Senator from Minnesota, January–November 1978.

842. Stuhler, Barbara. *No Regrets: Minnesota Women and the Joan Growe Senatorial Campaign.* St. Paul: Braemar Press, 1986. 127 p. Notes, appendixes, index.

Describes the contributions of Minnesota Groweing, a grass-roots women's group, to Joan Anderson Growe's 1984 campaign for incumbent Rudy Boschwitz's U.S. Senate seat. Focuses on the activities of the independent group, formed in support of a woman's candidacy, *vis à vis* the operations of the DFL regulars (largely male) conducting the official campaign. Written by a member of the founding committee of Minnesota Groweing, the book includes elements of collective memoir as well as political analysis.

843. *The Woman's Forum.* Minneapolis, 1920–27. Weekly newspaper covers child labor, politics, and educational issues on state and national levels. Founded by Estelle Holbrook and published under the title *The Community Journal,* 1913–20.

844. Ziegenhagen, Mary. *Running to Win: A Campaign Manual for Women Running for Office in Minnesota.* N.p.: Minnesota Women's Education Council, 1985. 64 p.

How-to manual provides advice on campaign organization, election strategy, fund raising, and public relations. Includes resource lists.